FUGITIVE PIECES

BY TADDY MCALLISTER

For Cem, part of the glue that holds our beloved Port Aransas together, from her fan and friend

Taddy
December 2007

Book and cover designed by Diahann Hill

Copyright © 2007 Taddy McAllister
All rights reserved.
ISBN: 0-9724050-2-X

Published by
Hightail Press
P. O. Box 90854
San Antonio, Texas 78209-9091
hightailpress.com

Other books by Taddy McAllister
Wander Lust
Beezie
Rut

FOR J.

TABLE OF CONTENTS

I. Letters from Prague 1

II. Poetry 71

III. Travel Journals 91
    A. South Africa and the Seychelles, 2000 93
    B. Denmark and Norway, 2002 101
    C. Cuba, 2003 113
    D. Norway, Greenland and Iceland, 2003 131
    E. Baja California, 2004 149
    F. Yellowstone, 2005 157
    G. Libya, 2005 165
    H. England and Scotland, 2005 183
    I. Prince Edward Island, 2006 197
    J. Jordan and Israel, 2006 203
    K. The South Pacific, 2007 221

IV. Editorials 237

V. Miscellany 253
    A. Excerpts from a Novel 255
    B. Speeches 259
    C. One Last Beezie Story, "Beezie and the Dogs" 267

INTRODUCTION

Readers who indulged me by buying one, two or all of my previous three books, *Wander Lust*, *Beezie* and *Rut*, have discovered that I have a short attention span at least insofar as each book was totally unlike and unrelated to the others. If this were bothersome to those who quiver at not being able properly to catalogue a writer, I am pleased to announce this new book, *Fugitive Pieces*, has reverted in part to the style of *Wander Lust* in that it is a collection dominated by travel journals, with a smattering of other, never-before-published "stuff." This includes poetry, op-ed columns, a couple of speeches and one last "Beezie" story illustrated by the author. If there were ever any doubt I was a writer not an artist, this will put that argument to bed, and if anything in this book cries out for the indulgence of the reader, it is my stick figures.

I would like to thank my fans for sticking with me, my mother for loving me unconditionally and thinking everything I write is wonderful, my book designer for her talent, and others, you know who you are, without whom my life would be very poor indeed.

Taddy McAllister
Washington, D. C.
2007

LETTERS FROM PRAGUE
January – June 1991

Introduction

In December 1988 I was the dinner partner of the new Ambassador from Germany to the United States at a fundraiser for the American Berlin Opera Foundation in New York City.

In November 1989 the German Ambassador was the luncheon speaker at the monthly World Affairs Council meeting in San Antonio, where I lived. I attended the luncheon and afterward invited the Ambassador and his wife to come for tea to my downtown apartment. Tom Pawel, their local host, brought them over. It was November 9th, the day the Wall came down in Berlin.

While Tom, the Ambassador's wife and I were all glued to the television, the Ambassador was on the wall phone in my kitchen talking to Washington and Bonn. Later I found his notes and scribbles on a cat-shaped scratch pad I had by the phone.

When they left I remained riveted by the scenes on the television, and wished I could go to Eastern Europe that very moment.

Two days later the "Velvet Revolution" happened in Czechoslovakia and the great playwright Vaclav Havel became the freely elected President of the country that had tortured and imprisoned him. All the other countries in the Eastern bloc except for Albania also became free that month. It was a glorious time.

I owned a restaurant in San Antonio that I ran myself; I sat on sixteen nonprofit boards and was the Development Chairman for more than one of them. My biggest fundraising job was for our annual music festival, the San Antonio Festival. I couldn't very well pull out and head for Eastern Europe.

In the spring of 1990, however, when some of my civic obligations were nearing their conclusions, I went to Washington, D. C. on a lark for a few days and before I left to return to San Antonio—in fact on my way to the airport while a taxi waited with my luggage—I met a real estate agent at the Watergate and bought an apartment. I told her I'd send her the money when I got home but meanwhile I had the taxi waiting and a flight to catch.

So that I could successfully conclude the fundraising for the San Antonio Festival, I didn't tell a soul except for my mother that I was leaving to move back to Washington, where I had lived before. Word finally got out mid-summer, right around the time I also managed fortuitously to sell my restaurant. I arrived in Washington on September 1st.

Tucked into the front flap of my calendar was a David Broder column from June that described an organization in Mobile, Alabama—Education for Democracy—that was sending volunteer English teachers to Czechoslovakia. I applied to them as soon as I got the boxes unpacked and the pictures hung. They accepted me to go with a cohort starting in January 1991.

Thinking it would be helpful, I went to Berlitz and took three courses in German. I talked to everyone I knew about Czechoslovakia and was passed along from one person to the next. The best contact turned out to be a new friend who worked for the Institute for East-West Security Studies. This think tank wound up "commissioning" me to consult (i.e., for free) on the restoration of the kitchen of a castle they had acquired from the Czech government just outside Prague, and where they had set up a European Studies Center. This is where I would start my Czech experience.

With this plan in hand I volunteered to Education for Democracy to help run their operation in Prague. I wanted to teach as well, but thought I would want more to do than that (ah, youth!). It was accepted that I would take over their operation when their current fellow left.

In Prague I did all these things with varying degrees of success. Along the way I wrote letters home, letters whose trajectory was meant to carry the ties that bind but were also calculated to suffice as my own written diary-like record of my time there. Even though I did not arrive in Prague until fourteen months after the Revolution, there was much to observe of both the old system and the potential new one. I wrote op-ed or feature columns for the San Antonio Express-News that addressed my observations of the transformation Czech society was going through and to some extent described my personal experiences as well.

My letters were not attempts at literary masterpieces, nor does this compendium of letters and columns parade as a literary masterwork. The Czech proper names are Anglicized and do not have their diacritical markings over them.

I.
THE LETTERS AND NEWSPAPER COLUMNS

Friday afternoon, 18 January 1991
IEWSS European Studies Center
Zamek Stirin, Czechoslovakia

Dear Family,

I have not put pen to paper since arriving here five days ago because, frankly, I have been in a state of shock. I have felt fear, joy, homesickness, terror, happiness and every nuance in between, and it has taken me until now to sort it all out and get my feet more firmly planted. I was so alarmed at my reaction actually to being here that I didn't want to alarm anyone else by writing home about it. I am more reconciled to my situation now and I think I am going to make it.

The trip over was a piece of cake unless you count having to deal with my luggage. I had four big heavy pieces and two heavy carry-on's full of cosmetics. I thought my back was truly a goner. Fortunately my bed in the castle is as hard as a board, and after one night in it my back felt fine. The plane left Dulles Sunday evening, landed in Frankfurt early Monday morning, the connection was made and I was in Prague at 10:30 a.m. Took a taxi to town to the Academy of Sciences Building on Narodni Street where my luggage was stored with the concierge and I was shown up to the offices in-town of the Institute for East-West Security Studies. There I met Stephen Heintz, the Secretary General, and other staffers. I called Grady Lloyd, the current head of the office of Education for Democracy, and left immediately to go meet him for lunch.

I took an instant dislike to him. In high school we would have called him a creep. He walked five feet in front of me, he had a negative personality and a jaundiced view of the Czechs and his job, he was whiny and ineffectual, and all in all I should not have met him for the first time after having been up 25 straight hours. The straw that broke the camel's back was when he took me to see the office—my future office—after lunch. It was small, crowded and chaotic. My reaction was, "oh my god I can't work here!" (I said to myself). I told Grady to get me a teaching job and let me evolve into the office position, and he said he had expected to do that all along. I fled back to Narodni Street.

It took every single person in the IEWSS office to get my luggage out to the street and into a taxi. They weren't going back to the castle until late so I decided to taxi out there myself. When I arrived, Matt Hirsch and Krzysztof Ners came out to help me carry things up to my room, and then Matt gave me a tour of the castle.

Arriving at the castle is auspicious after leaving the exurbs of the city and driving through farmlands and villages. It is smack on the road in the village of Stirin and looks like a chateau. It forms a "U" with its legs to the road and its entrance in the middle of the "U." Inside it is a combination of baroque and communist, with many beautiful flourishes but with some dreadful institutional carpet and furniture. The staff acts sometimes friendly, sometimes bureaucratically stern. The kitchen staff is particularly inflexible and the food is unimaginative and sometimes downright poor.

I had an appointment to meet with the manageress of the castle the next morning with an interpreter from the Prague office. I praised her and the staff lavishly but said that the Institute people longed for a more varied menu. The interview lasted two hours and had its highs and lows, but I reached some conclusions and made some recommendations to Stephen in a memo later that day. As for the kitchen, it needs to be nuked. A Swiss firm has drawn up a plan for it on spec so I don't have to tackle doing that from scratch. Next Saturday I will be part of the meeting at which the Swiss formally present the plan to Stephen and A.J. Land, a developer from Atlanta who has been helping with a master plan.

Here are my castle mates: Stephen Heintz, a tall, thin Connecticut Yankee with horn rimmed glasses and a boyish but diplomatic way about him—our leader. His wife is in Connecticut and won't move here until June. Matt Hirsch, 28, a scholar and assistant to Stephen, articulate and gentle. His girlfriend is either in N.Y. or Germany. Krzysztof Ners, a Polish intellectual who is Director of Programs. He is Stephen's age (late 30's), speaks good English, and works during the day at the castle along with Matt. He and Matt and I have been thrown together as a result of being here all day, and I couldn't wish for more interesting housemates. Krzysztof's fiancé will move here in March. Marie Lavigne, in her fifties, a French intellectual and economist who is the (intellectual) Director of the Center. She is delightful. Amy, an attractive Asian-American from their New York office who is here on a tour of duty as a word processor. And little me, from San Antonio, Texas. They want me to make margaritas for them. I hold my own with them in conversation, and they are all grateful that someone may make a dent in their nutrition problems.

Here is what we eat: breakfast has been a plate of ham, crepes filled with jam, uncooked oats over which you are expected to pour hot milk, served with bread and pate; eggs and ham; oranges and grapefruit. I gagged the first morning when I sat down to a plate of ham. I took a piece of bread back to the kitchen and put it on one of the plate-like burners of the coal stove and toasted it, much to the amazement, merriment, and consternation of the staff.

Lunch and dinner are meat in gravy and either dumplings (which look like slices of bread) or boiled potatoes. One morning at breakfast they were cooking spinach in the kitchen; we had it for dinner eleven hours later. That is the only green thing I have seen so far. Cabbage is about as green as you can get in the stores, and it's hard to find. It's going to be a long spring.

Matt and I got dropped at the subway out on the edge of the city on Day 2 and trained into downtown to have lunch with an acquaintance of mine, Tim Whipple, whom I had met in Washington and who is living here and working as a business consultant. He speaks fluent Czech and is going to help me find an apartment. After lunch (at which I ate cabbage salad and French-fries) we went to a lecture Marie Lavigne was giving, slipped out of that to go have a coffee at the Palace Hotel (which has a salad bar—I am going back!), then back to the office and a taxi ride back out to the castle.

Matt, Krzysztof and I stayed up late talking; everyone else was out. The quality of talk is wonderful.

Yesterday we were here all day except that Matt, Krzysztof and I went down the road to a restaurant for lunch, and wound up having a divine lunch of some kind of Chinese cooked meat and vegetables. We drank beer and were in a grand mood for not having to eat at the castle.

During the three days I have spent in the castle without going into the city I have taken long walks in the countryside. It is very cold but clear, there is frost on the ground, the ponds are frozen, the grass is crispy with ice, the fields are manicured, the trees are bare, and every couple of kilometers there is a village of stucco houses with orange tile roofs, and smoke coming out of the chimneys. Coal smoke. There is a romantic haze over the land which unfortunately is coal smoke.

Here is how low I have fallen nutritionally: today I walked to the store in the next village and the only thing I could find to buy was a bottle of vodka and two candy bars.

Next week I am going on a two-day orientation for Education for Democracy (EfD) somewhere out in the country. Next Thursday night I am invited along with the other IEWSS staff to Ambassador Shirley Temple Black's residence for a party. And I hope the week after that to start my teaching assignment, and as soon as possible to move into the city.

The castle is isolated, and this preys on everyone who lives and works here. Every one is separated from loved ones, the food is bad and the communications primitive, so there is a kind of low-grade depression that makes the nightly beers and camaraderie mighty welcome. I am the most isolated of all, and in limbo to boot, so I have been grateful for the friendship and attention of these special people. Stephen told me last night that I could stay here as long as I wanted to, but he also said he would watch with interest my machinations to get an apartment as he wants to get one, too—and get out of the castle and into town—like everyone else.

Those first couple of days I really woke in a state of terror thinking, what am I doing here? What am I going to do with myself between meals today? How am I going to stand this food for five months? Why am I not in the Bahamas snorkeling over a reef? Where is this grand experiment in democracy I wanted to participate in? Who will make love to me? I want my mama!

Followed by calmly rational thoughts like things will change next week, you'll be happier in the city, you'll be happier with a job, give it a chance, you can always read a book, and where's that vaunted courage of yours?

So far I have read three books in four days, and I feel a whole lot better.

P.S. (later Friday night) I gave Matt Jimmy Buffet's book *Tales From Margaritaville* and he got so bound up in it he didn't want to go out to dinner with Krzysztof and me (dinner was not being served at the castle tonight). So Krzysztof and I took off for the place we had had such a good lunch and—at 8:00 pm—they were out of food. Two other places in two other villages—also out of food. I have never been any place that didn't have any food. Marie Lavigne, when we returned, said she thought going hungry made you more metaphysical.

I will have to get used to it.

Sunday night, 20 January 1991
Stirin, Czechoslovakia

Dear Family,

Several things have happened. I changed rooms tonight because tomorrow the restoration crew starts on my old wing. My former room, where I was perfectly happy, was decorated by the old regime in communist/realist mode and by me in Chinese laundry mode. My bathroom was down the hall about ten feet, had a bank of sinks at which party apparatchiks must have splashed cold water on their underarms before reporting to their indoctrinations, a shallow tin shower with cold water which finally became hot, and a toilet with its tank up on the wall. Now I am in the master suite of the entire castle with my own cavernous bath. John Mroz, the president of the Institute, arrived today for a week stay. He normally stays in this monstrosity but he chose another room so I offered to move here and he thought that was fine.

We had no cooks all weekend so tonight Matt, Krzysztof, Amy and I drove 3 km. to Velky Popovice (the home of our local brewery) for dinner at the local café—the same place we had the good Chinese dish one day last week for lunch. The place was thronged with village men, one of whom smiled at me. No one ever smiles, usually, so I smiled back and he subsequently materialized at our table and said he was one of the painters at the castle. They were so noisy yesterday morning (Saturday) at 7:00 a.m. that I had opened my door and shushed them, and he teased me about it and told me how beautiful I was, and I was so embarrassed about it that I was too friendly to him and he clung to me throughout dinner and even bought us a bottle of Champagne. (This was all in Czech.)

The night before I had told Krzysztof, Matt and Marie Lavigne that I had figured out the reason I was homesick was because no one loved me, and when no one loved you it made you invisible. Tonight they teased me and said, now someone loves you!

Yesterday Krzysztof and I got all gussied up and mainly bundled up and drove into Prague for the day. First we took an hour to grocery shop. It's slim pick'ns and you have to wait in line in most stores for someone to wait on you. It's maddening. Everything is hopelessly bureaucratic here. We bought a bottle of scotch and as much as we could carry of salami, cheese, crackers, bread, fruit, wine, tinned tuna and salmon, tomatoes, and wilted lettuce. Last night we feasted on it all like people who had not seen a delicatessen for a year. None of this stuff do I eat under normal circumstances you understand, but after meat-flecked gravy and potatoes it tasted pretty good. It put us in such a good mood we sat up until almost midnight drinking and talking.

It was excruciatingly cold yesterday but after our shopping in the city we separated for a few hours and I went to the post office and walked around sightseeing, then met my young friend Tim Whipple at a coffee house to discuss finding me an apartment. Krzysztof came to fetch me and the three of us went to see Tim's temporary apartment, which I may be able to rent. Then we came home to the country to our picnic/feast and night of conversation.

Prague simply boggles the mind in its beauty and antiquity. Unfortunately when you are so cold in spite of everything you have managed to wear that your face feels like it will crack off and your hands burn (ironically) with the pain of frostbite it is difficult to become rhapsodic.

This afternoon I went out for a walk and it had finally been so cold for so long that the big pond in front of the castle had frozen sufficiently for skating. It appeared the entire village was out on skates, and one person was even pushing a baby carriage. Another was skating straddling a small child on a tricycle. The frozen pond had become their park. Around the bend two men with a basset hound and beagle threw a stick for them out onto another frozen pond, and when the dogs went down the embankment for it they landed in icy water, which caused great merriment (not on my part). No one ever speaks or smiles at me so it was nice to have a shared moment with the two men, and a sniff from the dogs. People are not too friendly in these parts. I like my castle mates very much. I shall miss them when I move into Prague but I will not miss the isolation of this country living.

I am listening to 'Madama Butterfly' and it makes me want to cry for all I have given up to have this experience. Sometimes I am washing my face and suddenly flash on driving my car, or I'm trying to coax some hot water and flash on my apartment at the Watergate, or I'm hoofing it along some country road and have a vision of Port Aransas. I really have to hang onto myself and savor the juxtaposition, the irony of it all. It's a terrible, exciting thing to be separated from all you know. I don't recommend it for the faint-hearted.

(Monday afternoon) The manageress of the castle was very upset to learn we had used the kitchen over the weekend and has banned us from it. That means my work here is essentially over and now I shall revert to being merely a supportive and charming house guest until I can get moved into town in the next ten days or so.

Krzysztof and I have been alone in the house today. I have organized my clothes and possessions after the chaos of changing rooms, and have done laundry, and have packed to go on my two-day Education for Democracy orientation tomorrow. I made us a picnic lunch to eat in the office.

Something serendipitous happens everyday. The evenings of drinking and stimulating conversation always send me to bed in a deeply comfortable mood, but no matter how quiet the day is something else memorable happens that affirms the reasons for being here.

Today I set out to walk after lunch and noticed that it felt ever so slightly warmer, and had become overcast. I was out of sight of the castle when a snowflake landed on me. I looked up to see that it was followed every yard or so by fellow kamikaze snowflakes, and within a minute the whole air was white with them. It was so delightful that in my aloneness I felt like it had started to snow just for me. Some hours later, sitting at my desk looking out the window, I am still in a state of euphoria.

Today is my one week anniversary of being here and so far everything I brought with me has been just right. This is some consolation for having had to deal with my luggage. Miraculously Lufthansa only charged me $84 for my overweight, but I did sort of throw myself on their mercy.

This morning I wrote a piece for the [San Antonio] Express-News which I intend to fax to Sterlin Holmesly [editor of the editorial page] if it passes muster around here. Keep an eye open for it.

It will be at least four days before I start another letter. I am well, and doing fine.

[The first op-ed piece for the Express-News follows.]

"THE VIEW FROM THE WINDOW"

"The hoarfrost is thick on the ground; the grass is crispy with ice. It is deeply cold, apparently too cold for snow. The neighborhood ponds are frozen solid and have become neighborhood parks. On a Sunday they are covered with a pickup hockey game, children playing, a mother pushing a baby carriage, a grownup straddling a child on a tricycle. A beagle and a basset hound chase sticks. Instead of shutting people in, ice opens whole new spaces for them. Watching from the road I feel the kind of envy a gopher must feel for a bird.

"I am a guest at Zamek Stirin, or Stirin Castle, which is indeed a castle but resembles more a French chateau. It is 30 kilometers southwest of Prague, and it is the new home of the European Studies Center, a brainchild of John Mroz, the founder of the Institute for East-West Security Studies in New York. The Czech government has leased the castle to the Institute, and it comes complete with staff. It is the permanent home to lots of other kinds of people including John Mroz himself for a few days, and me.

"While the other good people in the castle work to save the world, my job is to encourage the kitchen staff to serve more nutritious, balanced and imaginative food. There is beauty and comfort at Stirin but there is also an element of isolation, and the simple joy of mealtime can turn to low-grade depression when the food is discouraging.

"There is a second reason I am here, and that is to consult on the restoration of the kitchen. It is old and somewhat primitive by American restaurant standards, and beyond my ken to affect single-handedly, but I will participate in a planning session with the castle manager, an American developer friend of the Center, and a Swiss firm which has drawn a plan on spec for a new kitchen.

"What all these domestic arrangements have done is make me acutely sensitive to how things are done, what is available in the stores and, as a lifelong human watcher, who's doing what to whom, why and how.

"Krzysztof Ners, a Polish intellectual who is Director of Studies at the Center, has enlightened me considerably on the subject of communism in our conversations about Eastern Europe. For "enlightened" read: put me down. One night I said it was a shame that an ideology (communism) that had at its root an essentially humane philosophy had had to impose it in such a tyrannical way. He informed me that communism had not been an "ideology" for over fifty years, but rather was a system of power. Notwithstanding the Velvet Revolution of 1989 here, the bureaucratic imposition of control over the myriad aspects of daily life is alive and well in Czechoslovakia.

"Examples: the castle staff, who are actually employees of the Ministry of Education, must cook a certain number of meals each day to justify their existence. I have been wandering in and out of the kitchen but this weekend when the staff was off and I used the kitchen to organize a cold supper for my cohort I learned to my sorrow after the fact that to do so again I would have to pass a health test and be certified by some agency. When you go into the shops you stand in line to be waited on by a person who gets the things for you and doesn't release them to you until you have paid. There is no self-service.

"For some people a system exists to be beaten. In a country with an oppressive political and social system, everyone would be a participant in the game. They may appear to stand stoically in line at the post office or in the meat market but when they are finished they walk right through you to get out. Disrespect for the system in all its thousands of insulting, irrational manifestations breeds discourtesy and indifference. And fear.

"The change of regimes may take place overnight but the revolution, the real revolution, the turning away, the re-creation of government, takes much longer. And the evolution in attitudes perhaps longer still. One does not transform a lifetime of cynicism into gushy good-naturedness with a change of Presidents.

"So I bundle up in high tech cold weather clothes to walk the country roads and ponder the seemingly limitless amount of work before these people. I savor the landscape—the tree-lined lanes, the manicured, frozen fields, the stucco villages with their orange tiled roofs and busy chimneys, the occasional barking dog—and I smile and nod and raise my hand in greeting to those I encounter on the road. No one smiles back.

"But I am a creation of the American volunteer spirit, and I have the zeal of the missionary that comes from my old-time liberalism, so I'm going to keep right on smiling. They may not be glad to be here, but I am."

Saturday afternoon, 26 January 1991
Stirin, Czechoslovakia

Dear Ones,

I have had a stimulating several days and I am feeling happy to be here. Tuesday morning I drove into town with Krzysztof to the office, took a taxi to the Education for Democracy office, hooked up with Grady Lloyd and took another taxi to another part of town where 25 other EfD volunteers were waiting to be picked up by a bus to be taken to a conference center in the town of Loucen for a two-day orientation. The other volunteers had spent from one to three nights in a construction workers' dormitory—a sort of hostel for foreign workers—and it was as dreary as it sounds. I mentally crossed myself and thought, there but for the grace of God go I. If I had landed in Czechoslovakia and been taken to that place I would have lost it, plain and simple. Of the 25 volunteers, 23 were scruffy looking young people who became attractive and interesting as they came into focus. There was one woman older than I, and well dressed, and there was me, another well-dressed rara avis.

The bus was on time, clean, big and comfortable, and the trip into the countryside was interesting. With the snow on the ground and the trees bare one could dispense with color film in taking pictures of Czechoslovakia; it is a study in black and white. The air, thick with pollution, fog and moisture, is also white, and where the white curtain of air meets the white ground it appears to be the edge of the earth.

After less than an hour's drive we arrived at Zamek Loucen—Loucen's castle—which is a conference center with many similarities to our castle (note: "our") but with some major differences, namely that it was tacky and dreary and our castle is elegant. We were four to a room and there was one shower, two sinks and three potties for probably sixteen people. It was really not bad, although I certainly would not choose it as a lifestyle. I got along with everyone, and was good-natured and friendly and helpful. In fact I took two girls who were having problems under my wing. I also made a couple of nice new friends—one a volunteer and one the seminar leader, a woman with English as a Second Language background whose husband is the head of the Citizens Democracy Corps in Romania.

I was glad to be at the orientation when the talks got under way because it was really interesting and helpful. Teaching is complicated. Especially when you have no materials, Xerox machine or curriculum guide, and are just out there on your own responsible for filling the school time of your students with something new and meaningful everyday. The small group sessions were conducted by a couple of bright young men who have been here teaching for several months, and who were full of ideas and suggestions, every one of which I wrote down.

I had a car and driver (someone recommended by Liana Barenblat) pick me up a half day early to take me back to Prague, and I took with me one of the other volunteers, a young woman with a severe kidney infection. I kept the driver until I got her squared away, which took some doing, then landed at the Prague office of IEWSS to go with the others at the end of the day to a reception in honor of IEWSS at the American Embassy residence. Ambassador Shirley Temple Black greeted us at the door, and I later had a nice visit with her. She is small and not as attractive as I wanted her to be. She smokes. Her dog, a boxer named Gorby, was walking around with a partially deflated basketball in its mouth. The residence is magnificent and the celery sticks were out of this world.

Five of us had to cram into one car for the trip back to Stirin, which put us in such a crazy mood that we started drinking in earnest when we landed safely. There was a new face in the crowd—Peter Volten, a Dutch intellectual who is the Director of Research in the N.Y. office—and I came to find out that he was sleeping in my room, which I must say I did not protest. I sat up for awhile and listened to them plan a conference, who would be invited, etc. These people know everyone in every government in Europe, and it is heady business to be in on their machinations.

Everyone on the staff went into the Prague office on Friday, leaving me alone in the castle. I never got out of my bathrobe all day long. I napped and did laundry and talked on the telephone for hours. Peter called and invited me into the city for the night—he had moved to Villa Lanna, a mansion used to accommodate guests related to the Academy of Sciences, where the Prague office is, and I found a way to get into town to join him. Villa Lanna was huge and elegant and empty except for us. We went downtown for dinner and walked through the narrow streets until we found what turned out to be a good restaurant with real, tasty food. We stood out in the middle of the Old Town Square and marveled at the incredible beauty of the city, then walked into the old Jewish ghetto before succumbing to the cold and hailing a taxi.

This morning, Saturday, A.J. Land and his wife Lynne picked me up at Villa Lanna and we drove out to Stirin. A.J. is a wealthy developer from Atlanta who is overseeing the restoration of the castle as a volunteer. He and Lynne have grown kids and are living in Europe for six months. When we arrived at the castle we went straight into a meeting with Stephen Heintz, the reps from the firm which has drawn the kitchen plan, the castle manager, and the castle consulting architect, a handsome type in tweed jacket and turtleneck who also acted as interpreter. The firm is trying to sell the Institute $250,000 worth of equipment(!) so we had a bit of discussing to do. I think I was helpful. Armed with blueprints and accompanied by the big bosses, I got to see the storerooms and other places I had not seen yet. This is a big damn place.

After the meeting and lunch everyone sheared off and I took out walking. It is as usual close to excruciatingly cold, and it was drizzling, so it was an inauspicious walk although I did see two pheasants running across a snow covered field. The air is so bad that, while I am sure it is good for my legs to be out walking, it is probably bad for my lungs.

Stephen has gone to town for dinner so Krzysztof and I are dining alone tonight. I have enjoyed him very much. He has just told me he is going to Poland for a week, and I felt crestfallen because I shall miss him. These people have really become like family to me.

(Sunday Evening) We have had a quiet Sunday. I have been reading and working on the kitchen plan. Krzysztof is going to leave me his car and he took me for a check out spin around the neighborhood with me driving. It was fun to be behind the wheel of a car. I felt liberated.

Wednesday, 30 January 1991
Stirin, Czechoslovakia

Dear Ones,

I have been here for 17 days and basically have not done anything for these good people except entertain them, but this past weekend after we had the presentation of the kitchen plan and it was clearly not what we wanted, I went into hibernation over the blueprint, switched brain sides and came up with a plan that could solve all the problems. Stephen, our leader, and A. J. Land, the developer, are both pleased and want me to confer with the castle architect. The architect is handsome and charming but terribly self-important so we shall see if he can stand being one-upped by someone Stephen says he was attracted to. My mini-success has prompted me to decide that I must go to Germany to look at restaurant equipment, and when I mentioned it to Stephen he said, oh, and could you get us a file cabinet, a case of Xerox paper, 15 in-boxes, 33 mirrors and some bottled water? So I am going to rent a car and go to Munich for a couple of days as soon as I can arrange a guide there to help me. Renting a car and driving to Munich is not like running over to Houston.

My deadline in the guest book to be out of the castle is February 1, and I am going to come close to making it. Yesterday I learned that I can indeed rent Tim Whipple's apartment as of Sunday the 3rd. It is clean, cozy, secure and near downtown. I will pay $300 a month for it, and the landlords will do my laundry. It has a phone. I will have an address at which you can write me, although I don't know what it is. I may move Sunday the 3rd or I may go to Munich Monday the 4th and move when I return.

I have had three really interesting days. Monday, Stephen and A.J. invited me along to go house hunting in the neighboring villages for houses for staff families who cannot or won't live in the castle. A very slick Canadian real estate agent/hustler businessman and his lady friend partner picked us up in a Cadillac limousine (we just about fainted at the sight of this car) and took us down the road to see a man in the next village. This guy lived in a really handsome compound of buildings in a house full of antiques and with a garage full of collector-quality cars, including a Corvette. We were mystified how someone in such a poor society could have accumulated so much wealth, but obviously he had found a way to beat the system. He had a couple of rent houses. When the Canadian hustler dropped us back at the castle we fell to like a gaggle of geese laughing and speculating about him and the car collector. Then we got in one of our cars and drove around the countryside looking at property, winding up in Velky Popovice at 11:00 a.m. for a courtesy call on the mayor there (we had an interpreter with us).

Stephen then took me into the city with him to pick up Krzysztof's car which he was leaving with me for a week while he went to Warsaw. I drove it back out to Stirin all by myself and thought, I could get used to this.

Tuesday morning I spent writing another piece for the Express-News and answering the telephone. My huge master suite is next to the office. At noon, Lynne and A.J. Land arrived to have lunch with us and the mayor of Stirin, who was adorable. He looked like a sophomore in college. These visits with neighboring mayors are for social, political and ulterior reasons. Stephen wants to be a good neighbor but he also needs to acquire some neighboring properties without rubbing anyone the wrong way.

Today I had a free day with nothing to do so I drove Krzysztof's car into Prague to go sightseeing. I stopped at the Forum Hotel on the way into downtown. Stephen and the other men on the staff play squash there and I wanted to see the health club facility. It was closed until later in the afternoon so I went into the coffee shop and ate a ham sandwich, drank two cappuccinos and had a big slab of cake (all for $4). As I sat there staring out the big windows at the city I lapsed into a reverie that included thinking about old lovers, wondering what was really happening to my system as I dump all this junk food in it, wondering why it is that when you have a rich life of the mind you sometimes don't need other people so much and yet you crave them when you want them, and generally putting myself in an exotic and emotional mood for the sightseeing ahead.

The weather was nice today—a little dab of blue sky, and not excruciatingly cold. I parked near the office and walked up the river to the Charles Bridge. The river was full of ducks, swans and gulls. The river is quite wide and is as integral to the vision and life of the city as the Thames, the Seine, the San Antonio or the East Rivers are to their cities. I remember when Linda Adelman Gintel first came down from N.Y. to visit me in Washington years ago. As we came in from the airport and she surveyed the Potomac and the city she said "oh good, you have bridges. I just wouldn't live in a city without bridges." Prague 1 is the old core of the city and it is on both sides of the river. The castle which is the seat of government is on the left side along with the ancient neighborhood of Mala Strana, which is built on the side of the hill with the Castle at the top and the river at the bottom. I climbed the hill to Hradcany Castle, which is actually a complex of buildings, some ancient, some just old. I walked around Hradcany Square (Hradcanske Namesti) and was struck by the utter silence and desertedness of it. It would be as if there were no cars or people on the street around the White House. I walked into St. Vitus Cathedral on the castle grounds. I may be a heathen but this thing did take my breath away.

The whole city takes my breath away. It is stunningly, indescribably ancient and beautiful. Through narrow cobbled streets, up hills, down avenues and sitting in side streets one sees countless elegant buildings, incredibly romantic doorways, outrageous architectural decoration and endless embraceable antiquity and form. Words do not do it justice.

I walked and walked and gave myself up to it and could have been smiling or crying, but mostly I was stunned and breathless. I kept thinking, each step makes it more mine, each step takes away the mystery and danger and infuses this foreign place with comfort, each step makes it more understandable by making it retraceable. I was invisible in black boots, black coat, black ear muffs, black sunglasses and black gloves. I could have been from Leningrad, Lake Louise or Lahore. I was an invisible person. I was at home. I was alone with history.

One thing I have learned here is that it is unnatural for us to have been in the same place for so long (150 years in San Antonio). You would think that in this ancient bed of history the generations would go back to Biblical times, but the order of European history has been dispersal and disruption and not stability. All my castle intellectuals are amazed at my history. They come out of floating stock that crosses borders and languages willy-nilly. One thing I hope to come to understand is how people live with so much tragedy. I have had one tragedy in my life—the loss of my father—and I can still come undone over that. Europeans have lost countries, generations, races, borders, regions, families and freedom and yet right here is a whole population of them plugging along living in this wildly opulent, decayed city as if it were the most natural thing in the world. I want to know their secret—the secret of how to live with sorrow. This fascinates my existential soul.

When I came back down the hill into Mala Strana I suddenly found myself staring at a sign in a window that said "Price Waterhouse." I went in to the building, found their offices, introduced myself to two young American men who reacted as if I had just dropped in from Mars, and left a note for Geoffrey Upton, the managing partner, saying I was a friend of the San Antonio Price Waterhouse crew. Then I drove myself back to Stirin.

Yesterday I called Prince Schwartzenberk, President Havel's chief of staff to whom I had an introduction. I could not decide how to use the introduction, whether to wait until I needed him or go ahead and make a social call. I did not want the introduction to get stale, so I went ahead and called him. He was not there but his secretary said, "Oh, Miss McAllister, we have been trying to call you." I thought, well if that doesn't beat all. We are going to try to make telephone connections tomorrow.

Everyone is in town tonight so I am going to eat delicatessen, listen to some Pavarotti and read. Here's what I have read: *Tales from Margaritaville*, Shelby Hearon's book *Group Therapy*, *The Third Life of Grange Copeland* by Alice Walker, and now *The Mambo Kings Sing Songs of Love* by Oscar Hijuelos—all good. I do not recommend *Tales from Margaritaville* if you are homesick, though.

✦·┈┈┈┈·✦

[The following is the second op-ed piece sent to the Express-News.]

"THE FLY ON THE WALL"

"As a guest in the castle of the Institute for East-West Security Studies Center, I'm sometimes invited to tag along on expeditions where I have experiences I might not otherwise enjoy.

"Yesterday Stephen Heintz, the Secretary General of the Center, and A. L. Land, a wonderfully civilized, unreconstructed capitalist developer from Atlanta who is the volunteer overseer of the castle restoration master plan, allowed me to invite myself along to go house hunting in the neighboring villages. A real estate agent picked us up in his Cadillac limousine and took us a few hundred yards down the road to meet one of the local squires who was looking to deal some property. The initial part of the meeting consisted of sitting around the Squire's dining room table politely drinking coffee and listening to the real estate agent, an American who has been doing business and prospering in Czechoslovakia for the past ten years, complain bitterly about having to adjust to life under the new democratic regime. As he delicately but revealingly put it, it was easier to "organize" things under the old system. Obviously his friend The Squire had found it so, ensconced as he was in his beautiful house full of antiques which had clearly not been acquired on the standard Czech salary of $120 a month.

"This pretty countryside is full of vacation homes which are only used by their owners in the summer. The phenomenon of second homes is apparently fairly common in Czechoslovakia. The contradiction that such a poor society could afford what we would consider an outright luxury may be explained by the fact that everything is so cheap here, or at least it used to be before this wretched democratization started!

"Last week I enjoyed some reflected glory as a guest, along with the rest of the Center staff, at a reception given by American Ambassador Shirley Temple Black in honor of Marie Lavigne, the French intellectual who is the Director of the Center. The other guests were ambassadors from the other European countries as well as ministers and other representatives from the Czech government. I tried to be a friendly, charming fly on the wall while I surreptitiously ate all the celery sticks. I had a nice long chat about "Republicans We Have Known" with Mrs. Black, who is small and smokes. She has a boxer named Gorby who slobbered his way amongst the pinstriped legs carrying his old leather bone.

"I also had an interesting conversation with an attractive young woman who works for and was representing the Minister of the Environment. Now this is a man who has a big job. The air pollution is, in my humble opinion, terrifying, and the ground water is probably not much better. There is something eerily disconcerting about moving through air so thick and visible it seems to have a corpus of its own. When I go out to walk the country lanes for exercise I know I am making a doubtful tradeoff between my legs and my lungs. But back to the pretty girl from the Ministry, she is representative of the new breed of bureaucrats running the country, or trying to: young, inexperienced and happily arrogant from the headiness of their newfound power.

"On a more local note, I have been the silent third party in meetings which Stephen and A. J. have had with the mayors of Stirin and Velke Popovice, the nearest large town (1800 souls). The mayor of Stirin was young and cute and school-boyish; when asked how he came to stand for election, he said no one else wanted to do it. This brought knowing laughs from all us old pros at democracy. The mayor of Velke Popovice has a major employer in his town: a large regional brewery. Like dominating industries in towns everywhere it is a mixed blessing.

It creates jobs, but it pollutes. Its huge smokestack belches black coal smoke, and whatever kind of mess it is that comes out of the other end of a brewery goes into the ground. Natural gas and a wastewater treatment facility are coming sometime, someday. The mayor, formerly an electrical engineer, looks like he has the weight of the world on his shoulders.

"Soon I will leave the security of this castle and my adopted castle "family" to move into an apartment in Prague. There I will start my real job as a volunteer English teacher with the Education for Democracy program. It has been my good fortune not only to have this safe haven in a strange country, and to have made these new friends, but also to have been exposed to these and many other slices of life in this emerging democracy. Emerging in this case by breech birth. No one is having an easy time of it."

Saturday, 2 February 1991
Stirin, Czechoslovakia

A full moon was still hanging in the tree tops when I went out to start Krzysztof's car Thursday morning at 6:45 a.m. I had to meet Lynne Land at the Intercontinental Hotel in Prague at 7:30 for breakfast and a trip out to a school where a friend of hers, Nancy Painter, teaches English to Czech military officers. Nancy is the wife of the American military attaché. It took forever to get the car started—in fact it took going back in the castle and asking Stephen to help me and then it took some scraping to get the ice off the windows (inside & out), and finally I was on my way, spluttering along, barely able to see out. It was 9° F.

It is about 6 km. from Stirin to the highway, and then it is about 25 km. into Prague on an interstate-type freeway. About 10 km. toward Prague there was a muffled "pop" under the hood and a cloud of white smoke or steam came out. It scared the liver out of me but the car kept going. Then about 10 km. later the car started to lose power so I moved way over and was well off the highway when it finally stopped. Now black and grey smoke was coming out of the hood. I stepped out of the car, put my thumb up and was instantly picked up by a man in a van who did not speak any of my languages. I asked him to take me to a hotel but instead he dumped me on the side of yet another freeway on the outskirts of the city and pointed across a field at a place that said "Auto Skoda" and said, 'mechanika'. I said "gee thanks pal," and hiked over to Auto Skoda

(Skoda is the Czech car). There I threw myself on the mercy of two old dispatchers to call me a taxi. They finally had the bright idea to ask a taxi driver who had brought his car in for repairs to take me, which he did, to the Intercontinental. He had a country music tape on playing Patsy Cline and other oldies which really made me want to cry. I walked into the hotel at 8:35 a.m. Lynne and Nancy had gone on but A.J. Land was there and he bought me some breakfast and took me under his wing. I was ravenously hungry from relief.

I basically followed A. J. around for the rest of the day. He and Peter, his interpreter, and I went back out to Stirin for a meeting and to make the arrangements to have the car picked up. Then we went back to the city, leaving Peter with the car on the side of the road to meet the wrecker. Back to the Intercontinental; I struck out to run errands but got too cold and went back to the hotel coffee shop where I wound up having my second meal with A.J.—his lunch date had not shown up. Then we went to another hotel to renew the lease on his rental car so I could keep it (they were leaving the next day), then to the Forum Hotel to drop him off to play squash with Stephen, and at that point I was back behind the wheel of a car by myself heading home and it felt damn good. I'd had enough adventure for one day.

Stephen and I dined alone and talked and talked. After dinner we scoured the castle bathrooms for toilet paper, as everyone was running out and the staff did not show any signs of replacing it. The quality of talk I have enjoyed in this castle has been unparalleled. I shall miss that part when I move, although there will be other things I won't miss, for instance the food.

Friday morning, yesterday, I woke up feeling puny and after breakfast I went back to bed and slept most of the day. I think it was digestive. It's about time. Today I feel better. My apartment should be available this weekend. I'm basically ready to move when I get the word. I'm excited to have my own cozy nest but I am also facing one more adjustment with all its attendant ups and downs, highs and lows. I hope I don't weary of being brave before my life here takes on some definition, before the reason I am here, the plan, becomes manifest. There is a reason I am here beyond seeing how brave and patient I can be. I am not good at waiting for things to happen to me. Perhaps I had to come all this way to learn loss of control.

Marie Lavigne and I had a talk at breakfast this morning about American idealism. She is French and does not understand it. Czechoslovakia is a great example of the worldly and cynical meeting the brash and idealistic.

Thursday, 7 February 1991
Prague, Czechoslovakia

Dear Ones,

    I spent a quiet last weekend at the castle and then on Sunday afternoon Marie Lavigne drove me into town to my new digs. There I met my friend Tim, who had just moved out of the apartment and into a permanent place, and the landlord, Mr. Trso, who is funny and speaks English. We went over the whole place, and they showed me how everything worked. When they left I unpacked in a wildly happy state of mind, I was so happy finally to have a nest.

    The apartment is darling. It is two rooms—a bedroom with a desk and stereo and a great record collection, and a kitchen with a table that seats four. The kitchen is basically the living room. There is a little entrance hall, and a nice bath with a separate loo. Everything is clean and modern and works. The heating is good, the doors and windows are secure, there is always hot water, the linens are beautiful, but the building itself looks like a slum. Most buildings in Prague look like slums on the inside, although an overwhelming number of them are beautiful on the outside. Mine is plain on the outside.

    I like the neighborhood. Three blocks away there is a grocery store, and within six to eight blocks are all the other shops—butcher, greengrocery, bakery, paper store (where you buy your stationery, toilet paper, napkins, anything made of paper). Tim came back around that first Sunday evening and walked me two blocks to a beautiful Vietnamese restaurant where we pigged out.

    I am still in the stage of being fascinated by it, but shopping is a time consuming chore. You have to wait for a basket to enter the grocery store. Once in there is so little packaging that you just lay your bare loaves of bread in the bottom of the basket. They do deign to put the eggs in flimsy little paper bags. I have taken to buying things even if I do not know what they are, just to see what they are. I bought what I hoped was sour cream and it turned out to be bacon fat. I bought what I could have sworn was going to be mayonnaise and it turned out to be horseradish sauce. You carry your mineral water bottles back to the bottle man and get your deposit back. There is a certain charm to the process, as primitive as it seems, and of course after living with the dreadful waste in America one hopes they never get hooked on excessive packaging and throwaway containers.

    My ward from the Education for Democracy orientation—the girl who was having health problems and whom I brought into town with me to go into the hospital—got out of the hospital over the weekend and called me. We agreed to meet on Monday at lunch downtown. She needed a place to crash and so is staying with me. Her name is Joadie Newcomb, she is from Nova Scotia, she is 26, a playwright, and I am enjoying having her here. I cooked for her and another orphan Monday and Tuesday nights, then fed them leftovers last night (Wednesday) because I was invited to a dinner party.

    It was exciting to get dressed up and go out. The hosts were Nancy and Dan Painter. He is the American Army attaché. We had made friends on the phone via Lynne and

A.J. Land. They have a big beautiful house and the dinner was elegant. There were some Czech guests, two Brits and four Americans, including the cultural attaché who works with the EfD program. We had a long visit about the program.

I have gone into the EfD office everyday to start establishing a presence there, and I am telling everyone I meet that I am taking over the American part of the administration. It remains to be seen how easy this will be when Grady Lloyd actually takes his leave.

It is so cold here that it is beyond cold. Right now it is snowing. I have developed a passionate attachment to my boots, my earmuffs, my gloves and coat. If anything happened to any one of them I would simply go to the airport and fly home.

I finally talked to Prince Schwartzenberk, Havel's chief of staff, on the telephone, and I have a date to meet him next week.

I met a man from Houston at the ticket window at the National Theatre. We are going to go to the opera together. I was buying tickets to see "King Lear." The tickets were $1 apiece. Opera tickets are $2. It is no wonder these people are so poor.

―――――――――――

[The third op-ed piece sent to the Express–News follows.]

"THE CLIFF DWELLER"

"After an adulthood spent globetrotting, the contemplation of spending five months in one of the grand old capitals of Europe seemed deliciously but manageably exciting. Right? Wrong. Prague is one of the grand old capitals, it is delicious, it is exciting, but it is not always manageable. To be more precise, perhaps it is manageable but my reactions to it are not.

"Prague is the most gorgeous slum you will every see. It is dirty, dreary, dank, dreadful and tacky — on the inside. On the outside it is an outrageously beautiful architectural confection.

"Flower shops, shoe shine stands and drugstores are housed in buildings of such antiquity and beauty that the Conservation Society would blow a decade's budget to preserve just one of them. Yet leave the street and step through the door of any one of them to find someone's office, for instance, and you might as well be in the South Bronx or, more accurately, in pre-war Eastern Europe.

"The fact that everything is sadly dingy and poor-looking prompts one to wonder how these attractive, otherwise civilized people could have settled for so little for so long. Obviously it was an evolutionary process. It would not be like taking someone in, say, Kansas City and making them live in Moscow suddenly. But that is what happens to expatriates like me, and it is a thought-provoking process.

"After spending the first three weeks in country in rural Czechoslovakia, I have now become a householder right in the middle of Prague. I have a cozy, comfortable, warm, safe apartment in a building which, if you walked into it in San Antonio or New York City, you would call a slum. The neighborhood is nice, the shops are good, the transportation is excellent and the location is handy. But when I enter my building I think to myself, I hope my mother never sees this.

"An American friend who has done advanced Slavic studies both here and in Moscow says he wishes everyone could see Moscow first and then come here. He is amused as he watches the various little shocks register on me with each new experience. His lesson is that the Czechs have it good compared to the Russians, but this only helps me in a remote intellectual sense because my relativity "relates" in the opposite direction, that is toward the great wealth of the United States. It is this relativity that I must transcend in order to burrow successfully into this society.

"Here are some observations from a newly created Prague householder. One goes to the grocery store and waits in line until a shopping cart becomes available. One does not enter without a basket. Same for the vegetable stores and department stores. The other system is, one enters the drugstore/butcher/fruit stand/delicatessen and simply waits in line to be helped by the clerk, no baskets involved. And don't forget to take your own bags — there are no others.

"Two excellent aspects of the city: the transportation system, and the prices. The prices make you want to cry. It costs 4 cents to ride the metro. It costs $1 to go to the theatre. It costs $2 to go to the opera. It cost me 7 whole dollars to fill a grocery basket the other day. It costs $6 a day to rent a car if you are a Czech, $45 if you are a foreigner. Now that makes sense. Why should these struggling people subsidize me?

"The subway system is very good if you don't mind heights. The Russians built it deep and the escalators are long, steep and fast. The trams (electric streetcars) actually run on schedule and go everywhere. Taxis are cheap and plentiful, at least while it's below freezing and there are no tourists around. One drove me 20 minutes across town and charged me $4. He had a country music tape playing that was like a stab in the heart of my homesickness.

"Everyday something scary happens. Everyday something serendipitous happens. Expatriation is not for the fainthearted. To describe what happens when you are being tested, provoked and excited everyday I think back to those Walt Disney movies of my childhood like "The Living Desert" where the camera was speeded up to show a blossom become a flower, an egg crack open to become a lizard, a rainfall create a carpet of grass.

"The camera inside me is speeded up, everything is cracking open and I hope everything is blossoming. It's a great life if you don't weaken."

Saturday, 9 February 1991
Prague, Czechoslovakia

Dear Ones,

This is going to be a non-newsy running compendium of unrelated trivia about life here in Prague. I will try to finish it up before it totally gags us all.

Item: I do all my laundry by hand. Usually I throw it in the bathtub with myself when I take a bath. The definition of dingy is going to be my clothes after being hand washed for five months.

Item: The river is full of ice. The gulls stand around on the ice floes distractedly pecking at themselves, but the swans continue to swim in the channels between the ice. It makes you cold just to look at them.

The bird butcher shop sells duck, goose, and pheasant, as well as chicken. The meat butcher shop sells pork and a variety of mish-mashed and mostly sickening looking sausage concoctions, but rarely beef.

The trams are dingy, but they win the heart for being always on time and going everywhere you want to go. It costs 4c to ride but no one ever checks for tickets. Sometimes when I am riding the tram, looking out the window like a little orphan girl, I remember when mother and I saw Governor Clements's stepson Jim Bass on a bus in Xian, China. There was something inexpressibly poignant about seeing that sweet young Texas face through the dirty windows of the bus, surrounded by all the dark foreign heads. My visage through the dirty windows of a Prague tram is not nearly so poignant since I look like everyone else.

Mother asked me, do you look like everyone else, or can they tell you are different? I said I look like everyone else. But I was slightly mistaken: I am the only person in Czechoslovakia who wears dark glasses.

The standard which I apply to everything is, what would Wilson think of this? Wilson is our ranch foreman. Particularly when I am in the subway, which is dug so deep in the earth that hell could not be much further.

I listen to the news on the BBC, and buy the International Herald Tribune and Manchester Guardian everyday, and buy Time and Newsweek when I find them. I read everything cover to cover, I am so starved for news without television. The news is mostly about the Gulf war but people here are far more concerned about Russia.

We sleep on linen sheets under comforters with damask duvets. The linens in this little apartment look like they belong in a palace.

The b.o. is palpable in public places. It is deodorantless armpit/unwashed clothes/cigarette smoke/dirty hair b.o. Sometimes it is rather sexy.

I stick relentlessly to my grooming schedule and grooming chores, almost in defiance of the way everyone else looks and smells. No one knows how well groomed I am, because I am dressed like an Eskimo just like the next person.

Speaking of the way people look, I find the Czechs very good looking. I fall in love several times a day. The women can be stunningly beautiful. No one is fat. The adolescents are adorable. People dress well, though in clothes of poor quality.

The National Theatre is beautiful, but it is a difficult theatre in which to be a member of the audience. It is a horseshoe-shaped well, not an expanding well but a straight up and down well. It is small, so the audience sits up the walls, so to speak. On my first two trips I have sat literally eight levels above the stage. If you dropped your program over the rail it would achieve enough speed to decapitate someone in the orchestra section.

One of the aspects of the architectural delights of Prague is its profile, its roofs. It has fascinating exotic roofs.

Carl Embry at the Art Institute taught me perspective. Here is the perspective from my side of the river: wet cobblestones; bare black branches of trees with snow frosting; the river full of ice and birds; the ancient shapes of buildings on the far side; and the roofs, their shapes undisguised by their uniform covering of snow.

I am in love with the city but I am shocked by it.

Sunday, 10 February 1991
Prague, Czechoslovakia

Dear Ones,

It occurred to me that I never mentioned that I did not drive to Germany after all. Stephen decided he did not want to spend the money to send me. I was not heartbroken; it would have been a hard trip. I know you all were wondering.

For the first time since I arrived four weeks ago, for the past two mornings I have not awakened in a state of panic and despair. The panic and despair always went away as soon as I arose and started moving around, but it was a horrible way to start the day.

What helped me over it were two things: one, I started a journal, a private journal just for me, not for you and not for the newspaper. Two, I decided I would go stir crazy waiting to see how my administrative position with Education for Democracy shook out, and I have applied for other teaching jobs. I realized that my low grade depression was from not being in control, from having to wait for something to happen. Taking some initiative instantly made me feel better.

Everything else is fine. I love the city—it's beautiful and easy to travel around in. I love my apartment and my neighborhood. And my EfD orphan, Joadie Newcomb, who came to crash with me for a couple of nights has moved in, so I am not alone. It's fun to have a room mate.

Thursday and Friday I drifted into downtown to go by EfD headquarters, buy the newspapers, and go by the IEWSS offices. I take the subway in and the tram home, and I always carry a bag because I shop constantly for food. Thursday night I cooked for us.

Friday night Joadie and I went to have dinner at the apartment of one of the doctors who cared for her in the hospital when she was so ill a few weeks ago. He is a gynecologist, probably in his late 30's, a bachelor, and wants to date her. We took the subway to the end of the line, he met us on the platform and walked us another ten minutes to his building. It was the usual dreary building and his apartment was pitiful. Coming out of a culture that honors people with his kind of education, I found it shocking. I thought, boy, I'd like to see the gynecologists I know live like this! Much less their wives. We cooked a chicken and some spaghetti and drank a bottle of wine, then it was back through the dark to the subway, home on the subway and back through the dark to our own slum.

Yesterday for the first time it seemed a tiny bit warmer. We got bundled up and went sightseeing around downtown and up to the castle. After a couple of hours we stopped for coffee and pastries and then split up—Joadie to go meet the teacher whose job she's taking over, and I to go home to change to go downtown to meet Paige Alexander and her fiancé, Steve Grand. They both are here doing projects for the Charter 77 Foundation, and the people at the Foundation in New York had given me their names. Paige is from Atlanta and her father is Elliott Levitas' best friend.

We met at 5:00 p.m. on the platform at a specified subway station downtown, went to a really nice place for dinner and had salad, steak and French fries, then went to the National Theatre to see "Richard III" (in English). We were in the topmost gallery above the light fixtures. There was nothing above us but the friezes. Someone was in our seats so we had to sit on the steps of the aisle. The play was fascinating—it was done in modern dress with people in tuxedos and army uniforms, but the first act lasted two hours and our backs had given out by then so we left and went across the street to a coffee house and ate ice cream.

Paige and Steve were both wonderfully bright and fun to talk to. They are in their 20's. Her project has to do with charities and non-profits, and is funded by the Rockefeller Brothers Fund. He is writing a dissertation on labor in Czechoslovakia. But they are both attached to Charter 77.

This morning Joadie and I have cleaned house and we are waiting for my favorite taxi driver to come get us to go find two dissidents to whom I have an introduction, but who do not have phones. More later....

(Two days later) We found the dissidents' apartments but not them. One of them, Jiri Wolf, I'm told was a cellmate of Havel's. His roommate and his dog greeted us and said he was "downtown." I left him a note and he later called me. He is going to call me again when he has a friend with him who speaks better English. We were interested to go to their different neighborhoods, and decided our neighborhood must be pretty nice. Also, the very slum–like appearance of the entrance of this building is quite common. I have yet to walk into a building, even an office building, that does not look like something in the South Bronx or Dresden after the fire bombing. Other peoples' buildings are even worse than ours, with sinks in the hall and trash cans right inside the front door. Even Tim Whipple, who moved into a 16th century building in Mala Strana—a beautiful baroque building with a great stag over the door—has dark cold halls and, in his case, a toilet down the hall and outside. I could not handle that.

Sunday night we went to see "King Lear" at the National Theatre, sitting again in the belfry as I had the night before. I rented opera glasses this time (16c).

Yesterday, Monday, I was all over downtown on foot, talking to the EfD people and applying for other jobs. Of the various jobs available I shall probably take one and start teaching next week.

Last night Tim took me to a gorgeous restaurant in Mala Strana which, based on the prices, has already been privatized. It was French and cost us $73/U.S. a piece. He was going to take me last night but when I saw the prices I insisted on paying for myself. It was good food but in light of how little one has to pay for food elsewhere the prices seemed definitely skewed.

The prices are a constant source of pain and amusement. Pain for them that so little value is put on things, and amusement for us, that I can buy a jar of marmalade or a bag of frozen peas for 16c.

Apparently many of the business people who swooped in here after the Revolution hoping to make a killing have gone home defeated by the difficulties inherent in such a bureaucratic and quaint system. The Czechs are starting to privatize but they are not selling to foreigners.

Tomorrow I am going to the castle to see Prince Schwartzenberk; that should be interesting. I am staying in today to do some writing. It is 0° but I am warm and cozy.

I was telling Tim last night that one of the reasons I left San Antonio was because I was craving the freedom of anonymity, but here in Prague I am not just anonymous, I am invisible, and maybe that was overshooting the mark.

✢ ✢ ━━━━━━ ✢ ✢

Sunday, 17 February 1991
Prague, Czechoslovakia

Dear Ones,

It is Sunday, it is cold, Joadie and I have done our house work, I am cooking beans, we are going to the park later, and two friends are coming for dinner. A nice day. Marred only by the fact that I have an inner ear infection and have to move gingerly to keep from blacking out. I secretly thought I was going crazy when the dizziness started a few days ago, so it has been an ironic kind of relief to decide that I am actually only sick.

Tuesday the 12th I finished two letters to you all and wrote my 4th newspaper column. Late in the afternoon I took the column to the IEWSS office to fax it to San Antonio, and to hook up with Vasil, one of the staff people there, to take the rental car back that I had rented for Krzysztof a couple of weeks ago when his car broke down on the highway. I followed Vasil to the rental car place, then he brought me back into downtown so I could go to a meeting the Canadian founder of EfD was having with a bunch of Prague muckety-mucks he had invited to sit on an advisory board. The meeting was conducted in Czech and I was hungry so I left and came home and had a cold supper by myself. I do not know where Joadie was.

Wednesday morning I put on something nice (mostly I go around in pants and sweaters–it's too cold for skirts) and went to Prague Castle, the seat of government, to visit Prince Schwartzenberk. He and his family had been living in exile in Vienna for decades but they always supported the dissidents and when Havel asked him to return he did. It was snowing as I walked across the Castle grounds, and there was such a hush over everything it felt like there was no government going on at all. I got through security and found the Prince, who clicked his heels and kissed my hand. After a few pleasantries I told him I would like to interview him for my newspaper, which I did, and in about 25 minutes I was back out in the snow. He's a funny looking man, terribly aristocratic with a sort of lizard-eyed way of looking at you. I found him personally repulsive but I was still impressed. I left with him a copy of Larry McMurtry's book *Leaving Cheyenne* to give to President Havel, or as I said, "to add to the mountain of gifts I am sure your President receives." I did not want him to think I was so naive as to actually believe Havel would ever see my book.

That night I went back to Nancy and Dan Painter's house—he is the American military attaché—for family style dinner around the kitchen table. That was nice, to get to be family with someone and eat their cooking.

Thursday I went downtown to get instructions on my teaching job, which starts Monday. Details to follow, after I have a few days of it under my belt. It was snowing like a sumbitch when I got off at my subway stop going home, and I was covered with snow when I finally reached shelter. It snows all the time. When it finally quit late in the afternoon, Joadie and I walked to a huge park that starts about two blocks from here and spent a delightful hour tramping through the winter wonderland and watching the kids sled down the hills. The dogs were crazed with the fun of the snow and activity and were tearing around playing king of the snowdrift. It was enchanting. Home to a good dinner and an evening of reading. I am reading Alice Walker's *Meridian*.

Friday morning I went to meet a friend of a friend of Bernard Lifshutz, a man named Jan Goldscheider, at the Intercontinental Hotel. His earlier appointment had appeared late so we agreed to try again on Monday. From there I went to meet my new friend, Michael Zargarov, "under the horse" in Wenceslas Square. Michael is from Houston, and he is the one I met at the ticket window at the National Theatre. He is a darling irrepressible guy who is here teaching. He teaches at a newspaper, and he took me to lunch with some of his "students" at a vegetarian restaurant. Lunch cost 50c—for both of us! After lunch we walked around downtown doing errands, then jumped on a tram and went to the American Embassy to register our whereabouts with the consular section. I stuck my head in to the USIS office to see if Tom Hull, the head of it, was there. I had met him at the Painters. He was there so we all visited at some length, mostly about the problems at EfD. He introduced me to the cultural attaché, who introduced me to the Consul, and while all this was going on the television was going with the news from Baghdad about Saddam Hussein's offer to pull out of Kuwait, so we all got momentarily excited about that. Finally we left and Michael and I parted on the street with his inviting me and Joadie to a party at his apartment that night.

I went home and cooked supper, then we bundled up and took the subway four stops to Michael's neighborhood, found his building, climbed the stairs to his apartment, stayed for one hour and left.

The party depressed me because it was all people who had made a home or found a home here, and I have what may be an irrational feeling that people who love it here and want to stay are misfits. Many of them are young, so the stakes for them are still relatively low; in any case they haven't had my 45 years in which to build a full life complicated by many friends and loved ones which one perforce must leave behind in order to have such an adventure as this. I do not like to be around the misfits. Either it strikes too close to home, or it makes me feel inadequate because I do not love being here. Anyway, I was depressed all day yesterday.

Yesterday was not a bad day, actually. We walked downtown (it took 45 minutes) and went to the movies to see "Valmont." It was a new adventure, to go to the movies. You get assigned seats. We did not know that, and just plunked ourselves down in some good seats. We could not figure out why other people were climbing over each other to sit in not very good seats. The movie was in English with Czech subtitles. I was not feeling too good so I lay down for awhile when we got home. Then I took a duck and some other fixings over to Tim's apartment, and he and I cooked for Paige and Steve. None of them had met. We had a good dinner but I was the first to leave.

Everyone in Czechoslovakia is sick, so I guess it's my turn. As long as I do not pass out in public from dizziness I think I can keep on plugging. Today the thermometer reads 3c, which is warmer than usual.

[The fourth op-ed piece sent to the Express–News follows.]

"RELATIVE VALUE"

"Some artists believe squalor is a desirable condition for breeding the kind of nervous energy necessary to creation. Certainly one cannot picture an obsessive neatnik stopping straightening long enough to write a novel. As an example of the latter, I am fascinated by constituents of the former. How do they reconcile squalor with their assumed interest in truth and beauty? How can they thrill to a field of wildflowers, then go home and burrow happily back into their dump? Why don't they take offense when their eye lights on a mess?

"Prague is messy. It is gorgeous, but it is messy. One thrills to the profusion of public art, the riotous wealth of architectural design, the ancient narrow streets, the great boulevards, the charming cobblestones. Yet internally, people live in squalor, or rather most people live in some degree of squalor. Including me.

"Vaclav Havel lives in a beat up looking old building. An old cellmate of his, Jiri Wolf, lives in an even more beat up building with sinks in the hall and trash cans inside the front door. An American friend who took some time and did some work to find himself a large permanent apartment lives in a 16th century building in a beautiful part of the city, but his toilet is not only not in his apartment, it is down the hall and outside. It is zero degrees here, by the way.

"I was the dinner guest of a Czech doctor, and I was profoundly touched by the poverty of his living arrangements. American doctors can be pretty self-congratulatory when it comes to living well, and there are many who think they maybe ought to live less well. But the basic reaction of this American was simply that this man surely must deserve more because of his accomplishments. It was a pure capitalist reaction to an abiding communist phenomenon: everyone is worth the same thing. Actually, the intelligentsia is worth less. Workers are worth more. Gad, how un-American!

"I was also the dinner guest of the American military attaché and his wife—good folks who have learned the language and make it a point to entertain Czechs and not just other diplomats. Now their house would fit right in to Terrell Hills or Olmos Park. It felt good to be in a big, nice house, but it felt wrong, too, and I was glad to get back to my proletarian neighborhood where no one knows I'm different.

"It is fascinating to be in a society where wealth simply doesn't seem to have a function. How do people measure themselves or each other in the marketplace? It might be comfortable to have that aspect of competition removed from human relationships, but removing it for purposes of taming the evils of selfishness and egocentrism also removes it as a natural goal or reward for superior behavior. If someone does a better job than the next person but gets no credit for it, then why bust a gut to do so well the next time? Just to be noble?

"On the other hand this appears to be a peaceful, non-warlike society with no visible crime. This makes it a nice place to live, particularly for nervous expatriates. But is it just a mediocre country that happens to have a stunning capital thanks to centuries of historical collusion? One month does not make me an expert. In fact one month of exposure has only broadened the mysteries—the more you know, the more you know you don't know...

"The National theatre is a magnificent jewel which may be the most uncomfortable theatre I have ever sat in. The orchestra section is a horseshoe with perhaps 200 seats in it. The rest of the audience sits up the walls, which are vertical and have seven levels of balconies. The chairs are small, the foot space is nonexistence and the drop to the stage is daunting. One wonders how 19th century ladies and their skirts made it to their seats. It sure is purty, though!"

[The fifth column also fell in this time frame and follows.]

"THE PRINCE IN EXILE"

"Snow was falling thickly, and with it the hush snow brings, as I made my way across the grounds of Prague Castle, the seat of government for the Czech and Slovak Federal Republic. My destination was the balcony, the porte-cochere under which was the entrance to the secretariat of the office of President Havel. Across the plaza from the lavender 18th century building loomed the Cathedral of St. Vitus, so awesome the rare tourist group out in the snow simply slammed on the brakes at the first sight of it. I tried to keep my head straight in spite of the enchantment of it.

"Security in Czechoslovakia is a rather simple affair, even at the American Embassy, and it was no different as I went through the process of being on time for my appointment with Prince Karl Schwartzenberk, President Vaclav Havel's chief of staff. Prince Schwartzenberk, as his name might suggest, is an aristocrat, and has lived out of the country for some decades. At Havel's request he returned last year to his ancestral home to assume the prodigious effort of running Havel's office. Even though Prince Schwartzenberk and his family had supported the dissidents from their exile, it was nonetheless an interesting choice on Havel's part: the bluest of blue bloods running the secretariat of a revolutionary government.

"He clicked his heels and kissed my hand and said bluntly, what can I do for you? When I told him I was in his country to teach English with the Education for Democracy program he said, 'good, they need to learn to speak English.' I gave him a sixty-second rundown on the program and, noticing his eyes glazing over, I changed the subject and asked him if I could interview him for my hometown newspaper. He perked up at that.

"The prices of things are so astonishing to foreigners that the first question that came to mind had to do with food prices and the new inflation. Food prices have been allowed to float to some extent even though everyone is still making the same wage, approximately $120 a month. Editorializing like a novice, I asked him how the people were taking the inflation in food prices, and he replied, 'with surprising understanding.' I then asked, 'when will you free wages, just before the riots?', and he smiled faintly and said, 'precisely,' then launched into an understandable explanation of why wages had to be tied to privatization.

"Privatization is nature's way of humbling the most formidable Eastern bloc economist or politician, and is the great mystery of how these countries will look in the future. They are damned if they do and damned if they don't with regard to foreign investment. Even local investment is viewed with suspicion because who is supposed to have accumulated enough money on $1500 a year to be able to buy anything? Either the foreigners own you or the former Party apparatchiks own you. Mr. Schwartzberg's last word on the freeing of wages was they won't be freed until the last moment because inflation must be avoided. I thought of all the housewives I see everyday looking in shop windows in consternation at the prices of their beloved staples.

"At the risk of sounding patronizing I said I myself was embarrassed to pay such low prices for food. His reply: why should you be embarrassed? You live in the system, so you should pay the same as everyone else. I let it go.

"I mentioned I had spent some weeks with the Institute for East-West Security Studies at their castle in Stirin, and that one of the things we had done while I was there was interview some of the neighboring mayors. I mentioned I was surprised that the mayors of these little towns were full time paid employees of the state. I said mayors of small and even big towns were not paid in the United States. His reply: if they are doing their job properly, they deserve to be paid.

"Finally I said I had been amazed and amused that communism was still in effect, and his response, through what I was now beginning to recognize as the grandfather of Long Island lockjaw, was: we've got to have some government, so we have the old government until we have the new government. I thought, may the new Ministers have the sheer force of will to wrest the government from the old Ministers.

"An interesting new friend of mine made the observation that what was amazing was not that they had finally made their revolution after forty years but that they had made it at all. The sheer weight of poverty and communism on the land, the people, the infrastructure and the way of life will not be easy to wiggle out from under.

"But high on a hill overlooking the capital sit a playwright and a prince trying to do it in the most humane yet concrete way devisable. Perhaps their unusual marriage speaks best to the task at hand."

✦ ✦ —————— ✦ ✦

Saturday, 23 February 1991
Prague, Czechoslovakia

Dear Ones,

I finally started what I came here to do, and that is teach. It's fun—I like it. I had an easy week of it because I was working with the teacher whose classes I am taking over. Next week will tell the tale. I have 3 classes—one advanced and two beginners. There are about 15 enrolled in each class but they do not all always come. Two classes are in one location and the third is in another. Both locations are downtown in the heart of things, which is nice. In both locations one enters the building thinking it must be abandoned or a flop house, and then there are these nice classrooms, and retired factotums with hot plates to fix coffee or tea at the breaks. I am finally getting over the shock of how squalid the buildings are on the inside, and now it does not faze me to walk into a dark, cold, dirty lobby full of trash cans and stuff piled around.

I have told the students about myself (not everything) and they have told me about themselves. I have to concentrate like mad to speak in a way the beginners can understand; the advanced class is really good, and will be fun. They all clearly loved the other teacher, a 23-year-old Canadian woman, and I could see why after following her around all week. She was good folks, and has left me with a legacy I shall be glad to have. I teach four days a week, Monday– Thursday, four hours a day.

The old news is that I am still suffering from my inner ear infection. The good news is that I am getting used to it. It only bothers me at night and when I arise in the morning, and when I lie on the floor to do my exercises. That is quite an adventure—I do not know if I am doing my crunches on the floor or the ceiling. As long as I am erect I am all right, although I sort of have to close my eyes on the escalators in the subway.

Early in the week I just lay low, because at that point I also did not feel too good, and stayed in at night and ate soup and leftovers. I met my classes every day, and ran my traps around downtown every day, but just did not feel real outgoing. On Monday morning I went back to the Intercontinental Hotel to meet Jan Goldscheider; our meeting the past Friday had been aborted. He is an appealing, sparkly-eyed, avuncular, 70-year-old worldly Jew. His only child, a daughter, works at the hotel. At his request I had a visit with her because her 14-year-old daughter is applying to Concord Academy for prep school. I am going to meet the daughter and talk to her in the next week or two. I told Jan I needed him to find me a boyfriend. He got this wonderful misty look in his eye but then decided he was too old. The next day he called and invited me to dinner with him and two other men the following night.

I put on real clothes and shoes (not Eskimo gear) and went with them to the Diplomat Club. They were all old, which I love; one was a businessman from Zurich who used to own F.A.O. Schwartz, and the other was an artist here in Praha. They were all golfers, and have played golf all over the world. I have given up trying to understand where they get the money. Jan is the business agent for various British interests. The artist invited me to his studio, and I went to see him a couple of days later. He used to do all the graphics for Laterna Magika, and said he would go with me to see it.

Friday morning I went to find Jarda, my favorite driver. He works out of the Park Hotel, which is three blocks from here. My goal was to track down a person in charge of a nice dormitory which Education for Democracy wants to use. I found Jarda, and we finally found the person after several false starts and an hour and a half of Jarda's time (he lets me guess what it's worth, as he usually does not turn on the meter—I am sure I always over-guess). Jarda has driven for the Barenblats, and he drove for Peggy and Lowry Mays last fall. Today he asked me who was richer, Mr. Barenblat or Mr. Mays?! Then I mentioned to him that I had become friends with Jan Goldscheider and he said 'the Jude who plays golf' and I said yes and he said he knew him and had played golf with him. He told me that Jan had been in Auschwitz; I was stricken. Later in the day when I saw the artist friend, Jiri Trnka, I mentioned this conversation and he said he was in a concentration camp, too, and was jailed again by the communists in the 50's.

I feel like a complete nothing in the face of these people's history. I get all dramatic over having broken my arm or lost my father, but that is like a mosquito on the side of an elephant compared to the terribleness others have suffered. I really go limp and speechless in the presence of these survivors.

I also put Jarda on the project of finding me a boyfriend. When I said to him, 'Jarda, I need a boyfriend', he looked horrified, put his hand on his chest and said 'I not enough.' He is very funny and speaks understandable but fractured English.

We are eating well in this little household. I keep wondering why I have not gotten fat, but I think it is because I walk so much, climb so many stairs, carry so many heavy groceries such long distances and work so hard to stay warm that I burn off the calories. Actually I am eating just what I should be (oatmeal, fruit, yogurt, etc.) but I have a drink every night and eat sweets—filling the void, so to speak. Along about 5:00 p.m. I am torn between a pastry or a scotch. Usually I have the scotch first and then the pastry, with dinner in between.

Joadie and I have been ships in the night this week, but tonight we are having another teacher over for dinner. We do not know her but she sounds charming on the phone.

Tomorrow will be devoted to housework, grooming and lesson plans. I hope I can figure out how to do what I have to do by myself. It will not be the first time.

◆◆────────◆◆

Saturday, 2 March 1991
Prague, Czechoslovakia

Dear Ones,

I faced my classes by myself this past week, and I enjoyed it. I do not know if they did, but they seemed to respond positively. The first day, Monday, after standing before students for four straight hours, I was so tired I could barely put one foot in front of the other. By the end of the week it did not seem so tiring. On Tuesday–Thursday, I teach only 8–10 a.m. I have to get up at 5:30 a.m. to get there, but when it's over I have a whole day for errands, shopping, reading, writing and lesson plans. But I am zonked by the end of the day.

Tuesday after my 8–10, I walked to the Diplomat Club (where Jan Goldscheider had taken me for dinner) to talk to the manager about teaching English in his club—to his staff or whomever. He said he would poll his people to see if and when they could or would do it, and he invited me for dinner on Friday night.

The Diplomat Club is in Old Town, where the streets are narrow and cobbled and if you blinked you could be back in the 14th century. When I came out of the shady, medieval, tunnel-like streets and onto the Old Town Square, playing on the Square was a Dixieland jazz band. People had gathered to listen and to drop money in the hat. I must have stood there for 15 minutes in a state of enchantment, my mind pulled every which way by the evocative American music being played on the stage setting of the incredibly beautiful, colorful square. The singer of the band had a deep scratchy voice like Satchmo, and he sang black-style but in Czech. It was wonderful.

The weather has improved—i.e., it is not so cold and the streets and squares, formerly deserted, have become rivers and seas of people. I do not like it. I want my city back. Gad I'm schizophrenic! Half the time I hate this place, half the time I love it. I do not ever actually hate it. I just get tired from it. It is physically demanding to live like a poor person.

I go to Wenceslas Square every day to buy the papers. I buy the Herald Tribune and The Guardian (a great paper which gives the European point of view, which p.s. is different from the American). It costs me 70 crowns a day ($2.80). This is a small fortune to most people. Yesterday I bought the papers at my usual stand and stood there in the middle of the square, people swirling around me, reading about the end of the war with tears running down my cheeks. Being so far away, and with no TV, the war has been (blessedly) remote to us, but I have read every word in every paper everyday about it, and I was touched as much by its actual end as by the unreality of my remoteness.

Sometimes I have sensations which are akin to being stoned. Last night I took the tram to a stop near the Diplomat Club, then walked in the dark along the river embankment on the cobblestones past the dark ancient buildings and doorways and passageways and then turned in to Old Town with my footsteps echoing. I was cursing, thinking I would rather be in a taxi, when all of a sudden I started laughing thinking, this is so glamorous: I am walking along in my black trench coat like a John LeCarré spy in this movie setting, the only sound my footfalls. I am in a fantasy and all I am is mad I'm not in a taxi!

Wednesday was Joadie's birthday. Before I knew that I had invited Vasil and Amy from the Institute staff for dinner, so I made it extra nice and bought a cake, and that is how we celebrated. 5:30 a.m. Thursday came awfully early, and I felt tired all day, especially since Thursday I have to lay in groceries to last until Monday or Tuesday. Friday the shops are too crowded and Saturday and Sunday they are closed. So I spend two or three hours Thursday on foot carrying groceries. I just buy everything that looks good because with these prices money is no object. Someday I am going to list what I pay for various things. It is so ridiculous. It takes me two weeks to go through $100 if I am extravagant.

Late Thursday afternoon after I had recovered from my marketing, I went to meet one of my advanced students, a woman lawyer named Irena, and one of her partners, a man named George (Jiri in Czech). As usual we met in a certain subway station, and went from there to a restaurant for drinks and supper. George wants to build a restaurant and Irena wanted me to talk to him. It was fun to be with bright, professional English speaking Czechs, and our conversation ranged far and wide. They want to do other things, so I think I have some nice new friends.

And none to soon, because I was starting to feel bored. This is a feeling normally alien to me, and I was concerned about it. I think it is a function of having a limited social life, a nonexistent romantic life, and no travel plans to look forward to. I have never dealt with any of these factors before, much less all at once.

Friday I substitute taught a class of beginners at the request of my employer. I work for the Canadian Club, and one of their teachers had gone off for the weekend. Her class was not as animated as mine are.

Friday night I dined at the Diplomat Club with the manager and the general director and his lady friend. They were all attractive and full of fun, and I had a good time. This morning, Saturday, we are doing housework, laundry, desk work, nails, etc., so that we can play all day tomorrow with my cute friend Michael. We are going sightseeing.

My secretary in Washington sent me a big envelope of mail and stuff, which I pored over and savored.

Joadie has put together a theatre company and I am one of her actresses! We are going to do "Crimes of the Heart." I will play the repressed older sister.

Next week I am starting to have root canal work done by an English speaking dentist at the diplomatic hospital. This should be an adventure. Every one complains about their teeth here. Probably the heavy metal in the water eating away at our enamel.

Joadie and I laugh because after teaching we have a tendency to continue to speak in the same slow precise way we speak to our students. Last night I was introduced to four Englishmen and because I could barely understand them, I noticed I was speaking to them in the slow deliberate way I would to a Czech.

The Czech people are really good looking. I admire them from afar, and walk around with a kind of shy downcast air because I don't want them to know I am a foreigner. This ploy fails me in the shops, however, when I am reduced to pointing and other forms of sign language. I do not want them to know I have money when they are suffering so many problems. Their average wage is $100 a month, and I can waste that much in my sleep. But within the confines of reason I am trying to live like them. I just refuse to scrimp on food. It is too vital to our sense of well being.

Friday, 8 March 1991
Prague, Czechoslovakia

My Dears,

Prague beckons and repels. Last Sunday I let it beckon me, and spent the day with Michael sightseeing in new places. We met in a subway station (where else?) and trained upriver to Vysehrad, the ancient fortress of the very first Slavs. The buildings in the ruins are different ages starting with about a thousand years old and getting younger. In the late 19th century a cemetery was established for poets, musicians and artists. The composers Smetana and Dvorak are there, for instance, and like many old graveyards it was beautiful, spooky and fascinating. The day was cold, grey and slightly damp—a good day for a cemetery.

We stopped for a coffee at the Forum Hotel, then went to the Technical Museum, which we loved. We spent over an hour in the Transportation Hall looking at ancient Audis, Mercedes, and Russian cars, trains and planes. Then to a wing on cameras, after which my back gave out. We left the museum and walked across the street, drawn by an old gazebo style pavilion. Inside we found the oldest carousel in Europe, 110 years old, and it looked it. The horses were covered with real (albeit moth-eaten) horse hair and saddles, and the music box would fetch a fortune at Sotheby's. We were hypnotized, and if the music had not been so repetitive we would have spent longer musing over this ancient contraption.

Over the weekend I had spent several hours in consultation on the telephone with Ann Gardner, the founder of Education for Democracy/USA, who lives in Mobile, Alabama. From these conversations the new shape of EfD/USA began to make itself manifest, with me "in charge." She has severed her relationship with the Canadian EfD people, who ran the Prague office along with her man Grady Lloyd in a not very organized fashion. She is coming here March 16th, at which point it will become clearer just exactly what I have to do. I want to keep my classes because I enjoy them so much, and I will probably keep two out of three.

On Monday morning I went to the EfD office, now manned only by Canadians, and had a little heart-to-heart in an extremely open and friendly way with them about who was going to do what, and received their cooperation. Made some other stops on the way to my classes—everything downtown is within walking distance of everything else, so I go to EfD, post office, newsstand, bakery, banana store, Institute, post-card stand—and window shop constantly to see if any new food has come in. One day I carried a cauliflower around all day because I saw one in a window and veered in. I always carry two canvas bags, one full of books and teaching material and one full of whatever treasures I encounter. I am so physically tired from always being on foot carrying things that I am a basket case at the end of the day.

Monday night I went to a surprise birthday party for Paige. Steve had arranged it at the flat of two women friends. The directions were, take the subway to the end of the line, then take bus #x 4 stops, then walk 3 blocks. I called Jarda and he took me and picked me up. I thought, I am too old for this poor public transportation bit in the dead of night, so I spent $4 and took a taxi. I love the public transportation all day, though. It is incredibly good.

The birthday party consisted of 14 people in their 20's and me. They are so sure of themselves. I guess they do not know any better but I surely admire them. One thing I have learned is that people without homes make better expatriates than people like me. Most of the happy un-neurotic people here grew up in military or diplomatic families. I had fun at the party—I always have a good time—but left early as I had to get up early for class the next morning. Oh, these women had broccoli. Everyone who walked in the kitchen said, where did you get the broccoli! We are so pitiful.

Tuesday I taught early in the morning, then met Jarda after lunch to go to the dentist. He was going to wait for me (on a taxi meter it costs about $1 per hour to wait), and the appointment was at 1:45 p.m. at this fancy hospital sort of far from downtown. The dentist was in the foreigners' wing. He spoke English, and put some stuff on my tooth to see if it would help before he committed to a root canal. He spoke English, so I asked him to show me to the ear doctor, which he did, and stuck around to translate and mediate my inner ear problem. The ear doctor could not see anything wrong, so he sent me upstairs to the neurologist (Jarda had come in and was with me at this point). The neurologist fooled around with me and sent me to X-Ray to have my neck X-rayed. By the time all that had been done it was after 4 and I was frantic to get home, but then we could not find our way out of the hospital. I got home at 4:40, threw supper on the stove, and Michael came at 5:00 to eat and go to the opera at 7.

The opera was "Don Giovanni" by W. A. Mozart. It premiered in Prague a couple of hundred years ago, and the quality and technique of the Prague Opera Company has apparently not improved much since then. The Smetana Opera House was a sight to behold, however, and worth the price of admission ($1.35 each, 8th row center) a hundred times over. Home on the subway with all the other opera-goers. I was pooped.

Wednesday I did the marketing, stood and taught for four straight hours, and had a nice quiet supper at home with Joadie. We sleep within two feet of each other but do not have a lot of just quiet eating, drinking and talking time together. She is only 27 so of course I dispense a lot of advice to her (mind you I like her and respect her) and tonight after hearing her talking to someone back home on the telephone I made a few helpful suggestions about how to deal with people and then said, "I'm going to get you raised yet." She laughed and said she was learning at the knee of the master. I said, yeah, I know how to run everyone's life but my own!

Thursday back up at 5:30 a.m. to get to my 8:00 a.m. class, then met the husband of one of my students for coffee. He is an artist, and an English businessman wants his designs for a T-shirt venture. I sat there dispensing advice on contract negotiations and intellectual property rights like I knew what I was doing. I would be arrested for fraud in the U.S. for practicing without a license but here I am a guru.

More marketing on the way home, then Jarda picked me up at 1:00 to take me out into the country to see Karstejn Castle—a medieval castle (14th century) built by the same "Charles" (Karlovo) of Charles Bridge, Charles Square and Charles University. If it is not called Charles-something it is called Vaclav (Wenceslas) something. If you can pronounce Karlovo and Vaclav you have got it made geographically. I had told Jarda I was sick of being always in the city and that I wanted to do something fun, so he took me to the castle, then delivered me downtown to teach a new class which never materialized. I killed two hours going to a department store (where I found a sympathetic person to help me figure out how to buy panty hose), by the Institute office and to the Canadian Club, then took the tube over to Prague 5 to have dinner with a couple from Maryland, Jan and Michele Klika. Jan works for my employer. He was born here. Michele is his miserable pregnant wife with two dirty-faced little boys, aged five and three, swirling around her feet in the kitchen of their messy flat. She is clearly hanging on for dear life, and I must say I was, too, after two and a half hours of chaos. We had a good dinner and I fled at 8:15 p.m. as Jarda had insisted on taking me home. I was so tired I could not put one foot in front of the other.

Every one talks about how tiring it is to live here. It is probably a function of doing everything by hand, on foot, in bad air, and with ones expatriation preying on one. I am not unhappy; in fact I would have to say I am in the positive quadrant of the graph. I love my teaching. I actively look forward to it. But it is strangely tiring—draining is probably the better word. Yet it appeals to my sense of drama, to my love of knowledge and to my abiding fascination with the language. It really is a perfect profession for me. I will keep that in mind when I have to decide what I want to be when I grow up.

Saturday, 9 March 1991
Prague, Czechoslovakia

Dear Ones,

I got up early this morning and wrote another column—my 6th. While I was fiddling around this semi-darkened flat I realized that I had neglected to mention in my letter of yesterday the resolution of my inner ear problems. I knew you all were waiting expectantly to know.

Well, it turns out I have vertigo. When the neurologist told me that I thought, no kidding. I knew I had vertigo every time I had to get on an escalator in the subway. But the source is not inner ear, it is a vertebra in my neck. So I start rehab next week, which will probably be with a chiropractor. I called mother and asked her to check with her chiropractor and also with Dr. Wagner to get their reactions, just to make sure I was not enjoying the ministrations of some voodoo doctor, and I felt relieved when she reported back they both had said it was a quite common phenomenon.

The other big piece of news that has occurred in the last eight hours is that Jarda brought us a television. It is an old black and white he had at home, and he is loaning it until summer. We get CNN early in the morning, at noon and at night. I wish we had had it during the war.

We are having a dinner party tonight, and I am spending the afternoon tomorrow with Irena, my lady lawyer student, and some of her friends. I am off now to meet a woman I do not know for coffee—another one of Liana Barenblat's contacts. I would still be groping around in the dark if it were not for Liana Barenblat.

[The sixth op-ed column sent to the Express–News follows.]

"STREET LIFE SPEAKS VOLUMES"

"The winter world is thawing out, and the narrow cobblestone streets and the great squares are becoming rivers and seas of people. Wenceslas Square, actually a great boulevard with wide sidewalks on either side and an island up the middle, looks at first glance like an impenetrable mass of humanity. It slopes up from the very heart of downtown to the foot of the National Museum, a typically wildly overdone, fabulously beautiful and extremely dirty landmark. Just below the Museum stands the famous statue of "good King Wenceslas" on his trusty steed. When someone says, 'meet me under the horse,' you know exactly where to go. The other place to meet is 'under the clock,' the astronomical clock which is a major attraction on the Old Town Square. Subway stations are also popular places to meet.

"Where more than one Czech stops to look in a window or browse over the periodicals at a makeshift stand, a crowd will soon gather. If Czechs see a clump of people, they gather. I think that if three people experimented by standing together peering in the same direction, they would soon have a crowd pushing to see over their shoulders. I have even seen people queue without looking to see what is being sold. This phenomenon has been explained as being the result of not being able to gather in the past and also not having anything worth looking at in the past.

"Perhaps the most important thing they have that is worth looking at is a free press. There are so many newspapers now that it is having an adverse effect on the book publishing business. They also have that old dark side of a free press, pornography. One goes to buy ones daily Herald Tribune and there on the same table smiling up at you are crotches selling toothpaste, movies and just themselves. There is no rhyme or reason to some of the things naked people are used to sell. There is no rhyme or reason to the fact that my favorite news vendor was selling margarine one day, either. Most civilized Westerners have been shamed by the women's liberation movement into understanding the destructiveness of pornography but women's liberation is a primitive concept here, so that tempering force does not exist.

"A police state does have the dubious virtue of making people terrified to commit crime, so this is a relatively law-abiding society. An example which floors me and the other expatriates is the fact that women leave their babies out on the sidewalk in their carriages while they go inside to shop. THEY LEAVE THEIR BABIES ON THE SIDEWALK! Most of the babies are infants asleep under piles of covers, but one day downtown there was a big baby sitting up in its carriage eating a piece of bread, and it was so cute that of course several people had gathered.

"Prague could use a pooper scooper law out in the neighborhoods. Dogs are always on leashes, and many wear muzzles, but their dear owners have not made the connection in their dog-loving minds that humans must use the sidewalks after their dogs do. There's lots of other 'stuff' on the sidewalks which attests to the health and attitudes of the people; suffice it to say you shouldn't walk to the subway if you have morning sickness. The other thing on the streets and sidewalks is dirt—plain ole dirt like you grow things in. I saw a street sweeper recently and thought, running that street sweeper is about as useful as trying to empty the ocean with a thimble.

"Life in Prague takes place on foot. The automobile traffic is so light you would have to work to get run over. Traveling on foot and by public transportation is both efficient and noble, but it is also tiring and time-consuming. One is physically tired at the end of the day just from being constantly erect and on the move, and usually carrying something. The other day I carried a cauliflower all over town because it was the first cauliflower I had seen in two months and I couldn't resist buying it.

"The Czech people are good-looking to this frankly Anglo-Saxon observer. They are snazzy, too, especially in winter with their pants tucked into their boots, mufflers wrapped dramatically and headbands across their foreheads and ears. The adolescents are adorable and all seem to be in love. But even in the middle of their smooching they stop to be courteous to older people on the trams and subways.

'People compete to give up their seats to older people, people with canes or babies. Yet there is an impersonal underlay of discourtesy in many transactions, and a definite lack of friendliness. There's no good ol' boy automatic trust in a stranger. One can hardly blame them after forty years of Soviet-style communism. Still, this expatriate would welcome a warm smile.

"A margarita wouldn't taste too bad, either!"

Saturday, 16 March 1991
Prague, Czechoslovakia

Dear Ones,

I was a busy bee this past week. Last Sunday afternoon I went to the house of my lady lawyer student friend to eat and visit. She had seemed rightly proud of the fact she had a whole house in a suburb—actually a small town incorporated into the city limits, but again it was one of these terribly shabby dwellings which they consider nice but which cause me to have to scramble around in my brain to adjust to. I always hope my face doesn't belie the kind of sad embarrassment I secretly feel for secretly having so much more than they. She and a friend fixed me a Slovakian dish of little squiggly potato dumplings tossed in hot bacon fat and covered with cheese and sour cream—everything so bad for me I was irrational for an hour afterward. The plan was to eat and then talk for six or seven hours. Visiting is a major form of entertainment, but I left at the end of the afternoon pleading that I had some writing to do.

Monday, I taught all afternoon, then met an English woman I didn't know named Hilary James for dinner. We had an introduction through a friend of a friend who thought we would like each other because we were both business women. Hilary is teaching management and marketing for some group here. We fell to like old friends and treated ourselves to an expensive ($20 ea.) dinner. I didn't have enough money so she paid and I am going to reciprocate by taking her to dinner next week. One of the things I liked about her was she was older than I. I have begun to feel like Methuselah after being around all these 20 year olds.

Tuesday I taught my early morning class, then fiddled around downtown before meeting another EfD teacher, Paula Schulz, "under the clock" (the famous astronomical clock in Old Town Square) at noon for lunch. My favorite Dixieland band was playing across from the clock so I got to listen to them for a minute. We lunched in a place nearby to discuss the possibility of her helping me with the administration of EfD. I had singled her out at the orientation in January because she was a calm, older good ole girl type who also happens to speak Czech. Home for a nap, then met Joadie at the opera to see "Madama Butterfly." Joadie had never been to an opera, so I thought this was a good one for starters. The Butterfly was good, and I cried at the end, but it was kind of weird because it was sung in Czech. The Smetana Opera House thrilled once again. To plagiarize Frank Lloyd Wright, it looks like the inside of a wedding cake.

Jarda was out of town so Wednesday morning he arranged to have another taxi driver take me out to the hospital for my first rehabilitation session on my neck for my vertigo. The doctor who saw me this time took my blood pressure, which was 95 over 60, and said it was too low and that was part of my problem. She did a few exercises with my head and then gave me a schedule of five therapy sessions. I skinned into my noon class at 12:05. Joadie and I had one of our rare suppers at home that night.

Thursday I had early class, then went to get my new artist friend, Jiri Votruba, to go for coffee and more conversation about his business venture with the T-shirt entrepreneur. I did my downtown errands (bananas, scotch, Herald Tribune), then met A.J. Land, the Atlanta developer from my days at Stirin, for lunch at the Palace Hotel. He was in town alone for a few days; Lynne was in Paris. Home for a nap, then up to meet Michael and three other people at the old Palace of Culture. (There is a new, modern, Russian-built Palace of Culture which is off-putting. You can just imagine the Party Czars erecting the new one and announcing, "Culture will reside here!"). We dined in one of the restaurants in the hall, then went upstairs to a grand and glorious rococo ballroom to sit concert-style and listen to the Original Prague Syncopated Orchestra play tunes from the '20's and '30's. It was so wonderful I had a silly grin on my face throughout, and kept wishing Mother were there. It was serendipitous, especially since Prague itself has not progressed much past that era. For that matter, in some ways it hasn't progressed much past the 14th century. This is a mixed blessing. Friday morning I went to see Tatiana Weisnerova, an acquaintance of Shifra and Jerry Rosen. She is a delightful old lady who still works as a guide. She has a wonderful house in a former stable in the courtyard of a former palace right downtown (decorated as usual in Eastern European Maybe). We decided to meet again after Easter. She reminded me of Aileen Goldstein. I went home and another strange taxi driver took me out to the hospital for my first actual therapy session. The therapist was a dear woman who practiced her English on me while she gently massaged my neck, head and shoulders. She took my blood pressure (100 over 50) and mentioned the connection to the vertigo. I said I had always had low blood pressure but I didn't have vertigo in America and she said, "Oh, it is because you are in Prague!" She was dead serious. Paige Alexander told me that she and Steve went to a doctor in Vienna because they had been coughing for six weeks and the doctor told them they had TB from being in Prague! I was in a pensive mood when I got back in the taxi, and as we pulled away from the hospital, John Denver came on the radio singing "Country roads/Take me home/To the place/I belong." I began to laugh. I don't want to go home yet. I want to see how it ends.

Friday night (last night) I went to Paige and Steve's for dinner. They had two women English teachers from Bratislava staying with them. We had fun but I get a little tired of the repetitious nature of expatriate conversation. It's always food, living conditions, the natives, etc. I'd rather talk about Yeltsin and Gorbachev. These are cute bright people here, though, and I do truly like them.

I was up at dawn this morning because Joadie and I had to meet the director and the other actresses who are going to be in "Crimes of the Heart" at 9:00 a.m. across town in one of their studios. Joadie gets up 30 minutes before she has to leave the house but I have to go through my ablutions or I just don't feel good. I'm not going to be the repressed older sister, I'm going to be the mean cousin, Chick, and although the part is (blessedly) small, it has the funniest lines. They all said I did great. Maybe I will be a movie star when I grow up! Speaking of movie stars, the girl whose studio we were in had some pictures of my old love Peter Falk hanging around. I thought it was ironic that he was looking down on the proceedings at the first read-through of my first acting job since 7th grade.

Speaking of firsts, I got my first paycheck since 1985 this past week: 1900 kcs, or almost $60.00. I was so proud of myself. Thank god for my dear dead relatives.

Ann Gardner, the founder of EfD from Mobile, arrives this weekend. I plan to spend some time with her. I am having dinner with A.J. Land and Nancy and Dan Painter tonight. The Painters have invited me to go to Salzburg over Easter. I am giving up my early morning Tuesday–Thursday class to a new EfD teacher who has just arrived. I won't miss getting up at 5:30 a.m., although I will miss those students. One bonds so quickly with the students. I have got the other three R's coming up this week: rehearsal, rehab and root canal. That starts Tuesday. I hope nothing else goes wrong with this old carcass. The price is right at the hospital ($0) but these $4 taxi fares are going to eat me alive.

―――◆・◆―――――――◆・◆―――

[The seventh newspaper article follows.]

"FORTY YEARS"

"Teaching English to adult Czechs from various walks of life is a revealing business. It reveals to me the complexity, the irritating irregularities and the sheer energy of our language. It reminds me how rich and complicated my own use of the language is as a native speaker when I have to rein myself in to speak and slowly and simply to my students. Even after hours I continue to sound like I am speaking to a small child even if the person I am addressing is from Atlanta, Georgia or London, England.

"What I learn from my students is even more revealing, particularly about the utter depths of ignorance in which they have been forced to live for the past forty years. Things that are second nature to us are mysteries to them. Money, for instance. One day without indicating I was about to abruptly change the subject, I casually singled out one of my advanced students and asked, 'Anna, what would you do with a million dollars?' This set hearts aflutter in the class as they all tried to imagine what it would be like to have a million dollars. Yet not one of them said they would invest the money and live off the proceeds. This glaring void in the list of options prompted a discussion on investment and banking.

"One evening I was wined and dined by a lawyer who wanted to build a restaurant. After prodding him a bit about his concept I asked him if he knew the basic economics of the restaurant business such as… and I began to show him, writing on a napkin, how he could figure if he would lose money, break even or make money. It had not dawned on him there was a relationship between the operation of the restaurant and the intake and outflow of money. Rather than guess at what his production would be in Czech crowns, I used some standard dollar figures which had his eyeballs popping out, and which I realized afterward had mistakenly given him false encouragement. The entire exercise was moot in any case since almost no one has accumulated any capital in the past forty years, including the banks. This single fact is the great white shark whose fin is getting ready to break the surface when the good ship 'Privatization' dumps its passengers overboard.

"An artist took me for coffee and pastries one morning to ask my advice on a business deal a foreigner had broached with him. It included selling some of his designs either for a flat fee or for a percentage of sales. What I know about intellectual property rights you could etch on the head of a pin, yet just by osmosis I knew enough to warn him away from certain dangers that had never even dawned on him. He thought I was a guru but I thought no, I'm just an American who's had her eyes and ears open during the forty years these dear people were forced at gunpoint to live in ignorance.

"I hate patronization, but there are times when I have to keep myself under tight control because I am swept with pity and a secret, sad embarrassment for the shabby poverty in which people live. Part of the embarrassment is fear that once they get out of this country and see how people in the West and particularly in America live, they will know how shocked we were even as we pretended to be equals.

"An energetic and irrepressible woman lawyer student, justly proud she had a whole house to herself in a suburb, invited me to lunch. I might as well have thought I was going to the Hampton's for the stupid surprise I felt on seeing her actual primitive and tacky living arrangements. I do not want to witness the deflation when these good people put two and two together and discover how little they've actually been proud of.

"I do not feel superior to them. I feel inferior to them. We should all feel inferior to them. As products of our history, a history based on a wildly inflated tradition of independence, we could not have patiently and deviously lived under their dictatorship conditions while we waited for history to run its course. We would have self-destructed with impatience. That is the difference between people whose history is only 200 years long and people whose history is 1000 years long.

"My students often explain things about their society by saying, 'you see, for forty years we were not able to ... ' They were not able to speak English, they were not able to travel outside their borders, they were not able to accumulate wealth, they were not able to compete on their merits, they were not able to read a free press, and of course they were not able to know just exactly what it was they were missing. Now they are starting to know, and now the real revolution will begin."

Saturday, 23 March 1991
Prague, Czechoslovakia

Dear Ones,

Spring is here, both on the calendar and in the air. As I walked down the street on Thursday the 21st with no coat on looking at all the people sitting on benches, feeling the palpable elation in the air, I thought I would not have given you ten cents for the chances of my making it to the first day of spring. It was the coldest, scariest winter of my life, yet here I am on the other side, safe and happy. It is a testament to the benefits of continuing to put one foot in front of the other, one day at a time.

Mr. Trso, our landlord, just delivered our clean linens. The linens would do the Habsburgs proud, although wrestling the comforters and 3-foot square feather pillows into crisply starched damask covers makes you feel like you have just gone three rounds with a huge furious marshmallow. Mr. Trso is attractive and always stands in the hall and visits with me at some length. I suppose it is a good thing he does not advance any further into the apartment.

Last night I cooked a feast for Joadie, Tim Whipple and Matt Hirsch from the castle at Stirin. The food at the castle has apparently deteriorated, if that is possible, and now enough people from the Institute have been here for dinner that the others are sending unveiled messages that they want to come, too. Tonight I am cooking for Joadie and Beth, one of the other actresses in our play. We are heavy into rehearsals and it is a fascinating process trying to act and remember everything. They think I am a natural, but I cannot comment.

Ota Sojka, the manager of the Diplomat Club, is hot on my trail. He had me for dinner last week, and lunch today. I do not know what to do with him but at the rate he is going he will probably get his English lessons for free.

Last weekend on Saturday night A. J. Land was in town and took Nancy and Dan Painter and me to dinner at the Intercontinental Hotel. It was horribly expensive and not great, and I was glad A. J. was paying. I asked the barman for a Chivas Regal, then noticed guiltily afterward on a table tent that the price was $11.60. So I had a couple more. Nancy invited me to go to the military language school where she guest-teaches every two weeks, and this we did on Thursday the 21st.

Nancy, as an agent of the government of the U.S.A., is a living breathing walking advertisement for the American way, and as such she comes across to her classes as kind of patriotic and patronizing—at least that's the way she came across to me. On the other hand, I operate on the assumption that I am the best advertisement for the joys of freedom and capitalism, and I do not browbeat students. I try to be more sneaky, so that the light comes on automatically and not because I have obviously flipped the switch. Also, I have an enormous native sympathy for these people trying to figure out how to do something they have never done before because that is the story of my life. So we had an interesting time at the military school. I taught five classes, then we had lunch with the muckety-mucks and came home. The school was about 40 km south of the city.

I had Nancy drop me downtown because I was determined to find some bananas. We had been without all week because there were none in the stores. Also no yogurt. I was so pissed off in the grocery store one morning when there was no yogurt, no frozen food, no cream and no veggies, that I walked up next to one of the commie robot grocery police people who stand silently in the aisles and said, in English, this is the sorriest grocery store I have ever been in, and kept moving. When my students want to talk about business I always bring up the subject of distribution. There is plenty of food here, but it comes in waves and is gone.

Anne Gardner, the founder the EfD, was here all week with her daughter and another woman from EfD, Bobbie Komisar, a gravelly voiced good ole girl. They came last Sunday night to dinner, we had lunch on Tuesday at the Palace salad bar, and dinner Wednesday night at the Diplomat Club. The upshot of all these meetings is that they are going to phase down their operation in Bohemia (that part of Czechoslovakia of which Prague is the capital) and operate more solely out of Slovakia. This means that I do not have to create a new administration here, but I will be the person any American volunteer can call for help or direction until the current crop of volunteers leaves or I leave, whichever comes first. This is a big relief to me because I have settled into a life I like and I do not particularly want a big new responsibility. I have my teaching, my play rehearsals, my food shopping, and a nice full social life, so I do not need anything else to do.

I went to the dentist, who drilled out my crown and filled the hole with nerve killing paste to kill the root. In a couple of weeks he will reopen it, ream it out and fill it permanently, and that is what they call a root canal in the good old CSFR. My vertigo treatment continues and is working—I hardly have it at all now. I love my therapist. I teach her English and she teaches me how not to pass out.

The English teachers all laugh about how they get used to talking "baby talk" in their work. It is a bit tiresome, but the challenge then becomes to say things in a poetic, perfect and a memorable way in simple declarative sentences. I love my classes.

Jarda, my driver, is a pillar of my life, particularly with all my trips to the hospital. He is a great guy, and funny, and always seems glad to see me.

One of the things I have had to do to cure my vertigo is to sleep only on my baby pillow. I cheat by putting a folded up Texas flag under it. Molly Mitchell gave me the flag from Jake Pickle's office before I left Washington, but instead of waving it, which would definitely be considered unseemly around here, I sleep on it.

Speaking of sleeping, one morning I woke up in the fetal position with my face in my armpit and I thought with a start, I smell just like them. I guess from eating the same food, drinking and bathing in the same water and breathing the same air.

I have not had a haircut since early December. This is the longest I have gone in my adult life without going to the beauty parlor. My hair has grown about three inches. By mid June I will have a mane.

I love you and miss you all.

Saturday, 30 March 1991
Augsburg, Germany

Dear Ones,

On the first day of spring, March 21st, we took off our coats for one brief glorious day; on March 22nd we put them back on, and it has even snowed again since then. Alas...

I was home one night this past week—Monday night. It was only recently I was complaining about lack of social life, and now I am as booked up as if I were in Washington. It's nice, but my chores become more onerous because I have less time to do them, or rather, less time to stand in line to do them. Every time I see the line down the sidewalk in front of the grocery store I think of Charlie Butt and what he would think of making people wait to get into a grocery store. This is such a sorry system. And the shops sell the dumbest things. You go into a shop and all they will sell is canned pineapple, canned mushrooms, fake coffee and Dewar's scotch.

Monday morning we rehearsed the play. I do not have to go to all the rehearsals because I only have four scenes. I have asked Stephen Heintz from the Institute to be in the play and he has accepted. This will definitely add a little caché to the proceedings. I taught my classes, stood in line in a couple of places, and cooked dinner for Joadie and me.

Tuesday I gave Ota his first English lesson and had lunch with him afterward at the Diplomat Club. Picked up a pay check (around $33), then Jarda took me to the hospital for my last vertigo rehabilitation session. I loved rehab and my precious therapist with the healing hands.

Tuesday evening I went to have dinner with the two dissidents I had sought out in early February. I had left notes at both their apartments, and one night Jiri Wolf came to my apartment when I wasn't there and handed Joadie an invitation for me to come to his friend Helena Furstova's for dinner on March 26th. Joadie had not let him in because he looked kind of wild and had a dog with him. The dinner was at Helena's and she and I visited before Jiri got there. She was an enormously sympathetic person whose soul was written all over her. Jiri was a burst of energy speaking pidgin English. He was in prison all during the '80's and was a cause celebre of Amnesty International. I lapped him up but studied hard to see what I could know of his ordeal. He had that kind of untouchable air which they say Havel has of a person glad to be alive knowing that nothing else that bad can happen to him. I am fascinated but I would not want to try it. Yet being around him and everyone in this whole bloody country for that matter makes me wonder constantly about the quality of my own mettle. It is interesting but it's tiring.

Jarda took me back to the hospital early Wednesday morning to be checked out and signed off on by (3 prepositions in a row there) the vertigo doctor. I am over it and only feel a little pressure in my head, which is extremely common in Prague because of the air. Then I discovered that my care had not been free when she gave me a bill for 1980 crowns (about $60). I gladly paid it, but when I told my classes about it later in the day they were outraged that I had to pay. They said I came here as a volunteer and I live like everyone else and therefore I should have free health care. I told them I thought I should pay; why should their government support me? I was touched by their concern, and amused at their horror over the prices. I told them I would have had to spend 10 times that much in the U. S., but they are becoming inured to my wild tales of what things cost in America.

I taught another teacher's classes plus mine that day and was tired when it was over, but nonetheless went with Irena, my woman lawyer/student friend, to hear the Verdi Requiem in a beautiful baroque church on the Old Town Square. It caused me to enjoy a welter of emotions ranging from this is the sort of experience that makes me glad to be in Prague, to thinking about our own Verdi Requiem at San Fernando Cathedral, to thinking that the San Antonio Festival was one of the things that drove me so far away I had to go to Prague to get away from it (I had been Development Chairman for two years in a row.). I also thought about lost loves, missed loved ones and a few other compelling subjects like that. We went to dinner afterward and I staggered home so tired I couldn't sleep.

Thursday was a freebie. Jarda took me and my dirty clothes over to Nancy Painter's and I sat in her laundry room for three hours washing clothes, inhaling clean smells and reading Time and Newsweek about the disintegration of Russia, the disintegration of Iraq, the disintegration of the entire continent of Africa and being aware, as if it were flypaper stuck to me, of the disintegration of Czechoslovakia and Eastern Europe. Good news passes like a stick on a flood.

I went to dinner at the home of Daniela Melicharova and her husband. They are both doctors and live in a nice house. I was fun to see a prosperous Czech home. She was one of Liana Barenblat's introductions. We had met for coffee once and decided to get together again. Her husband works in Germany and she wanted to have me over when he was home.

Last week in Parliament a list of the members who formerly had ties to the secret police (StB) was read, and these people had to resign or successfully defend themselves.

This sent a chill down the spines of Americans who remember when due process was suspended during the McCarthy era. I have been asking the Czechs what they think of it, and the consensus is ambivalence. My beautiful, soulful dissident thought it was terrible, which surprised me until I realized that would be the response of a noble liberal heart. My beautiful, educated lady doctor friend thought it was great. People have opinions here, obviously, and speak them (now) without fear. But the overall impression I get, as I dare to generalize, is that the Czechs have been forced by history to turn passivity and ambiguity into instruments for living and even now, 16 months after their "revolution," they are lying low, breathing shallowly and waiting to see what is going to happen to them. It is kind of maddening to Westerners, but I reckon they will be around long after we have self-destructed from activism.

Friday I was all over town running errands, buying theatre tickets, visiting Stephen, having lunch with Ota and coffee afterwards with my artist friend Jiri Vortruba. He works for a big organization called Albatros which publishes children's books. The company is situated on one of the best corners of downtown, and has a theatre in the basement, so he went with me to request the use of the theatre for our play, and I think we may get it. This would be a real coup, and I just thought of it when I went to meet him. Joadie and the other actress who are producing the play are neither one very high energy people and up until now I have been content to let them muddle along but we are doing the play in one month and the heat is on, so old Aunt Taddy has taken the reins gently into her own hands on a couple of matters and no one has protested.

Home from downtown to be picked up by Jarda and taken to the Painters' to drive with them for Easter weekend to Austria. This was my week to spend in the car with Jarda and he had never put the meter on so I laid some American cash on him and hoped it was appropriate. I get such a kick out of him. He is very funny.

Anyway, Nancy and Dan Painter and I drove to Salzburg through snow and rain Friday night, arriving at their favorite bed and breakfast near their children's school around 10:00 p.m. We had a quick visit with the children, then hit the sack to be back up and on the road again at 9:15 Saturday morning, this time with the children, to drive to Augsberg, Germany, which was a change in plans.

We stopped at a base in Munich to mail packages and eat at Burger King. No hamburger ever tasted so good. Then we drove another hour to Augsberg to a big base here, dropped Nancy at the commissary to do the month's shopping (with also a small list from me), went and checked into a ritzy officers' guest house with beautiful hotel-style suites and bathrooms with showers. I have had three showers in 36 hours. We do not have showers in Czechoslovakia. I struck out to walk; I was full of kinks from riding in the car. I stopped in a place called "Shoppette" to buy a breakfast roll and could not resist buying some Doritos, Tasters Choice, Crest toothpaste and Pace's Picante, then realized I had to have an ID to purchase these things, so I sweated bullets and decided to bluff my way past the cashier, and it worked but I felt somewhat guilty about it. I hid all the stuff and did not tell Nancy and Dan. We had dinner in the club—steaks and baked potatoes and salad bar. Their kids, a boy and a girl, are darling and voluble. They are starved for parental attention and talk constantly, but fortunately they are funny, so it is fun to listen to them.

(Sunday Morning) The Easter bunny found me, even in Augsberg, Germany. This morning in the private hall of our suites on the table sat everyone's basket including mine, which had in it Equal, Lawry's Seasoned Salt and Scope mouthwash—my shopping list. I was touched and delighted.

Easter Monday night, 1 April 1991
Prague, Czechoslovakia

Dear Ones,

I am finally, blissfully back in Prague after a weekend of being driven around eastern Europe like chattel until I was ready to scream. The Painters are nice, their kids are nice, but a trip which was represented as a weekend in Salzburg turned out to be a weekend on the highway with two teenagers talking nonstop about their school and listening to music on the car stereo. I am so burnt out and crazy I can not even talk about it—more in the next letter when I have chilled out. Suffice it to say it was fate's way of making me be extremely glad to get back to Prague. Home.

Saturday, 6 April 1991
Cologne, Germany

Dear Ones,

I came to Cologne to get some money, some food, some fresh air and a haircut, and I have succeeded in all those things. I flew here Thursday afternoon to visit friends but more importantly to enjoy a little R&R from the squalor and the kids in Prague. I am holed up in the Intercontinental on a spending spree enjoying not having to pretend I am poor. Yesterday I went to the fanciest food store I have ever seen, even in the U. S. When I entered I began hyperventilating, then I almost started crying, then my legs got weak and I felt like I was going to throw up. An hour and 240 DM later (about $160), I staggered out with caviar, tequila, breakfast cereal, pinto beans, spices, artichoke hearts, etc. etc. Today I went sightseeing and had a haircut; in between I have eaten Italian food, drunk margaritas and walked and read. Early tomorrow morning I head for home, laden with goodies and feeling refreshed. One thing I have noticed in the harsh light of the West (and of hotel bathrooms) is that I have gained weight, so I must face that when this R&R is over. But not yet.

Cologne, like all German cities, is mostly new because the Allies bombed it to smithereens in W.W. II. The old Romanesque churches still stand, as does the Dom, the largest Gothic cathedral in the world. Churches are a big deal architecturally in

Europe, and everywhere else for that matter, and apparently when we decide that the poor people who attend them are being led by unconscionable tyrants who must be bombed back to the dark ages, we piously leave those pitiful spires presiding over the destruction.

Germany does not look like it is disintegrating from here. It looks wonderfully prosperous. Cars which in America are symbols of wealth, i.e., Mercedes, BMW's and Audis, are here driven by everyone, used as taxis and common means of transportation. Things are gratuitously expensive, especially to one who has to work hard to spend money in Czechoslovakia.

Ironically, before flying here on Thursday, Ota took me to a special store just for communist big-wigs and there I bought 2000 kcs ($70) worth of things I have never seen in the stores, like white asparagus, Italian tomato products and aluminum foil. I felt like a hick turned loose at the county fair. After seeing the food store in Cologne it all came back into perspective. Actually, the lack of materialism in Czechoslovakia has its drawbacks but relative to the inflated prices of the West it is refreshing. I hope the Czechs find some happy medium between the gross consumerism of the West and their own enforced conformity to mediocrity. Their (formerly) state-sanctioned mediocrity in all things is such an insult to human nature. Sometimes I want to lash out in rage at them for being so cynically passive, and sometimes I want to hold them to my bosom and weep for all they have lost.

My root canal came to a climax of sorts this week. My dentist was sick so the hospital routed me to another dentist in the main (not foreigners) part of the hospital. He actually seemed more competent than my dentist, and after drilling into my crown to do the root canal he announced that he had to remove the crown to do the work. He had to take a hammer and chisel to it, literally, but afterward finally did reach the 'root' of the problem (I could feel the inflammation even through the Novocain) and now, two trips later, my tooth does not hurt for the first time in months. He is making me a new crown, which I get next week. I always tell my students stories about what happens to me, and when I told them this story I concluded with the line, "And now I shall take back to America a Czech crown." They loved this: the Czech crown is their currency.

Last weekend with the Painters was a bit of a trial. I figured out that in three days I was in the car a total of 25 hours. It was billed as a trip to Salzburg but degenerated into errand-running all over Germany with me as the witless and helpless passenger. You know how I love that. Especially with the kids playing their music on the tape deck interspersed with Nancy playing rock-n-rollers for Christ. I started out the trip being sweet and good-natured and friendly and helpful but by the time we returned to Prague on Easter Monday night I had resorted to plugging my ears with Kleenex and not volunteering a word unless asked. I thanked them sweetly and politely when they dropped me off and resisted the temptation to fall to my knees and kiss the ground. It totally changed my attitude toward Prague. Now I love Prague with a crazy happiness I never felt before. It may be a case of not knowing how much you love something until you almost lose it.

Tuesday morning after my return from this tiring weekend, I went to the Diplomat Club to give my weekly English lesson, then walked to Lufthansa to buy my plane ticket to Cologne. For months I have scanned the crowds for a familiar face; the crowds are now so thick that it seems incredible not to see someone I know (from elsewhere, that is; I see lots of people here that I know). Well, coming out of Lufthansa there he was: Charlie McBride, a friend from Washington. He was in town with Senator Bennett Johnston. We walked together for about ten minutes. I was glad to have my belief proved that you cannot go anywhere in the world without seeing someone you know.

Joadie had a terrible stomach bug and was sick from both directions starting about 2:00 a.m. that morning. When I got home after lunch I moved her over to the Park Hotel because our water had gone off in the neighborhood and she was too sick and it was too unhygienic to be without water. The water came on again that night but we spent the night at the Park Hotel.

Wednesday we rehearsed the play in the morning and I taught all afternoon. I cooked Wednesday night so Joadie could have some decent food and decent leftovers while I was gone. The best food in Prague is when I cook.

Last weekend when I was in Augsberg in the officers club with the Painters, they went to the movies on Saturday night and I stayed in and inadvertently watched a rerun of the Schwarzkopf interview with David Frost. I could see why the press loved him: his subjects and predicates matched and he could follow a thought from start to finish. But when he claimed that God was on his side he lost me. I was not a '60's antiwar demonstrator only to change my stripes and decide some bullnecked guy in fatigues could be made whole by speaking decent English. The circumstances in which religion is invoked are enough to make you puke.

Speaking of TV, I have been watching it this weekend. Yesterday, when Senator John Heinz was killed in a plane crash, I had this vision that Senator John Tower was killed, and today on CNN Senator John Tower is killed, and in a plane crash. I hate my ESP. It gives me the willies.

Daylight savings time began in Europe last weekend, a week before the U.S. Spring is also I think permanently here. Lots of trees and bushes have flowers, although nothing much has leaves, yet. It is quite a little triumph, Spring.

My guide today drove me down the Rhine to Bonn, 20 km south of Koln. Bonn is a graceful city, and I could see why the government might resist moving back to Berlin. It would be like moving from an easy-going, attractive place like Austin to New York City.

This Europe is a provocative place, especially if you think about it.

Saturday, 13 April 1991
Prague, Czechoslovakia

Dear Ones,

I had a desultory week because I had a cold which I picked up in Cologne. I was in a fog (and a funk) until yesterday, when suddenly I was fine again. It is my only illness so far and the reason I got it was because I bragged just days before that I never got sick because I ate properly, took megavitamins and practiced mind-made health. Pride goeth before the fall.

I came home from Cologne last Sunday morning, sniffing and suffering, barely able to put one foot in front of the other, feeling like hell. Jarda picked me up at the airport and took me home, then bid me farewell for two weeks because he was going to his country house for a week and to drive a Swiss lady around the country for a week for hard currency. He always leaves me in good hands but I miss the comfort of having him nearby speaking English.

Monday I taught my classes, then met Joadie and Stephen Heintz for Stephen's first play rehearsal. He is darling and a natural actor, and the girls were quite taken with him. Old Aunt Taddy just sits and watches and stirs the pot.

Tuesday I had no classes and felt at death's door but got up and went to the Palace Hotel to meet Irena, my lawyer/student, to edit a long contract she had written in English. Now in addition to posing as a business consultant I am also a lawyer. It is just amazing what I know, or claim to know. I stopped at the Smetana and bought some opera tickets (you can only buy them a week in advance so you have to time your purchase as carefully as the event itself), then came home to pad around in robe and slippers all afternoon. Instead I got inspired to make spaghetti sauce and wound up cooking and doing school work all afternoon. Fortunately Joadie appeared with Beth, so the cooking got eaten.

Wednesday I rehearsed all morning and taught all afternoon, and Joadie and I ate left over spaghetti for supper. I had so many goodies in the house from my recent shopping forays that I kept thinking I should invite someone to share them, but I did not have the energy.

Thursday I gave up and took to my bed for most of the day, which I hate. It makes my back hurt. But I guess it was salubrious, because I was well Friday. Thursday evening I went to rehearse a scene with Stephen—he can only rehearse after work—and took some curried turkey salad and a bottle of wine, which was welcome along about 8:30.

Friday morning a strange taxi driver picked me up to take me back to the dentist to get my new crown. All went well until the hospital cashier tallied up my bill: 4700 crowns, or about $175. I did not have enough money to pay it so I signed an IOU, and what I thought was my last trip forever to the hospital became the second-to-last, because now I have to go out there again and pay them. 4700 crowns is a small fortune. Even I have to go to the bank to rustle up that kind of money.

I had the taxi driver drop me downtown at the Institute office so I could send a fax. I wound up visiting there for an hour. Matt told me that Stephen has come home from his rehearsals in a great mood and I said, yeah, because he is surrounded by adoring females. I think Matt was surprised to think women found Stephen attractive. Typical man. Then I headed over to the Diplomat Club to see Ota, who had been out of town. On the way I saw some broccoli for sale in one of my vegetable store haunts, and I was so upset that I had forgotten to take my shopping bag with me that all I could do when I saw Ota was to beg him for a shopping bag and then sit and fidget until I could get back on the street and go buy my broccoli. How simple minded I have become. I am like a mama penguin who goes to sea all day to feed, then comes home at night to regurgitate my catch into the mouths of my 20-year-old babies.

Next stop the Canadian Club to pick up my pay—970 crowns, or about $35. I took it down the street and spent 330 crowns of it on Xeroxing things for my students. Then back to the Canadian Club to meet with the owner on the subject of hiring EfD/USA English teachers. Then I just kept walking around thinking up errands to do because I was so happy not to feel sick for the first time in five days, and also because it was Spring again and I was suffused with spring fever. Gee, let's see: that makes two whole days of spring we have had. I was in long underwear all week.

I cooked for Joadie, Beth and a new baby birdie last night—a 22-year-old looker (male) just arrived in the city who had contacted us after seeing a notice about our play. Stanford, Oxford, very bright, very polite, very young. I do miss decay.

It is Saturday morning. I have pared my finger nails, cleaned the bathtub, done my crunches and practiced my lines. Very soon I am going to burst out the door and go inhale some spring, pollution and all.

(Sunday Evening) We have real live glorious spring weather. Yesterday after doing everything I had to do, including some writing that was consuming me, I went to the river and walked and communed with the swans. Cooked a sumptuous dinner for Joadie and me, and talked and read in a very comfortable and stimulating mode. I like to talk to Joadie.

Today Ota took me out to the Diplomat Country Club—a funky little place by Western standards but quite nice and appealing. He played tennis, I had a massage and read my book. I am still such a wide-eyed hick that any new place is fraught with interest. Joadie and I walked in our park when I got home—the same park we had been so enchanted with in the snow is now enchanting with leaves (finally) on the trees. We have just had supper and now are both at our final desk work before the week begins. The count down to the play begins this week, and I as usual have multiple social plans including going to Berlin.

[The eighth and last newspaper piece follows.]

"THE CALM BEFORE THE STORM"

"There is a smoke-enshrouded calm hanging over Czechoslovakia. The smell of the smoke is imprinted in the memory the way the smell of a mother is imprinted on a blind newborn. When you go away and come back, the smell is the evocative greeting of home. But when you go away and look back, unable now to smell the smoke but still able to see it, the evocation is of suffocation, calm suffocation. When you go far enough over the horizon that you pass the curve of the Earth and you look back, all you see is a piece of a map puzzle, delineated from its Western neighbors by the smoke that hangs over it.

"The calm is almost as palpable as the smoke. It has been a year and a half since the Revolution and the people are still lying low, breathing shallowly and waiting with remarkable patience to see what is going to happen to them. Diurnal habits change imperceptibly with a price rise here, a price rise there. Sausage replaces fresh meat on the table, spaghetti replaces sausage. The occasional trash picker makes one gag with sorrow.

"One source of the calm is food. There is plenty of it, and the lines for it are stupid bureaucratic-system lines, not shortage lines. Another reason for the calm is the ample pauses between major price hikes, enabling them to be digested. This month it was transportation fares. They went up 400%, from four cents to sixteen cents. The scale may seem unreal but the relativity is very real. Next month utilities go up 400%, and the month after that rents go up 180%. At that point the calm could quite easily turn to terror.

"There is an almost universal disappointment with how slow change has come following the exciting change of government in 1989. People almost instantly got their civil rights and individual freedoms but the overriding difference between communism and democracy is economic and economic change has not come. Now it is coming and now we will see just how badly they really want democracy, and how much they are prepared to bear. The last rise they will have the pleasure of digesting is the rise in salaries.

"The smoke is a shroud of death for the Earth and the trees, and it is a harbinger of at least early death for the lungs of the people, but it is ironically a symbol for now of prevailing health for industry. If the outmoded industries of the old communist economy are not rescued, Czechoslovakia may wind up with a lot of hungry, frustrated citizens breathing mighty clean air.

"The current calm may also come from exhaustion. It may seem supercilious to say, but the expatriate community certainly suffers from mental exhaustion because they know how broad the leap over the chasm is going to have to be and they are secretly, profoundly worried it can't be done. Yet they are charged with being unofficial cheerleaders because they are representative advocates of the desired goal. They may be more tired than the natives, who have an idea what they are facing but no experience on which to base a formulation of it. In any case exhaustion is endemic.

"Yet people continue to walk around this stage setting called Prague as if doing business and carrying out daily life against a thousand-year-old backdrop were the most natural thing on Earth. On particularly serendipitous days one can get the crazy notion that the whole ancient rococo mess is an hallucination.

"In a recent speech in the United States, Margaret Thatcher said that the democracies of Eastern Europe would be different from Western democracies because they are being founded on so many layers of previously undemocratic history, and that they will in particular not be like American democracy because American democracy was created from whole cloth and based from day one on an ideal. Or words to that effect. This was construed in Europe as pessimistic.

"But when the smoke clears, if these new democracies even come close it will be a remarkable achievement and testimony to their calm and ancient staying power. They've already proved that ideals can prevail over history."

Saturday, 20 April 1991
Prague, Czechoslovakia

Dear Ones,

There is a chicken in the oven and my old pal Krzysztof Ners from the castle is coming for dinner. I have not seen him in weeks.

I have just returned from two days in Berlin, where I had a really lovely, interesting time. Berlin is a place which entered my consciousness thirty years ago; I distinctly remember where. It was at the Blue Angel bar in Chicago; I was 16 and I was out on the town with Bill Hallahan, an S&L friend of mother and father's. He told me about the Blue Angel and about Berlin, and it sounded romantic to one with an overheated imagination. The years since conspired to ensure that Berlin the place and Berlin the idea would continue to reside and grow in my nascent memory, and as I left it today I was in a pensive reverie.

It started out in a rather amusing way. I flew CSA Airlines (Czech Airlines), which is slightly quaint but just fine. When we landed I remarked to myself that there certainly were some exotic airlines represented on the tarmac—Bulgarian, Cubana, Mongolian, Condor. Then I thought the terminal was an awfully pissant little terminal. Then I got in a taxi with a driver who did not know where the Intercontinental Hotel was, and had to get out of the car and ask directions as I felt a growing alarm. He laughed self-consciously and explained in German that we were in Ost Berlin (East Berlin), and then the pieces of the puzzle fell together. Forty-five minutes and fifty-five marks later I arrived at the hotel.

The next two days I spent visiting old and new friends and sitting in on talks of the biennial meeting of the Atlantic Bridge, a German-American membership organization of upper level types from business and government. I also went shopping for food in another heart-stopping, staggeringly fabulous food emporium even more incredible than the one I found in Cologne. This one, KDV, was the Bloomingdale's or Neiman-Marcus of grocery stores. People were there because it was an event. There were beer bars, raw bars, espresso and pastry bars and every kind of brilliant above average food known to humankind. I have not been to Jamail's in Houston in years but some American entrepreneur ought to copy these places. I bought a couple of bags full of stuff and trudged back to the hotel to store it all before closing my suitcase.

Berlin is hopping. I thought it would be cavernous like New York but it is not. It is all new and of quite manageable scale. It was bitterly cold and snowed the whole time I was there. It was bitterly cold and snowing when I arrived here, too, this afternoon. The daffodils have little white beards.

So the Berlin spell is broken, and the reality begins. It is kind of a relief.

Yesterday I went with a bilingual friend in a taxi to see the Brandenberg Gate, the Wall and Checkpoint Charlie. At Checkpoint Charlie I was overwhelmed by the utter banality of it all. I hate communism passionately after being here. I get mad, I hate it so much. It was such a humiliating insult to people, and it was so stupid, so utterly stupid. Imagine sitting around thinking up a system that would force people to be mediocre, that would insist that poverty and squalor were the best they deserved. I want to scream sometimes.

I flew back out of the funky, goofy, tacky little East Berlin airport and back to my beautiful, shabby Czechoslovakia feeling ambivalent indeed.

It had been a short but busy week. I made six stops on foot all over downtown before meeting my classes Monday. I walk my feet off every day. Tuesday may have been a record for walking though—I must have walked 17 miles, and it was freezing cold. I went into a meeting at 8:30 a.m. to represent my artist against his T-shirt "partner" and had a two hour knock-down-drag-out during which we prevailed thanks to me but following which I could not decide whether to throw up or get drunk. I did neither, because I was too busy. I went to see Ota to get some money changed so I could pay my dental bill, to Lufthansa to pick up my plane ticket, to Tim's to fetch him for lunch, home to shop for a dinner party the next night and then it took me one hour and fifteen minutes to find ice cream. Back downtown to meet Daniela M. and her daughter to talk about sending the girl to the U.S.; to the Palace to grab a bite before going to the opera to see "Cosi Fan Tutte", before which and during the intermission of which I studied my lines for our play. Home through the cold and rain so tired I thought I would collapse, but I have got insomnia and have had it for a couple of weeks so there is no delicious slipping away—just tossing and turning. I think it is because of the play.

Early rehearsal Wednesday morning, ran errands on the way to class, taught all afternoon and home to cook for two hours for my dinner party. I served caviar, then goose, wild rice and asparagus with hollandaise, and ice cream with blue berries and chocolate sauce for dessert. My guests were Paige and Steve and a friend of theirs, and

Geoffrey Upton, the head of the Price Waterhouse office here. I only have four chairs, so I sat on the trash can.

Peter Volten, my old 'roommate' from the castle, came late for a drink, and when he left I tackled the dishes and finally fell into bed at 1:00 a.m. Jan Goldscheider woke me up the next morning on the telephone asking me to come help him edit some letters, so I flew into action, got myself and the rest of the kitchen cleaned up, packed, had my substitute driver take me downtown and wait for me while I helped Jan, then it was off to the airport and my rendezvous with Berlin.

I have reached a point in this crazy adventure where I am starting to love it. Sometimes I will be driving along or walking along and I will feel this rush of love. I do not want to love it. It is almost as if my pride of accomplishment will evaporate if I realize I love it. Part of the energy that enables me to live with this place comes from the adversarial nature of life here. I have never lived in a place where society is pitted against the people. I always thought society was ordered to help the people. So to learn to live here successfully, which I have done, has taken a Herculean effort and I may not be ready to give up that adrenaline. My brain is tired, though, I must say. I am about ready to go sit on a beach and drink rum. But I will give in to the love. I always do.

✦·✦——————✦·✦

Sunday, 28 April 1991
Prague, Czechoslovakia

Dear Ones,

You will be pleased to know that I have not had a profound thought this entire week. Our play is next week and I cannot think about anything else. In fact I had an uncharacteristic fit of pique this week which represented all my fears about the project, and after that I had a warm rush of feeling during which I finally realized this whole thing was supposed to be fun, and I had been approaching it as a burden, and since then my acting has improved immeasurably. Our pony-tailed director even clapped, shouted bravo and congratulated me on one scene today. It is Sunday evening and we have been in rehearsal all weekend. We are pooped, we are crazed but we are happy and each proud of the other. We have wrought a hell of a play out of the script in seven weeks of half-assed rehearsals during which we have run the gamut of human emotions. Our theatre troupe is called Studio Theatre but I call it in my own mind Ragamuffin Theatre after its founders (Joadie and her friend Beth). We have spent our rehearsals in Beth's studio in a wonderful old part of the city, near a subway station called, I am not kidding you, JIRIHO Z PODEBRAD. Pronounce it if you can. This language has been the bane of my existence.

Monday we rehearsed Act III, and I taught all afternoon. I felt unnaturally tired and went to bed early and slept 12 hours. I was fine; I just craved a random night of sleep.

Tuesday, Jarda picked me up late morning and took me back out to the hospital to pay my dental bill, for which I had written an IOU. They remembered me. Then he dropped me downtown to have lunch with Irena at the Jewish Town Hall, only my dear Jarda left me at the wrong place and I waited for 25 minutes in vain. Finally I gave up and moseyed over to the Intercontinental to get a sandwich. I bought the papers in the lobby, went into the coffee shop, shucked off my layers (it was very cold outside) and settled into a booth to eat and read when a voice across the aisle said "Taddy"? I looked over and there was A. J. Land. I moved to his booth and we ate and talked for two solid hours. Then I had to hightail it back out to my neighborhood because I had just received confirmation early that morning that Helena Furstova and Jiri Wolf were coming to dinner, and I had to shop.

At 6:30 the beautiful soulful Helena, her grizzled old man Slavek and her nimble daughter Monica arrived, followed by Jiri, wild and wonderful. Joadie was home and full of phlegm and fear over rehearsals and scripts, but joined the party and contributed considerably. I fried pork chops (Monica asked her mother what I was doing—she had never seen meat not smothered), but when I trotted out the chocolate sauce she was long since muted, having chewed the bone of her pork chop down to the marrow. We had a wild half-Czech, half-English conversation which everyone understood. It is amazing how I can listen to these people jabber away in Czech and not understand one single word they say and yet understand them.

Wednesday I went to collect on Geoffrey Upton's pledge to give to the Studio Theatre 2000 kcs from Price Waterhouse. I frankly thought he was a major horse's ass when he was here but he was peaches and cream at his office and it just reminded me for the umpteenth time that everyone is more than one thing. If this rule ever penetrates, I will have the patience of a saint. Then to teach all afternoon and home blessedly to do nothing socially for dinner.

Thursday, I went to the American Embassy to peddle tickets, to the Institute to peddle tickets, to see Mr. Hornik, the owner of the Canadian Club, about free office space for Education for Democracy, and then to a (to my mind) premature celebratory lunch with my T-shirt artist and his partner at a very fancy restaurant. They are both doe-eyed and handsome and naive and totally edible but they do not know it and I would hate to spoil a beautiful friendship by intimating it. Home to shop, shop, shop in a nasty rain for a very long weekend of rehearsals and feeding the baby birdies, and then cooking into the evening to be ready for our rigorous rehearsal schedule.

Friday I went to Act I rehearsal—my other act—then to see Hornik and see the possible EfD space, then back to the American Embassy to pick up birthday candles which Nancy Painter had brought us from Germany for our play, (we have made up since our disastrous journey through Germany and Austria Easter weekend—I wrote her a conciliatory thank you note because I really like her), by to see Ota to pick up some opera tickets he had gotten for me, back home to change into sweats and sneakers and back to the rehearsal studio for coaching by our 22-year-old Stanford/Oxford beauty.

All day Saturday and all day Sunday (today) doing run-throughs—I provided the lunches and our nerdy little actor who plays the lawyer told me the two lunches were the best two meals he'd had in Prague. Last night I went to dinner to celebrate Steve Grand's birthday. Paige had assembled the usual 15 25-year-old overachievers, and I felt hopelessly old and realistic. I have got to work this out.

My time here is drawing short and wouldn't you know I am starting to dig in my heels. It would be wonderful to want something when you have it instead of when you are about to lose it or have just lost it. That would be too easy I reckon.

✥✥ ———————— ✥✥

Saturday, 4 May 1991
Prague, Czechoslovakia

Dear Ones,

Well, I am bereft because Joadie is leaving on Monday to return to Canada. Three months ago when I invited her to live with me I made a calculated decision that over the long haul it would be more important to have a constant companion than to have the privacy I might otherwise sometimes desire. I have indeed sometimes desired that privacy, usually for some nefarious purpose, but when it has not been there I have simply weighed the inconvenience against the joy of her company and friendship, and the frustration has melted away. She was having trouble getting a flight out so I took her ticket to KLM to throw myself on their mercy, only to discover that a seat had opened up. I acted so pleased but I suddenly had to put my dark glasses on because I started to cry sitting there waiting for the ticket to be written. I am still in a highly emotional state. There is something about this entire experience that has made each event or turn of events seem to be vividly outlined in Day-Glo in heart or mind or both. I hope it is not unhealthy to have such strong feelings.

I will be alone for eleven whole days after Joadie leaves and then mother arrives. I quit teaching on May 15th, mother arrives May 17th for ten days, then she leaves and I may go traveling. Then I fly to Washington on June 10th to start summer. Summer will be richly appreciated this year. It is May 4th and it is still cold here. Cold and rainy.

I am having a myriad conflicting reactions to leaving. I do not want to stay but I hate to leave, if that makes any sense. I keep thinking I want to see how it ends, but of course ideally "it" is not going to "end." I have left so many people, places and things that my heart sometimes feels unnaturally old. It must be a comfort to be satisfied with one person, place and life.

Our play opened to acclaim Thursday night. It was not wild acclaim to be sure; rather the audience seemed genuinely to like and appreciate it. They laughed a lot. We were dark last night, so we all went to another play, "Look Back in Anger," a dreadfully depressing play done in English by Czech actors. It was hard to understand and we left at the half. We had had a good looking young man named Peter Krogh over for dinner. He is starting a theatre company and we were curious about him. He was pretty tough and self-assured but Aunt Taddy softened him up with good food and we wound up enjoying him. He went to the theatre with us.

Our first night was pretty nerve wracking but we all did fine and no one flubbed anything. We have two more performances, tonight and tomorrow night, and then we are having the cast party here at our flat. Joadie leaves the next day and I mop up.

This past Monday morning bright and early Jarda picked me up to take me to hire a taxi van to move our props to the theatre. The van picked me up at 4:00 after class and we went to a famous theatre here, the Realisticke Divadlo, to pick up some things they loaned us, then to the studio to get the rest of the props. I left the driver with Beth and Joadie to finish up, and went to the Palace to meet Michael for a quick supper and to go to the opera. We saw Dvorak's "Rusalka," which was one of the most beautiful, enchanting things I have ever seen. Why it's not in the American repertory I do not know.

Tuesday I got to sleep a few minutes late, then spent most of the day at the theatre in dress rehearsal.

Wednesday was a holiday, May Day, and there were no classes. Jiri Wolf came to get me to take me sightseeing. We climbed the highest hill in Prague and went to the Strahov Monastery, which has a spectacular library and for some strange reason a collection of ancient dried up fish. Living in Prague has not been an unalloyed joy but sightseeing is always serendipitous.

Thursday morning I went with my artist and his partner to pick up the money from the British businessman who had tried to screw them. If anything, this meeting was more acrimonious and depressing than the first one. It makes me physically ill to deal with hateful people. I was in a black mood afterward, and my next stop was KLM where I started crying, and I walked around crying for an hour. That night at the theatre, when everyone else was in a state of agitation about going on stage, I was almost perfectly calm because I thought, nothing else can happen to me today.

Friday I had a nice day. I foraged downtown, then met my lady doctor friend Daniela and her dear old friend Carlos Erhlich from New York, at a coffee house. Carlos is Viennese and is Liana Barenblat's uncle. He is a sweet-faced, handsome old soul who walks with a cane. We had a charming visit, then I headed home to cook for the baby birdies.

Jarda came to opening night, and took me home. When he dropped me off I went in, put on my nightgown, poured myself a vodka and then because it was a special occasion I opened up a precious bag of Fritos I had been saving for a month and ate about four handfuls. Joadie was still at the theatre, so I was alone, and I got this crazy happy feeling because the Fritos tasted so good.

(Sunday Afternoon) Last night the audience loved our play so much that we had three curtain calls, and as I was leaving the theatre three people spotted me and said, "oh, look!" like I was a celebrity. It was fun! Joadie and Stephen and I came home and celebrated a bit overmuch, and today we are chastened and ready to face our last performance tonight. The cast party is here afterward, and then it is back to reality tomorrow.

Sunday, 12 May 1991
Prague, Czechoslovakia

Dear Ones,

It is May 12th and it is cold and rainy. Global warming appears to be the only environmental depredation that has not been visited on this country.

Not only is it cold and rainy, it is Sunday and cold and rainy, and I am alone because Joadie left last week. I have got company coming late this afternoon for supper, and plenty of domestic concerns to occupy me, but I must say that when one gets used to having another soul around, it is pretty empty feeling when they go.

A week ago on Sunday night we had the last performance of our play, then cast and crew came here to our flat and partied until 2:00 a.m. Beth stayed over and we straightened until 3:00 a.m., then passed out for a few short hours until I had to get up and get ready for work. Joadie and I had our farewells and I cried all the way downtown—Jarda was taking her to the airport while I was in class. Beth and a taxi van were waiting for me when I came out of class at 4:00 p.m., and we went back to the theatre to pick up our props and drop them off back at the Realisticke Theatre and her studio. I had the truck take me on home. I cooked a pork chop and drank a glass of wine, then put my terribly tired soul to bed for a long sleep.

Tuesday I slept until I woke up, then finished cleaning up after the party and doing bottle duty (everyone recycles). Jarda came after lunch to take me to check out a couple of potential living places for a new EfD volunteer who was arriving that day to take over my 'job' as Prague administrator. I told Jarda I longed to just sit under a tree and drink beer. It was too cold actually to sit outside so he offered to take me to his flat for a beer. He and Dana, his wife, had been making noises about having me over and I had not really encouraged it so I took the opportunity to see his flat and off we went. They live in a fairly new socialist block of flats, and have a fairly nice though relatively small apartment that was pleasantly chaotic due to the fact they have two little boys aged five and three. They were just home from kindergarten and they sat on the arm of my chair looking at a picture book and giving me the names of things in English. It was so cute. The little one says "I'm a little Indian boy." Dana is 32 and exhausted. She works 12 hour days at the Park Hotel, then of course has to deal with all the stupid shopping we are all forced to do. From the way Jarda talks, I think he helps with cooking and child care.

Home to another quiet supper, using food as consolation, and another long sleep.

Wednesday I ran around all morning, taught all afternoon, then came home and cooked furiously because Stephen, Vasil and Tim were coming to eat Mexican food. I had promised them to cook Mexican food ever since I arrived and I had accumulated the necessary ingredients on my shopping forays in Germany. Then it took weeks to schedule everyone (mainly Stephen). I served margaritas, guacamole and chili con queso with Doritos, Spanish rice, chili and black beans (no pintos in Germany), with Paces and jalapenos for condiments. Also chopped lettuce and tomato with cilantro to put over all of it. We pigged out and then they stayed and stayed, which flattered me. It did mean that the incredible mess in the kitchen got rectified in the wee hours, however.

It did not matter, because Thursday was a holiday to celebrate the day the Russians liberated Czechoslovakia from the Germans in 1945. Naturally everyone feels ambivalent about this holiday now. There is an old Russian tank that sits up on top of a big stone monument to commemorate this event, and last week in the dead of night an artist painted it pink. I had the good fortune to see it on the one day it remained pink before it was hastily repainted by the powers that be (who do not want to irritate Russia, who is grouchy enough as it is). It was hysterical.

I spent the afternoon with Jarda trying to get the new EfD person situated. His name is Joe Vosoba; he and his wife Cathy look like they are in their early 60's. He is a retired banker from a Czech community in Nebraska and he has some money, which I have spent the last few days trying to spend on a temporary dwelling for them until they take over my apartment later in June. Jarda took me to meet them. They are staying in a nice Army officer's hotel for free (he is going to lecture at the Army Language School I once went to) but they have no kitchen and are antsy to get settled. I won't bore you with the details but we ran around some more following leads on flats the rest of the afternoon until I got sick of it and had Jarda drop me at home.

This was my week to spend with Jarda. Friday morning he and his boys picked me up and we drove to Karlovy Vary (a famous old spa town known to the West by its formerly German name, Carlsbad). He has a cottage there where his mother is encamped, and we dropped the babies off with her before going into the town to look around. It is a neat old city, with gorgeous fin-de-siecle buildings and crisp mountain air. From there we drove another 40 km. into Germany to a small town where Jarda bought some Deutsch Marks with some other hard currency he had. He has a D.M. account where he puts all the hard currency he makes from people like me. He is saving to buy a new taxi. Then we drove back to Karlovy Vary, and back to Prague—a nine hour day altogether. We were beat. He dropped me off and I came in to discover I had no water. At that point I had the choice of blowing my brains out or pouring myself a martini and saying to hell with it. I chose the latter course of action. The landlord came over, and while he was here the water mysteriously came back on. I washed myself, my hair and my clothes as fast as I could for fear it would go off again, but so far it is still on.

I was longing for some exercise Saturday so I got all bundled up, took an umbrella and a bag of stale bread and walked to the Intercontinental to buy the newspapers and down to the river to feed the swans. I spent one and a half hours out on foot and felt much better. I went to Tim's for dinner. He had Mr. & Mrs. Trso, my landlords, over. I had never met her. She does not speak much English but I did my best to thank her for all the beautiful linens she had supplied me all spring. Mr. Trso was his usual irrepressible self.

I have started a list of all the things I have learned from this experience of living in Czechoslovakia. It is already fairly long.

Mother arrives at the end of this week. I cannot wait to show her this grand, crazy old place. I shall be curious to see if she has strong reactions to this city which has created positively violent reactions in me, and does to this day, four months later. One would have to be blind not to respond to the wonderfully over decorated architecture. There is scarcely a window that does not have stone masks or cherubs protecting it, or a portal that is not supported by giant stone Nubians, or a roof without a minaret, or a doorway not made of ancient carved wood. Everything had to be beautiful, and stone, and permanent. Where did we lose that ability to project ourselves into the future?

I am happy, I am fine, but right now I am projecting myself into the surf at Port Aransas.

❖❖ ———————— ❖❖

Sunday, 19 May 1991
Prague, Czechoslovakia

Dear Ones,

Edith McAllister is sitting across the room from me, putting on her face. She arrived Friday at noon, and we have been sightseeing in the cold ever since. Jarda and I met her at the airport, and the only two minutes it rained all day were when we had to walk from the terminal to the car. I took secret delight in having affirmed my complaints about the weather. We zigzagged home, doing a little sightseeing from the car. On the day before, the Federal parliament had voted to change the holiday celebrating the end of World War II from May 9th, the day the Russians reached Prague, to May 8th, the day the Americans reached Pilsen (Plzen). Then a bunch of them crossed the river to the Russian tank memorial, which two weeks ago had been surreptitiously painted pink and then hastily repainted by the authorities, and boldly repainted it pink themselves. The whole city was ecstatic, and now the Pink Tank is enshrined as a new popular landmark. The day after it happened a man said to me, 'meet me at the pink tank,' as if it had been there forever. Anyway, that was our first sightseeing stop.

Jarda dropped us off and mother dropped onto the bed for a quick nap. Then we took a tram downtown to run some errands and walk to the Old Town Square and around the Jewish ghetto. We employed a guide to show us around the old Jewish cemetery, which is a jumble of ancient stones, aesthetically delightful and poignant at the same time. We tram'd back out to our neighborhood and went to see the recently opened Centennial exhibition, which is in 'my' park a couple of blocks from home. We were enchanted with the glass exhibition, which had spectacular examples of Czech crystal in both sculptures and household items. It was not the usual cut glass, dated stuff; rather it was mostly artsy and modern and for the most part breathtaking. Home from the park to a good supper eaten in jammies and robes, and then mother went down for the count, having been up over 30 hours at that point. She had been creaking pretty good all afternoon, and I had been walking geisha-style to keep from leaving her in the dust. I was a bit stiff myself from the different gait. This is when I think middle age is the pits. I won't comment on old age!

Saturday morning we left home around 10:00 a.m., all bundled up as it was unusually cold. We took the subway to Vysehrad, the ancient fortress home of the first Slavs to settle here on the Vlatava River over 1000 years ago. It is also where the cemetery for artists, writers and musicians is. It is a beautiful, fascinating cemetery which kept our attention a good while, particularly with its sculptures. It was almost excruciatingly cold and windy. We succumbed to the cold and wind and took refuge in the Forum Hotel near Vysehrad for a few minutes and a quick pastry and hot chocolate. Then onto the subway back to Wenceslas Square and the National Museum. I took mother's picture 'under the Horse,' bought the newspapers, then we wandered into the National Museum. A choir was singing in one of the rotundas—it created one of those light, unexpected moments that always seems to happen when one is sightseeing in Prague. We walked through the mineral collection, which was housed in cases from another century. We were charmed by the cases and the method of display.

Then by subway and tram to the Technical Museum, where we made quick work of the transportation hall, the clock section, camera section, astrolabe and sextant section—pretty dry. Across the street into the park for a quick snack at a kiosk and to meet at an appointed place and hour my friend Helena Furstova and her family. We got in their car and went to the farmers market, which was closed, then for want of another idea we went down to the river and fed the swans and ducks. That was fun. They dropped us at home at 4:00, by which time we had been on foot in the cold and wind for six hours. We felt like we had been beaten.

Had a nap, then met my friend Michael and his mother, Maybelle, at the Hotel Pariz for dinner. Afterward we walked in the dark and cold through the narrow cobbled streets to the Old Town Square, where we sat on a bench and marveled at the City until we got too cold and headed for home.

This past week, before mother came, I spent a lot of time with Joe Vosoba, the man who has come to take over my 'job' as EfD administrator in Prague. I am on the verge of acquiring us some free office space and a telephone, which is being donated by the Canadian Club (my employer, which is partly a private language school). Mr. Hornik, the owner of the Canadian Club, offered me the space and after conferring with the EfD ladies in Mobile, I accepted. The site of the space itself has not been determined but the commitment is made, so now we will have a home for the EfD operation. That prompted us to determine which of our volunteers had the wherewithal to be the administrator (and the money to live without a salary), and we picked Joe. I then talked him into it long distance, and he and his wife arrived a couple of weeks ago to take the reins from me. I have been carefully orienting him, remembering that feeling of floundering about that I had when I first came here.

Monday we went to look at a flat for Joe, and then he came and watched me teach my classes. That evening Michael came for left over Mexican food, then he took me to a special concert of Smetana's "My Country," which always opens the Prague Spring Festival. It was a lush, romantic symphony and quite beautiful.

Tuesday Joe and I met my friend Irena at the Jewish Town Hall for lunch, then he and I went to see my flat (where he and his wife will live after I leave), to the American Embassy to introduce him around, and back into downtown where we split up. I went to dinner with some of my old cohorts from the play at the Russian Cultural Center.

Wednesday I met Joe at the Canadian Club to see Hornik about the space, then went and taught my last classes. The advanced students took me to a pub for a beer to say farewell. I really enjoyed my students.

Thursday I had lunch at the Hotel Praha with John Streeter, who is here with Bell Atlantic working on the Czech phone system, and his wife. I really enjoyed them and we all agreed it was too bad we met just at the end of my stay. Joe and his wife came to my flat after lunch to go over a bunch of stuff.

Dull sounding week. But one is which I said many goodbyes to old friends, made some nice new ones, and ended my work in Czechoslovakia. And mother arrived. So it sounds dull, but it was anything but insignificant.

◆·◆————————◆·◆

Friday, 24 May 1991
Vienna, Austria

Dear Ones,

We are in Mittel Europe, especially if you consider that Russia and England lie in the same Europe. Mittel Europe is a literal place as well as a state of mind, a land of stolid burghers who are optimists if they are in front of the Iron Curtain and pessimists if they were behind. We are on the optimistic side, heading back to the other side. It is Friday morning; mother and I drove with Jarda all day Wednesday from Prague to Vienna. We turned a four-hour trip into a seven-hour one by stopping first at Stirin to show mother my castle, then stopping for a picnic (which did not last long—it was too cold), then going the long way through Brno and Bratislava (we looked at Brno from the windows of our speeding car; we stopped in Bratislava and took an elevator to the top of the handsome, modern suspension bridge over the Danube and looked down on that city). When we finally entered Vienna I for one was ready to get out of the car, which unfortunately took awhile because of course we got lost. We talked to a lot of nice Viennese people and saw a lot of pretty parks and architecture before simply abandoning the car and finding the hotel on foot in the maze of narrow inner city streets. Jarda left us and drove back to Prague, probably with relief. He is a dear precious man and mother is now devoted to him, too.

Our hotel was no great shakes but it was perfectly situated and for the first time in all our travels together on seven continents, I went shopping with mother without pitching a fit after we did the obligatory sightseeing. Even though I had been out of Czechoslovakia three times before, I was still kind of benumbed by the conspicuous consumption of Vienna, which is quite fabulous and wildly expensive, and so did not find my voice until I had trailed around passively for half a day, by which time it had ceased to be an issue.

We were in Vienna two nights. The first night we ate Japanese at my request. The second night, last night, we feasted at a self-serve market emporium with booths or kiosks for pasta, grilled meats, al dente vegetables, acres of salads and pastries. It was like going to an international cafeteria. We had to walk it off a bit before hitting the sack.

It is just plain cold in Europe; I think it is not usual. We have been whipped by the wind and bundled against the cold for the entire week mother has been with me. It is kind of wearing. This morning we are off to Budapest on a hovercraft which takes four hours on the Danube.

Last Sunday, Mother's third day in Prague, we went to Prague Castle for the day. First we went to a chamber music concert in Lobkowitz Palace. You could have blinked and Wolfgang Amadeus himself could have been playing the piano in this magnificent ballroom. My lovely lady doctor friend Daniela met us afterward and we went for lunch in one of the little places on the Castle grounds. Then she deposited us with a guide who took us into the major buildings, including the St. Vitus Cathedral and the Royal Hall (where jousting tournaments were held inside). Home by public transportation for a quick rest for mother, then I took her by subway to the Smetana Hall to see "Cosi fan Tutte" with Daniela—I had just seen it a few weeks before. I spent two hours drinking with and shrinking (back at my flat) a young acquaintance who had love problems with another young acquaintance. He was still there when mother got home from the opera, but politely left.

Monday morning I had to meet Mr. Hornik, the owner of the Canadian Club, to go see some space he was considering for our EfD office. I took mother with me, as we had to go on from there. It was kind of complicated but suffice it to say mother saw another little slice of Prague she definitely would have not seen otherwise. The space was not suitable.

Hornik dropped us off downtown and I took mother by to meet my friends at the Institute office, then we bought some opera tickets from a scalper across the street at the National Theatre for "Don Carlo" that night. I took her on my rounds (veggies, newspapers, etc.) in addition to taking her shopping for linen. We had lunch at the Palace at my favorite (and only) salad bar, then hoofed it back to my classes, or rather former classes. I had promised them I would bring my mother back to meet them, even though I taught my last classes last week. Both classes had bought me flowers, and we talked to them and joked around with them and then I had to accept their thanks and farewells with tears streaming down my face, all the time trying to be jolly and encouraging even though my heart was breaking, and I looked around and mother was crying, and it was pretty touching. I honestly did not know I was walking into any kind of ceremony, but I could hardly object to an accolade, even though it totally undid me, and undoes me again to think of it.

I took mother by the Diplomat Club to meet Jan Goldscheider and also Ota, the manager, whom I myself had not seen for awhile. Home for a quick rest and a bowl of soup before going back to the opera to see "Don Carlo", which we did not make it to the end of. The production was beautiful.

Tuesday was our last day of sightseeing in Prague, and we piddled. We started at the top of the hill at Strahov Monastery library (where I was satisfied to see mother have the same breath-taken-away reaction to the library as I had), then to the Loretto Convent, then down the hill into Mala Strana and a quick visit with Tim at his flat, then a mosey across the Charles Bridge, down Karlova Street and out into the Old Town Square, where we found a perch at an outdoor cafe (it was grey and windy but not painfully cold) and stayed for a good while. Home via more antiquities and more linen shopping, then home to rest, finally, repack, and have dinner in robes before leaving the next day for Vienna.

I try my best not to make these letters say, "and then", "and then," "and then", and I know I do not always succeed. I want to take this quick opportunity to thank those of you who are still reading them.

◆◆————◆◆

Saturday, 25 May 1991
Budapest, Hungary

Dear Ones,

We are in Pest; Buda is across the river. Buda is oldest and is built on a hill looking down at the Danube and over at Pest. Budapest looks and sounds like a busy European capital, in contrast to Prague, which acts like someone just lifted a bell jar off it after a hundred years or so. Budapest is quite beautiful but lacks that heart-stopping poignancy of the consistent beauty but weary decay of Prague.

We stepped off our hovercraft at 12:30 yesterday, and were whisked in 5 minutes to the Atrium Hyatt, where we hurriedly freshened up and got the guide book out before hitting the streets. The beautiful Chain Bridge with its stone lion guards is right in front of our hotel so we trucked across it to Buda, took a cable car to the top of the hill, and spent the afternoon soaking up Bud-ist antiquities and souvenirs. We even sat in a park and shared a bag of Hungarian Fritos and a Diet coke. When our feet, backs and shoulders gave out we came back down the hill and across the bridge to our Hyatt beds. We had dinner at a handsome restaurant called Gambrinus to which we had been directed by the concierge. Mother ate fogash, the Hungarian national fish. When she asked if it came out of the Danube the waiter screwed his face up and said with distaste, NO! The dear old Danube is apparently one of the major sewage systems of Europe, like the Rhine and some other romantically named rivers. The Danube current is so fast that mother and I could have put in at Vienna in a canoe and been here almost as fast as on our hovercraft. Back to dinner, I had grilled goose liver—not pate, but the liver itself. It was to die for.

This morning I was puffy-faced and irrational from eating junk and too much of it. This did not prevent us from sticking to our schedule of eating something bad for us every three hours. We ate a proper breakfast but then we ate at McDonald's for lunch and had pastries and coffee mid afternoon. Tonight we are going to eat Chinese food.

Today we did Pest in one morning foray and one afternoon foray. My irrationality did not mix well with the shopping today. I found it much more soothing to sit for a minute in each of several dimly lit, magnificent churches. As we walked out of each church mother announced that that one was her favorite one so far. They do just flat take your breath away, each one. We went into one where Liszt used to give concerts, and in its loft some musicians were practicing, so we got to listen to our own little truncated concert. We went to the museum and the parliament building, and got rained on a little, and finally plunked ourselves down in an outdoor cafe and sat for an hour, visiting and feeding the sparrows and listening to some musicians in the Square.

This has been a fun trip. We have not taken a profound historical dive into these cities. Rather we have walked and soaked up atmosphere and gleaned enough facts from our Fodor's not to feel like complete idiots. We have eaten and laughed and not spent much money. We have had good though cold weather. The architecture has been memorable. It just makes you realize how important public design is. This city is knitted together with good-looking bridges, which they could have made ugly but did not. There is 800-year-old and thousand-year-old stuff still standing in these cities and it is good looking, it is a gift from its creators to future generations. I wish Americans had more of that concept of long-range planning, so to speak. We need to make everything beautiful on the off chance there are a few more generations planning to be born into this beat up old world. We need to make everything beautiful for our own selves and own souls. It sure helps.

I will be back in Washington in a couple of weeks.

—◆—◆—————◆—◆—

Thursday, 6 June 1991
Prague, Czechoslovakia

Dear Ones,

I am in the last throes of this incredible experience and I am grasping at everyone and everything I can get my hands on as it slides away from me. I do not understand why I am so sentimental about leaving these people and this place after a mere five months when I seemingly waltzed away from San Antonio when I came here. Perhaps the difference is I knew I was not really leaving San Antonio, whereas I am most definitely leaving Prague. Also, in San Antonio experiences were part of a diurnal process which, while not altogether predictable, was nonetheless not fraught with the vivid strangeness of life here. Experiences ran together in a miasma of, ultimately, sameness, whereas in a mere five months here every experience is new and carried out in an extraordinary setting. I am actually in Elizabeth Kubler-Ross' stage of dying wherein all the people associated with the dying person are only each losing one person (me) but the dying person (me) is losing many people, and a whole world, and I am grieving, genuinely grieving. I knew even in the depths of my misery last winter that this would happen because I have not lived 45 years without learning that irony rules the world, but as much as one may heartily congratulate oneself on being prepared, one simply does not know what the future holds. This is a major reason why we are all still plugging away. Caution does not make for life, and besides, cautious people suffer surprise, too, usually worse so than wild people who have made a pact to accept the consequences of their actions, no matter what they are, so that they can have them. I would rather have pain my heart than boredom in my head.

Mother left two weeks ago and I have drunk whiskey, visited with all my friends, entertained, cried at least once a day, made even more friends, tied up loose ends and gone to a lot of concerts while putting off packing.

Nat Merrill from Opera Colorado was here—we saw "Abduction from the Seraglio" at the Smetana and "Rusalka" at the National Theatre. We left "Seraglio" and he was transfixed by "Rusalka." It is always a lesson to go to the opera with him. We also spent two nights in the audience of Stepan Rak, a beautiful (literally and artistically) guitarist who was compelling, and we were in a special audience on the last night of the Prague Spring Festival to hear Beethoven's 9th (Ode to Joy) which was stunning. I have initially a visceral response to music and when the lights go down and the music starts every thought and emotion kept in check by the exigencies of the day come to the surface of my nerve ends and that is that for me. I come unglued. Then I recover and have a spell of intellectual interest in how the horns are doing with the strings, and then I lapse into a reverie which can include everything from the hamsters we had in childhood to my latest desired conquest on the subway. I love music.

Nat and I did music, and some sightseeing. For two days the weather was nice and he said, 'gee, I don't think the air in Prague is so bad.' I could have screamed. Fortunately the weather got bad before he left, and today it is cold and grey again. I will probably miss it when I start sweating out the American summer. My class of advanced students was not content with the touching farewell they afforded me when mother was here and took me to dinner at a place called "Llano Estacado" which had "Western" cooking and even tequila. It was not recognizable (even the tequila) but we had a great time and I was profoundly flattered by their attention and affection. They all quit the class the next week because the new teacher was not good enough. I discouraged it, but they did it anyway.

My doctor friend Daniela arranged for me a meeting with Olga Havelova, President Havel's wife, and we went earlier this week to have a long conversation with her through an interpreter. I have it on tape, and I am trying to do something with it.

My gentlemen friends are acting properly sad that I am leaving and the phone rings constantly with them and others.

Today I spent eight hours on my feet at the airport greeting 200 people on 10-15 flights arriving for the annual meeting of the Institute. I just volunteered to help as a labor of love for my core 'family' in Prague. It was fun, really, but terribly hard on my back.

Knowing how many people read these letters has caused me to compose them with some care, although I have not ever really dissembled in them with the exception of some understandable omissions of sins. It has been a joy to have you for an audience, and I shall see you all soon.

(Almost) all my love,

Taddy

II.
POETRY

Disclaimer: I am only an amateur lay poet, not a real one, so I beg your indulgence as you read this smattering of poems which for the most part were written very fast at the moment of inspiration. With one exception I have not ever "worked" on a poem. After they are written in the frenzy to capture them, that is it, there is no editing. They would certainly be improved by some plodding, scholarly tweaking but that is not the way I have approached "poetry." Rather, the words fall out of the sky, are written on paper, then life resumes. Thank you for reading them. After you do, your life can resume.

After September 11, 2001, these little poems were inspired by the fear of attack on two special days in 2002, and were written upon waking the following mornings.

July 5, 2002

By dawn's early light
The sky was still there
Unpierced by the shells
Of Fourth of July.

September 12, 2002

The grey light untinged
The future lay crouched
The skyline still there
By dawn's early light.

BIRDS IN A HURRICANE

We swooped in pairs and dove for minnows
Back in the first memory of our wings
Until the vortex lofted us into green sky
Far from home and high above the world.
Spirals of fledglings sucked off their spoil banks
Joined us in the cruel and bully wall of wind.
We entertained the storm with our flaps and cries
And like a bully he enjoyed our torment.
Some resigned themselves to flying in circles,
Others died before we hit the wall of land.
Released from the giant's grip we fell tiredly
To Earth where once there had been a world.
Beside stunned humans we sat in bewilderment
Lost and wondering where everything had gone.
While they hammered and sawed below us we
Made tired mating dances to keep ourselves alive
And searched for the massive schools that migrated
For our delectation and regurgitation,
Far from home and high above the world.

                              Port Aransas 2003

TO JUMP

This poem is dedicated to all the people who jumped out of the World Trade Center.

The halls are blocked, the floor is hot,
Dark and dust the sudden landscape.
Crawling from their desks they look for holes and
Find none. They draw themselves a line
Before which is infinity.
Their minds step over the line in a
White wave of wonder, agreeing to
Their fates more easily than if there
Had been a decision to be made.
Now, fire lapping at their backs they
Think of pets unfed and love unsaid.
Pushed by gusts of heat they dance on
Sills too hot. They hug and make their choices
To trust the air, the summer sky.
A skirt, a shirttail, the pennant of a
Tie waft first like leaves then plummet.
Hearts of fear gain light and fly, then
Stop before they break.

Washington, D. C.
September 13, 2001

THE THIRD RAIL

A poem from a Woman to Her Married Lover

You're so close to me, just across the ties
An arm's reach, close enough to merge.
A passenger could look to the end of us and see
Us merge into infinity but we don't, ever.
It's an illusion.

Between us lies the third rail, crackling, dangerous,
Deadly to the touch, full of electric energy,
Ready to fry us if we reach for each other as
We long to do. We have kissed over her and
Felt the fear.

We have felt under her, groping toward each other
In our fearful respect for her love, her power.
We skirt her hard authority, her flying sparks.
But we are alike, and want to marry our sameness
Away from her sway.

We could enlist the ties that bind us to buck her off
And let us meet at the end of the line, in the
Station with the old clock and the water tower,
Dancing in the vaulted hall celebrating our oldness
And our oneness.

We could pray for drunken derailment where
In the confusion we could meld into one with
No one the wiser. Or we could meet in an abandoned
Yard and wind our iron selves into a twist of
Final love.

Unless it's our fate to feel only the dramatic
Longing that transforms the steely heart to poetry
And go to scrap with no one but ourselves
The wiser for the gnawing passion that hid
Itself in our bed.

                              Prout's Neck
                              July 5, 1997

When I was in graduate school at The George Washington University to get my Master of Education degree, we were given two minutes in a class one night to write anything we could think of about Christopher Columbus. This was my exercise. September 1992

COLUMBUS ARRIVES IN THE AMERICAN HEMISPHERE

Bearing illnesses their own bodies
Did not recognize
They came ashore and pressed
Their flesh to fit that of their
New friends.

Babies were held over heads to see
The shining metal
That covered the bodies holding
The illnesses they did not know
They had.

Old people fainted in fear only
Thinking gods had come
And did not know if they bore ill
Or good will, or secrets in
Their clothes.

The chiefs only knew that life was
Changed forever but did
Not know that life was ever over
They could not see behind the strength
The tiny killers.

This poem was inspired by a news story about an old timer named Mountain Bob who emerged from an underground mine where he had spent 227 days, breaking a world record. In pondering why anyone would want to do such a thing, it dawned on me that maybe there was an understandable reason.
June 1994

MOUNTAIN BOB

Mountain Bob entered the
Earth through the
Tunnel of her dark orifice
Saying this is mine.

For two hundred twenty seven
Days he held her in thrall
With his plunders of her
Dark tunnel and its every

Indentation space and place
For him. Exhausted and spent
He left his pleasures behind
To memory and emerged into the sunshine.

In August 2000 at Port Aransas, Texas I was the guest of Tony Amos, a naturalist at the University of Texas Marine Science Institute, on his every-eighth-day San Jose Island beach observations [San Jose Island is across the channel from Port Aransas]. In a John Deere Gator, a sort of heavy duty golf cart, we drove the 21-mile length of San Jose making "obs", counting birds, finding dead things and measuring the beach. Stranded at one point by engine trouble, I wrote this poem (with apologies to e. e. cummings) while waiting for Tony to fetch help. Every element of the poem refers to something we saw in the course of the day. An addendum to the poem refers to Andi Wickham, Tony's assistant, who usually accompanied him on such trips. August 2000

SANJobs

Seagull Pelican Sanderling Tern
Seagull Pelican Sanderling Turd
Seagull Leatherback Skeleton Skull
Seagull Skeletonback Broken-Wing Gull

Driftwood Sargassum Boat Ramping the Dawn
Center Console Motor Casing God's Gift Be Gone
Seaweed Plastic Cullers Buoys Bumpering Floats
Egg Crates Vultures Green Bottles Sea Oats

Genesis Exodus Levitate Wings
Rollers Updrafts Tossed Tidal Odd Things
Pelican Flotilla Tern Congeries
Wilson Snowy Piping Ploveries

Loggerhead Dolphinskull Measure Sand Soft
Fence Lines Bayous Ichneumon Aloft
Tevas SPF Little Egret Red
Great Blue Grey Sky Phone and Gator Dead

Deer Carcass in Velvet Fiddler Racing Crabs
Koozie Coca Cola Clorox Sandwich Big Red
Morning Glories Stories Dead Men What Went Dragging
Horizon Receding – No *Barrier* Island.

Seagull Sanderling Pelican Tern
Green Gator Green Water Sand Salty Sunburn
Eight Days Fishing Caps Washed Binary Change
Cumulus Street Clouds Threatening Haze.

—

Amos 'n Andi O'er Dune and Dale Bounce
Obbing and Looking and Laughing to Count
Beauty of Nature Disregard of Man
In Eons All Will Be Covered in Sand.

ROOSEVELT ISLAND

(As seen across the Potomac from the Kennedy Center Terrace, Washington, D. C., March 1995)

The raggedy winter edge drops into
Slate dirty water made magic by
Symmetrical ripples from shells knifing through
Night lights and shore lights in trees.

Peaceful anticipation is breathed in with
Smoke from forbidden mouths in the
Cool tender coatless air on arms and throats unmuffled.
The end of sunset is a closing exhibit through

The scrim of spindly inverted tuning forks,
The sere melancholy willows who wait
For summer to weep, now dainty and
Coy as they run their fingers to illude the

Raggedy winter edge.

ANDROS BEACH

A blue triangle of lapstrake shipwreck sticking out of the sand
    like a flying fish wing;
The royal whorl and promiscuous thighs of the pink labia'd conch;
The shivery meringue of foam blown off the wind-whipped bay;
The warp and woof of driftwood root systems laced with hawsers;
Bleached exoskeletal fingers and femurs of coral;
White confetti seaweed straw for the bricks of beach building;
Coconuts, pine cones, mangrove leaves and human detritus
    blown backward toward the surf;
A trillion trillion shells called sand under each footfall;
Dog paws, sneakers and splay-toe'd naked records of trespass;
Land creatures crossing the uncertain wavery line seeking
    the Other of the waterworld.

                            Andros Island, Bahamas
                            March 1996

JUST LIKE YOU

Old souls from past and parallel lives meet in casual but calculated
    conversation at the beach
And each thinks to itself the odd coincidence of finding someone
    whose valuable issues are the same.
The talk unfolds in chrysalis and there emerges a brightly colored
    new being in the convergence
Of two formerly isolated hearts that now know with four eyes staring
    into each other that they are just like each other.

After the story-telling and the note-comparing comes the dawn of the
    plan to elevate the relationship
By descending to the depths of physicality to see if that, too,
    generates a connection.
And when it does, when it is as dreamy and sweet as it is raw,
    one whispers You're Beautiful and
The other in a dawning of sensation that it is home and safe and
    unreasonably happy answers Just Like You.

Now they walk in a force-field aura of prickly desire and compulsion
    to say all the sweet things and touch
Each other in secret in public and frankly in private to know
    every centimeter of the other
So the heart will not fear loss when the exchange of body fluids
    and parts is over and the planes take off
To return them to parallel lives which now only look
    parallel but are really woven strands of the whole.

March 1996

ANDROS DIVE SITES

The Fish:
Mother Nature plays a joke on the fish by giving them countershading
    in neon stick-your-finger-in-a-socket colors
Not hidden are they but lures to admirers and enemies
    alike, in love with the palette and
Designs to rival the geometrician and artist.

The Coral:
Unseen but productive sculptors give off juices that harden dry in the water
    in shapes only intoxication could invent
Round wiggly wavy brittle soft squishy flat fat sting-y tickly
    smooth crusty purple plain
A landscape of boulders buttes plateaus hills and valleys.

The Water:
Ultramarine to green to turquoise to ink blue, waves piled on each other in their
    disruptive race that leaves the deep undisturbed
In the silent depths only fish sonar and hand signals
    communicate simultaneous movement
Memory of dry land fades and time is not counted in minutes.

Blue Holes:
Blue holes are full of clouds not ink and welcome the intruder with hostful
    uncharacteristic warmth
And in a place of no smells a recognizable sulphurous smell that
    spells the elemental beginnings of this
Trough and the very Earth it sinks its gouge into.

The Divers:
To see these things the clay figures wrench themselves counterintuitively into
    breathing underwater and forget they cannot
And go against their normal judgments of air and temperature
    to slip their Earth bonds
For the sake of the transcendent moment of being what they are not.

                                    Andros Island, Bahamas
                                    March 1996

The following poem was written at Port Aransas the week in August 2000 when the damaged Russian submarine Kursk was sitting on the bottom of the Barents Sea and the attention of the world was riveted on the possibility the men in it might still be alive. I wrote the poem in about five minutes one night just before bedtime. It was written to have the exact number of syllables in each line, and rhyming couplets. It was written from the point of view of someone making love on a boat in Port Aransas, thinking about the Russian sailors.

Somewhere beneath the sea
Lie mothers' sons who see
The end of life on earth
With not a grave in dirt.

Ten thousand miles away
I lie with you asway
A gentler warmer sea
Licks and laps at me.

Impressed and reluctant
Girls' lovers now are sunk
With short breath and fear stark
They pound metal in dark.

Ten thousand miles away
I pound your back to say
Don't leave stay where you are
Inside you've struck a bar.

Last thought the sailors scream
Don't kill the family dream
With water in their ears
They're deaf to all our tears.

Enwrapped but soberly
Their faces come to me
And in my ecstasy
My spirit floats to sea.

The following was a commission from my mother in the spring of 1997 to write a poem about turtles to be read at the dedication of the ARK, the Animal Rehabilitation Keep at the University of Texas Marine Science Institute in Port Aransas, Texas, where we live in the summer. Mother was on the Board of the Institute and had raised the money to build the ARK.

The poem took several months to write, and was finished on the deck of our house at Port Aransas that summer as a huge orange moon rose out of the Gulf of Mexico.

FROM THE TURTLES

In the beginning the sea was emerald and cobalt,
The littoral pink and gold. We swam in silence
Among clouds of cousin fish, smooth and fast.
We smiled at their quicksilver disdain as we ate them
When we wanted them.

In the countless time we watched bemused the
Fads of evolution come and go. The ocean was a
Stew of swimmers, no two alike. In seas
Full of bait and secrets we roamed and aged
And remembered.

From the quiet of the starlit beaches where we churned
The night sand for our nurseries, we returned
To dive deep and board at the bottom the daredevil
Murex sailors who manned our decks and gunwales
Like Armor we did not need.

Safe in our shells still we lost our share,
Our babies wolfed like peanuts as they toddled
To the sea. As we passed the strand in our
Stately slowness waiting for them we saw the Humans
Rise and walk on land.

For eons we didn't know of them. One circular day word
Echoed along the swim lines that a shadow had passed
Overhead, not clouds. Something else was in the air
Above us, in the world above us, on the water not of it,
In the air.

Our old ones foresaw doom. Basking lizard-eyed at
The surface we spied on the boat people and
Remembered their race from their time in the slime.
The old storytellers said they had returned in the floating
Cloud-makers to their first element.

They wanted us. So many mouths to feed with
Our puny meat, so many perukes to tame with our combs.
They drowned us and we sickened and disappeared, from home to
Net to cooking pot, losing our position in the chain of life
To these unlikely foes.

From their disappointing race came some who reached into
The sea to retrieve us, to run kind fingers over
The prisoners' numbers etched in our carapaces. Their
Beacon flashed across islands with flags and schools where they
Worked as their hearts hoped for us.

Like one Lazarus to another they spoke Come unto us
You tired you poor, and into the folds of their care
We swam, safe under their outstretched arm. Into the
Ark of their care we trundled, mossy and beaten and
Longing for succor.

They made us their partners in a future estranged and
Truncated by loss, no longer seamlessly webbed to our past.
In our loneliness we knew the first part of the world was
Over, and as we waited to see if there were a next part
We were not alone.

                                        Port Aransas
                                        August 1997

Introduction: This tiny poem was written after watching our naturalist friend Tony Amos, rehabilitator of turtles at the UT Marine Science Institute at Port Aransas, release a large loggerhead turtle on the beach. It swam into the water without a backward glance, although funnily enough with an antennae cemented to its carapace.

> To love a turtle is
> The hardest
> Because when they leave they
> Don't say goodbye.
> Charity at its purest reminds
> Not to care
> Only to thank the spangled heavens
> For the heartache.
>
> —June 2007

[WARNING: SEXY POEMS AHEAD]

HOW BIG

Syl tried to make her fingers go
around the upper part of her
forearm like a baseball bat
And said Taddy! You should
Have seen it! It was <u>this big</u>!

(I knew. I had seen it.)

Linda called me up and said
The stereo repairman had come
And one thing led to another and
Taddy! You should have seen it!
It looked liked a Hebrew National Salami!

(Umm-m-m-m)

I saw one attached to a bass player
Once and it does make you fall in
Love until that's all you can
Do or think about until it goes
Its merry way, it owner predestined

(Not to be yours.)

—1989

AFTER SEX

He labored over me until
He finally got my mind off the details
By mining the vein without the brain.
I screamed, and

To celebrate jumped in the pool.
Floating in the cross position staring
At an enormous sea bird floating
In a corresponding cross over me

Looking at me as food as he had
Plumbed me like a larder
A pantry to pillage practically
Licking the labels off the cans.

I soared with the bird and
Held its breast to me enjoying
The embrace without the threat,
The coming back together.

—October 1989

WHERE

Where's the craziest place
You've ever done it?

Under the piano in the maid's room
On a stair landing in the surf

On the tuna tower of a fishing boat
On the dance floor at Regine's

In a fleabag hotel near Elaine's
In a fleabag homosexual encounter
Hotel across from Julia's with a
British MP no less.

Under a table in an airplane
In a men's room in a baby's room
In my parents' bed with a terribly
Stiff friend, and once with a hood.

In a yacht in a speed boat
In a train backseat of a car
On the ground surrounded by
Bottle caps and condoms.

In a hospital room
In a hansom cab
In a hailstorm
In a hell storm

Covered with mosquitos covered with sweat.
Snowed in. With my lover's best friend.
In a shower. In the ass.
Any Where and Every Where.

Never enough.

—November 1989

NAKED CAME THE STRANGER

The book would be:
One chapter his,
One chapter mine.

The best craziest sex
We ever had, where
When and how.

The book wrote itself
And lay there before us
On the table at Martin's.

As real on that tavern table
As the booth, the smells
So titillating it was.

Lay there bestseller with
Money and fame all over it
And we savoured it

And the private stories
In the book but unwritten
Still secret stories

Causing us to break off, laugh
Thinking of them. But do
People care about other people's sex?

—November 1989

III.
TRAVEL JOURNALS

SOUTH AFRICA AND THE SEYCHELLES
INTRODUCTION

Sometime in 1999 my friend and sweetheart Leonid Romankov, the handsome Russian legislator whom mother and I met in St. Petersburg in 1997, invited me to meet him in the Seychelles in October of 2000. He had been helpful to a Seychelloise woman named Erenia Meriton who was studying for her PhD. in St. Petersburg and whose husband was in the government of the Seychelles, and they were going to import him for a vacation to thank him for his good offices. Naturally I jumped at the invitation.

One odd thing for me was that I was going to be the houseguest of someone I had never laid eyes on, and the schedule was going to be entirely out of my hands. There was a luxurious aspect to that as well as culture shock, since I always seem to be the one who makes the plan.

Without consulting a world map I directed the travel agent to route me through South Africa so that as long as I was in that part of the world I could stop and visit my old flame Armand Schonfrucht in Cape Town. We had had a romance for two consecutive springs in Washington, 1998 and 1999, when he had paid extended visits from his native South Africa. As it turns out, South Africa is not on the way to the Seychelles, a fact that caused me to do quite a lot of flying relative to the small amounts of time I spent on the ground in each of the places I visited.

Then it would not do not to return through London and see another old boyfriend, Lord Gilbert (John), whom I met in San Antonio at La Louisiane in 1968. This also caused me to go out of my way, but all these lovely men had gone out of their way to see me at one time or another, so it was my turn. It was mostly worth it.

Because of all this to-ing and fro-ing between swains, I did not write a trip journal for dissemination. There was nothing prurient about it but I didn't want it to fall into the hands of any of my other love interests, all of whom probably thought they were the only one. Now enough water has flowed under the bridge to come out of the closet.

THE JOURNAL

Tuesday, October 17. I leave Washington at 7:00 a.m., fly to Atlanta on Delta and thence to Cape Town (14 hours) on South Africa Airways.

Wednesday, October 18. Arrive Cape Town at 7:00 a.m. Armand, former sweetheart and now host, picks me up. He is spiffy in white ducks and a blue blazer; I am wrung out but healthy. In the car is Rollo, his Jack Russell terrier, who spends the next three days in my lap, his little back feet scrabbling on the tops of my thighs to keep his balance, his front paws on the dashboard. We bond.

I check in to a Holiday Inn because Armand's house is not ready for me. I'm just as glad, as I want a long sleep without interference at the end of the day. Armand gives me a couple of hours to freshen up, then picks me up. We go first to a park where he and Rollo walk everyday. I'm glad for the movement, and enchanted by the flora, particularly the proteas which we pay dearly for in the U.S. but which are the national flower here and grow like weeds. The temperature is perfect and the sky is clear.

I ask to be taken to Kirstenbosch, the famous botanical garden. I walk around it for an hour, barely able to put one foot in front of the other on the uphill parts, I am so tired. Armand waits reading in the car in the shade; a smoker, he doesn't make any pretense about being athletic.

We drive out to a suburb, Kalk's Bay, on the water and have a good seafood lunch in a restaurant looking out over the rocks and kelp beds. At the surface the kelp looks like dozens of sea lion heads bobbing, or else I am hallucinating in my fatigue.

By the time we get back to the city it is late afternoon. I go home to my hotel, force my eyes to stay open until 6:00 p.m., then sleep for twelve hours.

Thursday, October 19. Armand and I are going to meet at noon, so I am footloose in the morning to go to Robben Island and see the prison where Mandela was held for 27 years. Alas, the boat that goes over there is fully booked (Armand is amazed to hear this; he can't imagine why anyone would want to go there), so I have the hotel van take me to the waterfront, restored as a "festival marketplace" of the James Rouse school. I fiddle around idly wasting time in the shops until I discover there is an aquarium, which piques my interest. It is a lovely aquarium with among other things a Cape penguin display of the little darlings swimming around and stinking to high heaven. The van picks me back up and takes me to the hotel, where I check out and meet Armand.

Cape Town, from what I see of it, is a cross of Acapulco, Bermuda and Santa Barbara. It's pretty. Armand drives his Mercedes with a sense of masculine entitlement, fast and competently, and on the left, a hangover from the Brits. We drive forty minutes down to Cape Point so I can see the Cape of Good Hope, Rollo's little hard body and bright nervousness directing us. I'm wishing he had suction cups for feet, but I'm starting to adore him.

At the Cape Point Park they won't let us in with a dog. I convince Armand to go back to an ostrich farm just outside the Park and see if we can't talk someone into babysitting. Sure enough, one of the helpers is thrilled to take care of our Rollo for a couple of hours, and we are on our way back into the Park. There are wind-distorted trees and 'fynbos', a type of ground cover (actually several different kinds of flowering plants peculiar to the Cape that together make up the ecosystem called fynbos). At the Point itself there is infrastructure; we have lunch in the restaurant from which several busloads have just cleared out. It is still kind of chaotic, but we hunker down and order. Just outside the window bubble gum-bottomed baboons try to steal people's food from the terrace tables, one of which we have turned down because it is so windy.

After lunch we take a cable car to the top of Cape Point. Even from the top terminus we have to climb more stairs to the observation point, there to look down on the arrow of land cut into the extreme wind, separating the oceans. The pressure of the wind is like a hand pushing my face. My heart goes out historically to all the mariners who have rounded this dangerous Cape.

We retrieve Rollo from the ostriches and make a beautiful drive home up the East coast of the Cape, reefs of dusty sunlight pouring down the mountainsides as the day starts to end in the West.

I move into my guest room at Armand's house. The bed is too soft, so I make a pallet on the floor with makeshift materials. Rollo watches. That night I dream that Waring Partridge, Julia Jitkoff's husband who has the sailboat that has figured in my recent travels, to surprise us with a visit at Port Aransas has a foot of snow dumped in the driveway and slides in on his sailboat to rest at our door. I awake enchanted and deeply comfortable.

Friday, October 20. Armand, who is a bit of a sloth, is relaxing into a routine of doing things and with barely a whimper from him we drive up into the Winelands today for sightseeing and lunch. Rollo, who is now in total crush-dom, rides on my lap and even lies down some, giving the fabric of my pants a breather. The day and subsequently the scenery are beautiful. Cape wines are famous all over the world and there are many vineyards in the hills north of Cape Town. We go to one in Franschoek that has a good French restaurant, La Petite Ferme, and a porch where we can sit with the dog a la francais. We have a delicious meal following which a nap in a hammock is in order but we get in the car and drive slowly homeward instead, mellow and all too aware that I leave tomorrow and have not budgeted enough time for this visit.

Rollo

Late in the afternoon we pay a call on Rupert Ragg, a friend of Bernard Lifshutz (our friend from San Antonio), and Rupert's wife Leslie. They live in a beautiful house about two minutes from Armand, whose own house is not beautiful but is in a good neighborhood. Rupert is veddy veddy upper class English and gorgeous; Leslie is pretty and full of herself. Armand talks to Leslie and I talk to Rupert. Just before we rise to leave Rupert asks me about my reaction to the "sooties". I look blank. Blacks, he means. I graciously (for me) change the subject.

I have seen the miles of shanty towns on the highway, dense and artistic with found-object construction. I have seen the walls behind which everyone in the white neighborhoods lives. I look back at America (always a good practice when traveling) and I'll take integration any day. Apartheid may be officially over but it is alive and well until white hearts can be turned.

Saturday, October 21. I awake thinking about those people in their shanties and I think they will never be for one day as comfortable as I am at that moment.

I think I have to be at the airport two hours early because I am flying international to the Seychelles, albeit through Johannesburg, but when I am left at the airport by my fellows I learn it is only considered a local flight. I am left to ponder leaving Armand and Rollo earlier than necessary, a parting difficult enough as it was. Rollo came into my room as I finished packing, put his head down on his front paws and looked up at me reproachfully. I knew how people felt who stay together for the sake of the kids. Armand is not well; I may not see him again. I am pensive all day.

It is an hour and a half to Johannesburg. There I wait in the airport long enough to eat and get a lot of reading done. I have read *Country of My Skull* by Antjie Krog, a nonfiction book about the South African Truth and Reconciliation Commission, and now I am reading Susan Eisenhower's book about her love affair and marriage to a Russian scientist and politician, this in preparation for meeting my Russian, Leonid Romankov, in the Seychelles.

It is 10:30 p.m. when my plane lands on Mahe, the main island of the Seychelles where the capital, Victoria, is and where we will be staying with Leonid's friend Vincent Meriton. Vincent and I have been e-mailing about some things he requested I bring him from the U.S., and I know he is 39 years old, in the National Assembly of his country, and also the head of the government agency for Youth Programs. That is all I know. A tall, handsome black man with aquiline features meets me at the door of the terminal: Vincent. He has been let into the Customs area because he is a government official. We talk and wait for my bags, one of which is full of things for him: stereo speakers, soccer balls and dominoes, plus books I have brought for him and Leonid.

Leonid awaits me outside Customs and we have a happy reunion. By the time we get to Vincent's house on the mountainside above Victoria, it is late and we go to bed because we have to be up and at the airport the next morning at 7:30 to fly to Praslin, another island. Leonid and I have two rooms and a shared bath downstairs; I am desperate for sleep, which I don't get because the house is un-airconditioned and nature, the jungle outside, is so noisy. I am getting my ear plugs out.

Sunday, October 22. We get up, go to the airport and take the 15-minute flight on a Twin Otter over to Praslin, the second biggest island. On Praslin we take a taxi to a hotel and have breakfast in the open air. Our rent car arrives and we drive down the road a piece to Vallee de Mai, the home of the Coco de Mer palm trees. This primaeval forest is a preserved park; we walk through it. I am agape at the immense size of the trees. One palm frond could thatch a whole house. The characteristic coconuts are raunchy sculptures of human female sex organs, really torsos from the waist down. They are startingly lifelike, and then the mystery of their mirror image is heightened by the penile cylindrical thing that grows on the male trees. Mother Nature is making fun of us.

We go to a beach that heretofore I had only seen the likes of in advertisements. It is picture-perfect, turquoise water in a crescent of white sand bounded by mangrove trees, salt cedars, palms and huge granite boulders. I am into the water in a flash, and for the next two hours cannot get enough of the snorkeling and swimming. Vincent sleeps on the beach, his arm protectively flung over our possessions. I make myself get out of the water because I realize in my excitement I have gotten a classic snorkelers' sunburn on my back. I watch the scattered others who share the beach with us: middle aged couples, topless women, everyone moving in slow motion. A young woman goes by holding the hand of a small boy, and I think about how, when you see a grown person and a child walking together hand in hand, you can tell the child likes having a big friend and the big one likes having a little friend.

We go down the road to a restaurant on the water for lunch, then back to the little airport (where a sign instructs cars to stop on the road if a plane is landing, so as not to get clipped I guess), fly home and get cleaned up after a day spent mostly with sweat or salt water on our skin. When evening comes I sleep twelve hours with ear plugs and a mask—ear plugs for the birds, who are hysterically loud, and a mask for the daylight that comes at 5:00 a.m.

Monday, October 23. Vincent has to go to work today. He sends his agency driver, Innocente (whose name sounds like Inosha in the Creole they speak), to pick us up midmorning to go to the opening of a children's art show that is part of the Creole Festival that is going on. The show is in the lobby of the National Library, a building that also houses the National Assembly. I find a chair by the door as the lobby fills up, then there are speeches in Creole. Most everyone is Black except one older white man who kisses all the women he encounters. He turns out to be the French ambassador. Later he kisses me. I also meet the Cuban ambassador. This is a formerly socialist country that is now democratic, but in former times the Cubans and the Russians were big men on campus.

Innocente takes Leonid and me to Beau Vallon Beach, one of the many beaches on our main island of Mahe. While Leonid bakes on the beach, I go scuba diving with a group off a boat that leaves right from the edge of the water. We run for about fifteen minutes, then drop into the Indian Ocean. I see marvelous creatures I have never seen before, though it is murky and surgy.

That night we dine at home on the first of many meals prepared by Vincent's housekeeper, a skinny drink of water named Lorna who has an irrepressible smile. She comes early in the morning, cleans, fixes our breakfast, cooks and leaves the supper on the stove. It is Creole: various fish stews, rice, "chutney" (not like ours; a cooking process, really, having to do with dehydrating whatever it is first, then stirfrying it). One night we have mango chutney, the next shark chutney. It is not New Orleans Creole. One morning our sink is stopped up. I go into the kitchen to brush my teeth and there is an octopus in the sink: dinner that night. The food is good, but to love it would take an acquired taste. We rave about it for the benefit of our host.

That night we eat the dishes Lorna has left, and talk about government. Politics is the abiding thread through all our talk. Both Leonid and Vincent are in the process of building democracies, Leonid as a member of the St. Petersburg Legislative Assembly. I'm so proud to know these men, and humbled to think how easy we have it in our mature democracy at home. My Leonid and dear Vincent are both, for many reasons, men of great honor.

I like Vincent, too, because he is organized. He always has an earphone stuck in his ear, attached to his cell phone which is in his shirt pocket. His wife and children are in St. Petersburg, and his small mountainside bachelor keep is neat as a pin. We sit on the porch that dangles over the small driveway below, and look out at the ocean beyond the town below. Leonid revels in the view and the heat and the colors, knowing he returns to face the extreme cold and greyness of Russian winter.

On the way down the mountain this morning the first two lines of a poem come to me: "In blessed air we lived among The fruits of nature run amok ... " That's as far as I got, except for "Our cottage on a hillside tucked," but obviously there's a line missing.

Tuesday, October 24. Leonid goes in the morning to have a meeting with the Chairman of the National Assembly, and I read *The Hours* by Michael Cunningham. It is so good I think there doesn't ever have to be another book written after it; it will do. I am loving not having anything to do but read.

When Leonid returns we go to the beach at Anse Royale to snorkle and swim.

Leonid loves lying in the sand, which I do not, but I am polite and try to find some shade. It is his trip, after all: beaches, water and sand are not so difficult for me to obtain.

In the evening we have guests for dinner, Bernard, who is a government official, and his girlfriend Brina. We eat a Lorna-feast and talk politics, then tell some jokes to see if they translate to another culture.

Wednesday, October 25. Leonid and I are up early so Vincent can take us to the waterfront to catch the high-speed catamaran ferry to Praslin, there to take another boat, a schooner, to La Digue, a smaller island. It's a total of almost three hours of boat riding, and we're still on La Digue by 10:00 a.m. We take a taxi (and not one of the famous ox-carts, after we watch a driver beating his ox) from the little town at the docks up the coast road to a hotel called Patatran, down below which we establish a sand nest on a pretty beach with big granite boulders and great snorkeling. We each take turns snorkeling while the other guards our possessions. Everyone is theft conscious, which strikes me as antithetical to our surroundings. We loll and swim until we are hungry, then go up to the hotel and have lunch on their terrace (Creole, not as good as Lorna's). We walk back to the little town, maybe a kilometre, under a high canopy of trees shading the raised roadbed. All the roads in the Seychelles are raised about a foot but have no shoulder or guard rail. They are quaint but do not allow for mistakes.

There was the long boat trip home then, getting cleaned up, which always feels so good, and dinner and conversation on the porch. We love our evenings with Vincent because he is smart and fun to talk to.

Thursday, October 26. We have reservations to take a boat over to a Marine Park to snorkle and have lunch in a group, but as we are sitting at the dock waiting to get on the boat, I am hit with turista and decide I am better off at home. I call Vincent at his office, he sends Innocente to fetch me, and I spend the day asleep at home by myself. At the end of the day the men are there and want to eat, but I just watch and tongue some rice into my mouth. We watch a James Bond movie, "The World Is Not Enough", that Vincent has on DVD. He is as gadget crazy as every other man on Earth.

Every evening when he gets home from work we take turns on the computer, checking our mail. I have even checked my voice mail—heaven only knows how expensive it is—and have talked to Mother and to my editor.

I'm reading *The Night Inspector* by Frederick Busch—another great book.

Friday, October 27. This is my last day. Innocente takes Leonid and me to a beach we wanted to try, but the tide is out so far there is no water. In the ensuing trip around the island to find a beach with water, we are treated to some rare unspoiled scenery on the back side of the island. The road is shaded much of the way, and giant granite boulders lie hidden like lost temples in the creepers. These granite Seychelle islands are more dramatic than volcanic or coral islands. Some of the boulders are as big as office buildings.

Finally we land back at Anse Royale, where we have been before, but there is water and poor Innocente is getting nervous from all the driving. He has to come back and get us in a couple of hours, and we pick a beach close enough to town that he doesn't have to make the whole huge circle of the island again. I snorkle and say goodbye to the wonderful fish. We have a snack at a cafe on the beach, then return to Vincent's for one last evening.

We have a party, as it turns out, several friends of Vincent's who come for the farewell feast Lorna has cooked—some seven dishes. We have a hilarious evening around the table after much political talk because Vincent insists we tell our best jokes. Everyone thinks mine are funniest, which makes me feel good and sends me off to bed in a warm mood.

Saturday, October 28. I am flying on this trip on a reasonably priced consolidator ticket, but as always I get what I pay for, and the itinerary is not the best. This morning the men leave me at the airport (Leonid is not leaving until the next day) and I sit in the open air cafe for two hours waiting for the Air Seychelles flight, which is late. We take off for Johannesburg (I have to go back the way I came, even though it is out of the way) where I have a guide waiting to take me out of the airport for a tour in the hours before my next flight. In Johannesburg the guide and I get me checked in for the South African Airways flight to London, my next stop, then we go out and get in a white Mercedes and take off to see the city. As we approach the city I remark on huge yellowish sand dunes off the road. They are gold tailings from the mining of the great vein of gold that was discovered here and runs (ran) for 500 kilometres.

Downtown Johannesburg does nothing for me. I ask the guide, who is Colored, how far away is Soweto? Twenty minutes. Let's go there, I say. He's enthusiastic. Soweto turns out to be a huge exurb of three million people, most of whom live in little brick houses with tiny yards and cyclone fences around them. There are some nicer parts, mostly brick houses with the occasional palm tree. We drive by the Mandela's house (where Winnie ran her Mandela United Football Club gang) and see where Desmond Tutu formerly lived. Everyone is on the street. There are two bad areas, one the long lines of former miners' shacks, still lived in but pretty dreadful, and "Mandela Town", a shantytown of colorful shacks full of the poor ignorant rural people who flooded in when Mandela was freed from prison and they thought the Millenium had come. We drive up and down the streets, and the guide shows me where he grew up adjacent to Soweto where the Coloreds lived. Back at the airport he laughs gleefully and says in his singsong Indian accent that he doesn't think he'll tell the office he took me to SOWE-TO! I jerk back and say, you mean we shouldn't have gone there? Oh no, no, he assures me, but he has given me pause.

Sunday, October 29. The overnight flight to London is fairly comfortable. I have an exit row seat and actually sleep some. At Heathrow I check into the Hilton, get cleaned up and spend the day with my friend Lord Gilbert, whom I don't see enough. After an early dinner I sleep a long sleep.

Monday, October 30. This should be a simple day. Bus over to Gatwick, get on the plane, fly home. But no, England is having the worst storm in 13 years, trees are toppled, motorways are closed, flights are diverted. I get on the high speed bus to Gatwick for the 45 minute trip and four hours later we arrive. I read a whole book from Heathrow to Gatwick (*Dusklands*, an early book by J. M. Coetzee, the famous South African writer). At Gatwick my plane is still there; it leaves four hours late, but at least with me on it. When I walk into my apartment in the Watergate that night, I have been up for 24 hours and finished another book, an Elizabeth George mystery. I feel like I have flown as many hours as I have been on the ground on this trip. But all the things I have seen and done, and the people I have connected with, cumulatively have made the traveling worthwhile.

DENMARK AND NORWAY
JUNE 2002
INTRODUCTION

Mother, who has been almost everywhere and now just goes back to places she remembers fondly, called me over the winter to say there was a cruise she was interested in but she was afraid it sounded too tame for me. It was to the Norwegian fjords. I'd always wanted to see the fjords, I exclaimed to her surprise. The ship was one we knew, the Marco Polo, and perhaps because we had met them on that ship, we invited Peter and Lynnette Springberg to go with us to Scandinavia. To our delight they accepted. Then I asked my buddy Elliott Jones if she wanted to go, she of the great spirit of adventure, and she too accepted saying she had always wanted to see the fjords. She had never been on a traditional cruise before and thought she should at least try one. Thus we were five on this brief but altogether enjoyable trip to northern Europe.

Wednesday 19 June 2002
Onboard the Marco Polo

After listening to some 25 hours of Boswell's Life of Samuel Johnson this month, he is much on my mind. His aphorism about a place being worth seeing but not worth traveling to certainly would not apply to Copenhagen, one of the most attractive, nicest capitals in Europe and therefore the world. As tired and shell shocked as we were upon arrival after overnight flights from San Antonio, Fort Collins and Washington, D. C. respectively, we hit the street Monday afternoon to walk and work out the kinks, winding up in the irresistible Tivoli Gardens near our hotel. Tivoli is so fey, so eccentric and so delightful that we perked up considerably and at the end of the afternoon picked a restaurant there and ate before going home to lie down and sleep for the first time in 32 hours.

The world was a brighter place the next morning after a long sleep. Peter and I found a series of lakes to walk along for our 6:30 a.m. athletics—even the ducks and swans weren't awake yet although a fuzzy pile of cygnets eyed us with interest. This prompted bird talk and a discussion about trans-species friendships and human responsibility for animals. Peter can talk about anything and can also be silly, making him a valuable companion.

Our hotel, the SAS Royal, was designed by the famous Danish designer Arne Jacobsen and we appreciated its flourishes without necessarily wanting to transplant them. It was a museum of 'Danish modern' rhomboids of color, handles so subtle one had to study how to turn on the water, courses of color up one wall or on a closet door, some shapes pure and some brash but all clean, the whole appearing designed but not adorned. We loved it.

The morning was spent with an intelligent, laconic female guide who took us on a superficial but pleasant city tour. We rode around getting oriented, listening to Danish pronunciations we then matched with the written word: Nyhaven, Langelinie, Christianborg, Christianhavn, Glyptotek. We got out at a couple of places: at Langelinie to see the Little Mermaid (when a vandal decapitated her some years ago the police treated it as a murder case); at the Royal Palaces (where we raptly sought to understand the people's love of their monarch, Queen Margrethe); and at Christianborg to see the Queen's Reception Rooms, palatial and not much distinct from other palaces until one huge room filled with modern Goebblin tapestries of outrageous wit—ex: the Queen and her consort depicted as Adam and Eve—that made me, anyway, begin to love this liberal Queen and patron of even controversial art.

When we returned to the hotel a friend I had never met, Birte Lindell, was waiting to take us to lunch. A volunteer with Amnesty International, she and I share a friend in the Czech Republic about whom we corresponded when she was in prison. Birte had short no-nonsense hair and an air of determination. She is one of those volunteers who actually put themselves in harm's way, and had the calm good nature of one who has seen it all. She directed us to an ancient place called Den Lille Apotek in the Latin Quarter, and taking advantage of being with her we managed to keep the conversation on a fairly high plane (no 5 D's—disease, diet, deity, domestics, descendents). I think we all parted from her feeling we'd been with someone special, and braver than we. She is now working in Iran, a country of interest to Elliott and me especially because we went there last year.

At the hotel we napped quickly to be ready to go in a prearranged taxi van to Charlottenlund, a suburb "out on the beach," to Rydhave, the official residence of the American ambassador, currently a friend from Washington, Stuart Bernstein. The house was situated on the side of a hill looking out at the sea, and was full of Wilma and Stuart's 19th century American Impressionists as well as a cornucopia of Art in Embassies borrowed masterpieces of some of the great modern and still-working artists like Frank Stella and Christo. Stuart had just flown in from a meeting of Scandinavian and Baltic DCM's in Riga and had been enchanted by that beautiful city. We visited for an hour and came away impressed by his dedication to a job for which he was not originally trained but to which he has taken in a serious and impressive way.

Thursday 20 June 2002
At sea

Bags out at 8:30am for the cruise line to pick up; ourselves out at 10:15 to walk across downtown to Nyhavn ("New Harbor", new in the 17th century), a canal lined with schooners in the water and restaurants on the quai, there to board a low-profile tourist canal boat for an hour ride through the waterways of Christianhavn (the part of Copenhagen on an island across from the center of downtown—Copenhagen and most of Denmark takes place on islands) and downtown. We saw the huge public works project that will become the new opera house, a gift from Mr. Maersk McKinney Muller, as in Maersk Shipping. This may make him draw even with the Carlsberg Beer people, the largest philanthropists in this country of 5 million.

Upon disembarking we sat down in the first sidewalk cafe we came to that had a table big enough for the five of us. An hour later we got our lunch. The people watching enabled us to while away the time; we admired the buff, palomino-colored girls and their buzz-cut fellas. Many people travel by bicycle in this health- and environment-conscious country. We were constantly watching straight-backed beauties with scrumptious tushes go by on their way earnestly somewhere. Not everyone is beautiful but the overall effect is one of handsome vitality.

We ate with despatch, then took a taxi to the Ny Carlsberg Glyptotek, a gorgeous museum with a glass-enclosed winter garden in the center of it, and zigzagged among a city of Rodin sculptures that were a staggering testament to the artist as well as the Carlsberg person who had amassed them.

There was much else to see but Mother (and admittedly I) were growing weary, so we two sheared off, walked back to the hotel, retrieved our hand luggage and took a taxi to the ship where, because we hadn't arrived in a busload of fellow passengers, we were able to breeze through security and walk right up the gangway to be escorted to our stateroom.

We were unpacked and stretched out on our beds when Elliott and the Springbergs boarded. Elliott was in the room directly across the hall from us, and the Springbergs were nearby. There was nothing left to do but have lifeboat drill and our first dinner in the dining room at a table with two empty seats. We didn't miss having company, especially during an argument about the merits of George Bush as president. Like any good political argument among civilized people, it ended and the conversation resumed its cheeriness.

We have sailed all day today with nary a responsibility, an experience so rare I took two naps, morning and afternoon. We came out of the strait between Denmark and Sweden, then the strait between Denmark and Norway and turned right, north, into the North Sea sometime late in the afternoon. The ship finally rolled in time for the Captain's welcoming soiree. At the party we danced with the dance hosts along with other couples on the stage and had to engage our sea legs along with our dancing feet.

At dinner we were pleased to have at our table at the two empty places a delightful, lovely couple, Margot and Norman, from Australia, handsome, sophisticated and well-traveled, and the talk resounded on politics, monarchy, extraterrestrial life vs. carbon-based life forms, the merits of our respective homes and, at the end, almost apologetically, two funny jokes. We couldn't believe our luck, landing these two.

Margot and Norman, our "finds"

Friday 21 June 2002 — The Summer Solstice
Sognefjord

Even Elliott was up early this morning, a day that dawned sometime in the middle of the night here in the land of the midnight sun on the sight we had come so far to see: a fjord. Mother came unreluctantly off her pillow with little prodding when she saw the steep green cliffs out the window from her angle below on the bed. We hung in the windows, Elliott from across the hall in her nightgown, myself unable to lie down and do my exercises for fear I'd miss the next waterfall. Sixteen hours and hundreds of waterfalls later, I turn to my tablet sated.

Peter, Lynnette and I burst out onto the Promenade Deck to do our laps, and sucked in the freshest air I believe I have ever smelled. The ship had slowed in the emerald glacial water and again, we could barely finish our laps for stopping to watch the docking procedures in Flam, a storybook town with a big asphalt dock and unisex stevedores obviously not surprised to have a ship as large as the town itself appear at their doorstep.

We walked off the ship at 9:20 a.m. for a day trip excursion and boarded about a block away an old-fashioned train with high ceilings, panelling and velvet seats. We had struck up a conversation with Lawrence Rudner, a mariner and Viking expert who was one of our lecturers, and sat with him and his wife Marlene on the 2 1/2 hour trip. Basically the day took us on a route shaped like a long narrow triangle: by train through spectacular scenery via Myrdal to Voss, where we had a stress-inducing lunch of smorgasborg, vying for space at the buffet line as well as on our plates; then by bus via Stralheim back to the ship which had moved into another arm of the fjord, Naeroydfjord, and was now at Gudvangen.

Elliot, Lynnette, Mother, Peter on train to Voss

The town of Voss was full of tourists, all of whom were being fed in the same Park Hotel as we. I can feel either competitive in such a situation, or resigned to being jostled. Both are stressful, and today I felt both. From Voss we went to Stralheim, a hotel situated impossibly high over a steep, beautiful valley. In World War II the Germans commandeered this place to use strategically as well as sexually: it was a baby-factory in their super race eugenics scheme. It was even more crowded than the hotel in Voss so Mother and I rebelled, fell away from our group and did our own thing in the hotel shops until we could leave.

Mother had watched "Grand Hotel" on the TV in between naps yesterday and I had watched for a little while before peeling off to go to a Viking lecture. I managed to see Greta Garbo say "I vant to be alone", and by the end of this afternoon I knew how she felt. We came down from Stralheim on a tiny, spectacular road of hairpin turns and 20 degree grades to Gudvangen, and the tenders couldn't ferry us out to the boat fast enough. We've had another sparkling dinner with Margot and Norman and I am blissfully alone, the walls of the great fjord going past as we return to the sea, now the Norwegian Sea, to turn north once more.

Let me hasten to say that one would have had to be flayed alive to ignore the thrill of the scenery by which we have all day been surrounded. My intuitive reactions to our logistical situation may not have been 100% in check but my eye didn't miss a thing. Even in my exasperation at being herded I could smile at the vistas. I'm probably irritable from eating too many desserts. Manana...

Saturday 22 June 2002
Geirangerfjord

At 5:30 this morning it was overcast and we were still at sea, steaming north with Norway to starboard. At 6:20 as I lurched on the treadmill with the rolling of the ship, we turned right, east, and entered the stunning Geirangerfjord, even more knee-buckling than the one yesterday. In the calmer water the boat smoothed out just as Peter came to fetch me to do laps with him. As we stretched out we were mentally falling all over ourselves watching the unbelievable scenery of high, sharply-profiled blue and green snow-topped mountains coming down into water that is a color of green only Nature could have invented.

One reason for the richness of the color is the great depth of these glacially carved fjords. They can be thousands of feet deep. The captain just announced that we were approaching Hellesylt, where we will drop those passengers who are going on an all-day excursion (not us thank goodness). He said he had cut the engines to drift toward Hellesylt, where we would continue to drift offshore using the thrusters because the water was so deep that if we used the anchor "we'd never get it back".

Samuel Johnson said on the treadmill this morning (via tape; my witty friend Marshall de Bruhl asked if it were read by the author) that people like to read of travel to places they haven't been but they don't like reading about places they have been. This may not bode well for me as a travel writer. He also said people need four things: knowledge, the words to express knowledge, imagination to make something new of it, and presence of mind. I pass that along for our mutual edification only.

After a morning of rest, i.e. being able to do whatever we wanted, we 'docked' (again drifting offshore) at Geiranger, the town at the terminus of the fjord. This fjord had afforded us jaw-dropping scenery all morning with the sheer cliffs plunging into the water (water so deep the Empire State Building could have sat on the bottom and still not poked through the surface), waterfalls cascading from extreme heights, snowy peaks marching off into the hinterland and forests growing out of stone.

After lunch we took the ship's tenders ashore, boarded buses and drove up a road that had been a 19th century engineering marvel and was still pretty amazing with its 70 hairpin turns on the way to the summit of Mt. Dalsnibba, not so high in the pantheon of world mountains but vertiginous for us whose ship now looked smaller than a mouse far below out in the fjord. There is so much snow here in the winter they have to use GPS to find the road in spring in order to clear it. It was sharply cold on the mountaintop and raining (or we might just have been in a cloud), so we didn't mind the obligatory hotel stop where Mother wisely opted to pay for some hot chocolate in the bar rather than watch me get the heebie-jeebies being herded into a refreshment area with a couple of hundred other people. We were picked up in the bar by an apple-cheeked toddler who crawled then stumbled serendipitously right for Granny's lap. Elliott and I left her and Lynnette with their adoptee and walked fast downhill the rest of the way back to the dock, pausing to take a picture of a sod roof with a mama and baby seagull nesting on it, and another one totally sprouted in daisies. When the sod needs mowing they put a goat up on the roof to do the job.

This evening we went to a 'party' after dinner and danced on the stage again. This time it wasn't too rolly. As I prepared to turn out the lights at 9:30 and close the curtains against the still-light day, the pilot boat pulled up against the ship and took off the two pilots who had been with us in the fjord. They had on bright red parkas and backpacks, and waved back at the ship as if they'd had fun. We were back at the confluence of the fjord and the sea, and as the pilot boat headed away from us toward some unseen village on the far shore I was hypnotized at the window thinking of how far apart people live, and their connections.

Sunday 23 June 2002
Bergenfjord

In the grey early morning the Bergen fjord seemed to start with windswept sand dunes not cliffs, and the sky was wet and lowering as Peter and I went out into the wind for our daily constitutional. We made one foray across the bow and even yours truly who is built like a brick privy almost took flight. We retreated to our promenade deck.

At the dock in Bergen, some miles inland, we boarded the usual buses and went off to see the town. The old totemic Hanseatic houses on the harbor jumped off the pages of memory and into the present; anyone over the age of four has seen these houses in a picture somewhere. It was raining lightly as we drove around, peered down cobblestoned alleyways between blocks of narrow, pitched-roofed row houses, and admired miles of rhododendrons and statues of local greats.

The greatest of all was Edvard Grieg, to whose house we went, and I personally was transported to tread this ground sacred to music lovers. His house was Victorian outside and solid pine inside; it sat on a promontory above the fjord. Below it was a music conservatory with a sod roof that hid its modern interior concert hall. At the bottom of the steep hill the remains of Grieg and his wife lay in a tomb in the side of a clifflike rock, sealed by geometrically fitted stones. It reminded me and Elliott of the tombs in Iran carved high above the earth into sheer cliffs.

It was pouring rain as we walked back to the bus and continued to pour to such an extent that even the Bergen guide, who lives with 200 days of rain a year, admitted it was a bit much. Despite the rain we stopped at an open air market where I bought Norwegian salmon caviar and reindeer sausage, and saw my first monkfish, a hideous creature after seeing which I shall never order from a menu again. Mother and I left the bus near the end of the tour to shop the boutiques in the storefronts of the Hanseatic houses before walking back to the ship under umbrellas. As we sailed away from Bergen the sun came out.

After lunch our lecturer, Larry Rudner, gave Elliott and me a history then a practical lesson in the use of the sextant. We did fairly well on our first sightings: I was 3.9 miles off and Elliott was 6. He claimed he had been 40 miles off his first time, but that may have been his way of being politic with his students. Later Elliott and I sat in the Jacuzzi on the top of the ship, the cold sea air around us and the great rough ocean on all sides. It was so rough we all had on patches by dinnertime.

As it turned out, I stood corrected on thinking the Bergen fjord was bounded at its entrance by dunes. They were on closer perusal in the late afternoon sun low rounded rocks sculpted like sand dunes.

Last night the ship's trio, three young men from Romania, gave a classical music concert. The tunes were recognizable but the playing left something to be desired. My theory was these guys can't go home to Romania and are condemned to ply the seven seas like the Flying Dutchman, screeching away at their instruments innocently unaware they're getting farther and farther away from the original sound.

Our highest point of latitude on this trip was 62 degrees. This is a long way from San Antonio, Texas (27 degrees) and a short distance from the Arctic Circle (66 2/3) and the top of the world (90 degrees). It has been mild but it is not hard to imagine how wild the weather could be in winter. If one could venture to speculate, there is a social cohesiveness that may to some extent be weather-induced. I was asking our cute young bus driver in Geiranger some personal questions. He said he lived in a small village near Geiranger (itself pop. 200). I asked him if it were lonely and he grinned and said no, it was wonderful. De gustibus, etc.

Monday 24 June 2002
Oslofjord, Norway

The Oslo fjord was wide and low. We had worked out and eaten breakfast when the captain announced we were taking on the pilot at the entrance to the fjord. We were back around on the southern end of Norway, out of the North Sea. It was warmer and calmer.

Three hours later we eased up against the bulkhead of the Oslo cruise ship terminal in the shadow of the high ancient stone wall around Akershus Fortress, and without ado left the ship for a city tour we hurried through due to the fear of the tour company that we would get caught in an expected anti-World Bank demonstration. The lovely old city seemed calm, orderly and beautiful to us; later, independently afoot, Elliott did get into a demonstration.

Our group trip made three stops. The first was Vigeland Park (also known as the Sculpture Garden), a landscaped park full of purposely placed bronze and granite statues by Gustav Vigeland, whose life work was these incredible figures depicting the aspects and phases of human life, the overall effect of which was sad, somehow, and also a bit horny-making as they were all naked. They deserved more study than we gave them but the impression should linger forever, so special it was, and touching.

Second stop the Viking ship museum, another place to have ones mind rearranged in the presence of their magnificent works-of-art ships, ships that carried them such immense distances. Elliott reminded me of the jolly archeologist we met on the plane to Tehran who had found Viking coins around the Caspian Sea, and of course our own North American continent was known to them when the Southern Europeans who got so much credit for discovery were still picking their noses and being afraid of falling off the edge of the horizon.

Third stop a well-designed museum housing the Kon-Tiki, Ra II and some Easter Island artifacts, representing the major parts of the life of another impressive Norwegian, Thor Heyerdahl. The boats prompted the appropriate awe. One could walk along flush with the side of the Kon-Tiki and also under it, where swam a great whale shark and other taxidermed creatures of the deep. It was well done and again made one think of these crazy men and their boating adventures—modern day Vikings trusting to the sea, a sea that would rightly terrify any normal person. In fact this entire trip by sea has done what any sustained contemplation of the ocean does, and that is generate a profound and humble respect for all the sailors who have gone down to the sea in ships, or gone down in the sea in ships.

My theory is the Vikings felt as familiarly at home on water as we sand crabs feel on land. They knew it as we know our yards, balconies or ranches. It was theirs. We respect the rocks, crevasses and cactuses; they respected the wind and waves. It didn't occur to them to be afraid of their main medium any more than we are afraid to go abroad in our dry spaces.

After the bus deposited us back at the ship Elliott and I lit out at a fast clip to walk back into downtown because I wanted to case the Grand Hotel, which features in my novel. I needed to see if I'd gotten it right, never having seen it or Oslo itself for that matter. A nice desk clerk showed us the ballroom and the Henrik Ibsen Suite (Ibsen drank coffee in the hotel everyday), and told me when the Herald-Tribune was delivered—all details I had guessed at as I wrote. Elliott left me and went on to ramble; I walked back to the ship through the battened down streets, wishing I'd come upon a demonstration. Alas, I made it home safely.

Tuesday 25 June 2002
Aarhus, Denmark

As I write there is a tug boat captain outside my window, pushing his ship against ours to dock it at Aarhus, Denmark. I could reach out and touch him if the windows weren't fixed. On the p.a. system Mimi and Rodolfo are ecstatically singing. The juxtaposition is delicious.

The day started rough and grey, so rough I had to hold onto the treadmill to keep from lurching backward then forward; the seas were running perpendicular to the ship. Peter fetched me for an hour of shouting at each other in the wind on our daily forced march past the deckhands drying everything off from the night's waves and moisture. We were out of sight of land as we crossed back to Jutland, the land peninsula part of Denmark located at the top of Germany. We were headed for Aarhus, the second biggest city in Denmark (.5 million v. Copenhagen's 1 million).

We had already had lunch when the tug appeared at my window. Shortly we walked off the ship to the tunes of a girls' band playing on the quai. It's sweet when there's a band on the dock; it's welcoming and they always seem so earnest. These were little blonde pubescent girls in quasi-military mini-skirts and white boots looking cute and smiling shyly, playing martial tunes under an American and a Danish flag, and for some reason it reminded me of the outpouring from Europe after September 11th and made me want to cry.

The excursion was a ride out into the Lake District. It was not a tour to fire one's engines but it was pretty and the magnitude of the sights just about fit the magnitude of the country itself: small, orderly, fitting—a world obviously cared about by its people. There were lakes—Ice Age remnants—and villages of half-timbered houses with thatched roofs and rose bushes. There were chunky, bushy-maned horses, farms of coniferous baby trees destined for the Christmas trade, and dark overarching forests of beech that made one realize why the fairy tales that sprang from here were so terrifying. In Norway we had learned that trolls were used to threaten children with dire consequences if they weren't home by dark, and it takes only a small exposure to these northern forests to understand why that would be critical.

Our first stop was Himmelbjetger, the second tallest "mountain" in Jutland (160 metres; Denmark is flat). There again simple local pride prevailed over common sense in considering it special, as pretty as it was; the scale was small, but the feeling was sweet. [I wondered if I took a bunch of Danes to the Hill Country of Texas and showed it to them with pride, if they would think me equally rustic.] There was a monument to the Danish constitution, another to women's suffrage and a third to Hans Christian Andersen, all worthy of honor and placed by the Danes here on their sacred mountain with obvious purpose.

In the town of Silkeborg we went to the local museum to see Tollund Man, a 2400-year-old male figure dug out of a nearby bog. He had a rope around his neck, whiskers still visible and a calm expression on his face. He lies now for eternity in a relaxed fetal position, as burnished as if he were bronze, for all us present-day tourists to contemplate, thinking of our own mortality and probably all hoping we don't have to spend eternity on display in a museum.

Then home to Aarhus where we drove past the Queen's summer house. She and Prince Henrik (Henri when he was French) are neighborly in Aarhus and can sometimes be seen on the street.

Anyone with animadversion toward monarchy should come to Denmark and Norway. Here the monarchs are democrats who are loved and honored by their people. Of course they each only have 5 million 'people', which might go a long way to explain the social cohesion we have observed everywhere. It has felt positively serene to this American who spends a chunk of every day thinking about the political and social problems in the U.S. Then again maybe the serenity is from my not having seen any news for over a week. I recommend it.

We had a farewell dinner with Margot and Norman, who were the finds of the trip. If we had sat the first night and devised the perfect couple to fill the two empty chairs at our table, I doubt we could have imagined better than they. The dining room staff marched around the room with flaming Baked Alaskas and the cooks were introduced ("And in charge of sauces and frostings, RICKY ROMERO!"). It went on a bit too long but they had done a bang up job and deserved applause.

Wednesday 26 June 2002
Over the North Atlantic

Below us have passed the Shetland Islands. It was clear enough to see ships far below, and an oil rig, and even a rainbow. The trip is over and already today Mother and I have discussed the logistics of the rest of the summer. This talk took place at lunch in Tivoli Gardens, where we bided a couple of hours before heading to the airport. Elliott, Peter and Lynnette were on earlier planes; we had our farewells on the ship this morning.

It was a beautiful, fun, relatively easy trip. I didn't study for it, I only had some local currency in my possession one day, I traveled first class and some might say I was carried along like a leaf on the tide, so what could come of such a trip? Only the expansion that comes from seeing something new and knowing something else. Peter started a club with some bright youngsters he mentors called S.O.B., Stretch Our Brains. That's what I've been doing within my own poor powers, and it has been a pleasure. Most expansion doesn't come with a cruise attached; I've just been lucky this time. I want a lifetime membership in the S.O.B. Club whatever the initiation and requirements. In the meantime I shall happily remember Denmark and Norway and not think of them as boring countries up near the Arctic Circle. They are sui generis and very special indeed.

    Iceland is out the window now. Maybe it's next. Something is next.

CUBA
MARCH - APRIL 2003
INTRODUCTION

In January 2003 my good friend and traveling buddy Elliott Jones and I went to dinner in Washington to discuss planning a trip. We wanted to travel together in calendar 2003 and we had an intense desire to get the hell out of Dodge—Washington was unusually cold and uniquely grim as war loomed. War prevented us from considering some destinations on our wish lists, and in fact we narrowed down the decision to the Western Hemisphere. When she mentioned Cuba I jumped on it, and the decision was mutually made.

I executed the plans through a travel agent in Mexico, as we would be defying our government and traveling illegally. It seemed timely, as we were in revolt against our government for every other reason as well. The Iraqi war indeed officially started two days before we arrived in Cancun to start our trip, but we pressed on in spite of the shaky state of the world and our attendant nerves.

Carrie Myer, a pal from San Antonio, joined Elliott and me. She signed on three weeks before we left. Her mother had just died. All in all we were about as stressed as we could be in the run-up to a trip abroad.

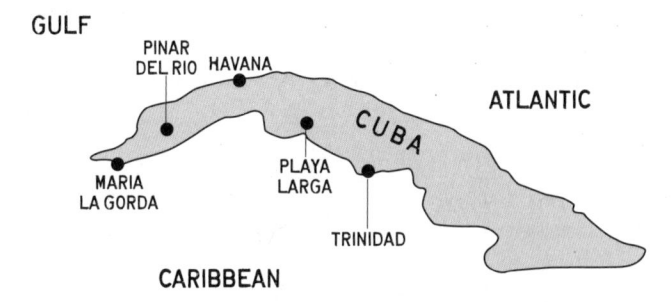

```
        GULF
              PINAR
              DEL RIO   HAVANA
                                         ATLANTIC
                              CUBA
                       PLAYA
              MARIA    LARGA
              LA GORDA
                              TRINIDAD
        CARIBBEAN
```

Sunday 23 March 2003
Hotel Santa Isabel, Havana

To fly from Cancun to Havana one flies straight up, levels off for a few minutes over the Strait of Yucutan, then descends to land at Jose Marti International Airport forty minutes after take-off. The airport serves a city of four million and had only six airliners on the ground when we landed. We were bused at least a mile around the airport to the building housing Immigration, and there a friendly officer did not stamp our passport ("No selle mi paseporte, por favor"—yeah yeah yeah, he nodded). My bananas were confiscated, the only contraband I indulge in. We watched two cute friendly dogs sniff everyones bags and put their snoots and entire heads down in open totes. Everyone was smiling and no one was arrested.

A taxi driver whisked us into town, speaking in Spanish to Carrie and me—Elliott doesn't *habla*—and we began to focus on the old American cars which we'd heard about and were everywhere. Most were decrepit, as well they should be at age 50, and I cast back in my mind to that period when we were growing up, the automobile manufacturers retooled every year and everyone knew a '54 from a '55 from a '56 from a '57 Chevy, Dodge, Pontiac or whatever. I thought about my brother Bo, the car nut who is the reason I can still tell the body styles apart.

We got excited about the architecture when we reached Habana Vieja, Old Havana, the East end of downtown and the original part of this 500-year-old city. When the taxi stopped we had to hoof it across a plaza with the luggage; our beautiful hotel had no motor access. A process had started as we came upon Havana Vieja, continued across this plaza and through the front doors of our hotel: we were falling in love. Everything—our huge room with 18-foot ceilings, the kind staff, the music down on the plaza, the shutters onto the balcony, the patient bellman, the rain briefly falling into the inner courtyard of the hotel, watering the potted plants from out of the sky—combined to cause us to give ourselves over to this gorgeous shabby place.

We made our nest, then hit the street to walk for awhile in the tiny bricked streets, looking into doorways at family life going on in full view, gaping at the colonial architecture and beginning the process of absorption. We wound up on the roof of the Hotel Ambos Mundos, where Ernest Hemingway lived for some years during the '30's, and had a token rum drink before walking home. Elliott has gone honky-tonking and Carrie and I are in the sack. We had yucked it up with the women on the front desk when we came in; they sent the poor dear bellman out to find me some bananas. We tip American style and don't feel it. I hope it makes a dent in their poverty.

Monday 24 March 2003

At 6:30 this morning I opened one set of the floor-to-ceiling louvered balcony doors to see what the day looked like and tumbled again, not over the railing but further into love. Our corner room must be the prettiest corner in all of Havana. Directly across from us is El Templete, the spot on which Havana was founded. We can see the ship channel beyond that. The panorama as we fan around the balcony is fortress walls, church, plaza, lush trees and, at 6:30 a.m., a streetsweeper with his rush broom and a few early birds going to work. The buildings we can see are constructed of coral stone, fine square blocks of organically eroded limestone from the sea. A sudden shower washed and cooled us, and the sun began to rise, turning the stone to gold.

At breakfast on the patio on the plaza we had to listen to a table of businessmen regale each other with tales of their nightclubbing and whoremongering of the night before, and describe development they'd like to see in this old city. As a sparrow pecked at the remains of our toast I thought, Castro in his irrational way has managed to save this glorious place from the rapacious West, and I felt a bemused, temporary love for him, too.

My silly love for Fidel had gone the way of all such temporary insanities by the end of the day, replaced by a head-scratching bewilderment over why the man has not perished of embarrassment to have to imprison the Cuban people on a floating island to keep them from fleeing his rule. Over and over I was reminded of my half year in Czechoslovakia when I would get mad at Communism over how poorly my crummy commie carpet sweeper worked, or how ignorant my adult students of English were of economics, nutruition and a host of other concepts. Communism treats people evilly, as if they have no value—the so-called greater good for which it stands having no idea that a whole is the sum of its parts.

We stayed awestruck by Havana all day, though, and had a marvelous time sightseeing even as we commiserated with the victims of misery in paradise. [I am not so naive not to know that many Cubans love Fidel and still believe in the Revolution.] With the help of our hotel desk people we had arranged for a guide, who fetched us at 9:30 a.m. He was young, smart, had an MBA, spoke colloquial English, had relatives in America (they all do) and was indefatigable.

We set out on foot and went from wonder to wonder in our neighborhood of Old Havana. We walked in and out of many buildings to admire their inner courtyards; discussed the extensive renovations of several buildings (but still not enough) being bankrolled by the government from tourist revenues—we were happy we were helping; peered into the 17th century tunnels in which the people hid from pirates; admired the squares and blocks of scrumptious architecture, some about to fall down, the wiring all exposed looking like a tangled afterthought, laundry hanging outside on fragile, shuttered wrought iron balconies; walked into the store where everyone lines up the first of the month with ration books to get their inadequate share of food, the store empty of customers now at the end of the month while everyone goes hungry until the new monthly ration book is available (at this point we made the group decision to give money to anyone who asked); went into the pharmacy museum to ogle the old apothe-

Carrie interviewed by "CNN"

cary bottles and polished wooden shelves; and when we stepped out again onto the street had a few hilarious moments with a clever kid who had built a TV camera out of a cardboard box and written "CNN" on the side, had rigged up a microphone and a headset for himself out of cut-off plastic bottles, and proceeded to "interview" us. Pictures were taken, dollar bills changed pockets. [Elliott subsequently saw him the next night at a baseball game, working the crowd. He was probably raking in more money than a medical doctor.]

Outside one museum we were given the grand but tiny tour through a presidential railroad car from the turn of the last century. The wood and hardware were fine and meant to last, the little beds and baths would not hold modern *homo fatticus*, and the whole effect was adorably minature. Lastly we stood in yet another handsome square and encouraged with dinero some old Black musicians to cut loose. When they did we were transported back to a lost time, and to top it off up moseyed very slowly an ancient Negro in an ice cream colored suit with a cigar in his mouth. Sergio said he must be 95 years old still to be wearing a suit. He stood tapping his cane to the music, quite alive. [Come to find out from a New York Times Travel Magazine piece that he was "El Dandy" and only in his 80's.]

Street musicians and "El Dandy"

We jumped in a cab with several destinations in mind, leaving Havana Vieja behind. We saw the Capital, built in the 1920's to look like ours, and drove through Chinatown toward our first stop, Sergio's 3-year-old daughter's day care center. He had told us they lacked for simple things like cleaning supplies, and the teachers were so poor they sometimes took home food intended for the children. They even didn't have enough drinking water. We wanted to see this slice of life.

The 3-year-olds were cute and noisy. We messed around with them, got them to say their names and sing a song; the 2-year-olds were en masse at some activity and didn't know us so stayed put; but the 1-year-olds were eating their lunch of rice and looked so vulnerable I lost it for a moment in one of those 'life is not fair' fits and shed a tear for all the helpless creatures of the world. Cuba of course is not the only country niggardly toward these 'hope of the future' statistics.

At the vast and famous cemetery, the Necropolis Cristobal Colon, we hired a guide to tell us about the incredible city of tombs. The architecture housing the sarcophagi was eclectic: toy chapels, mini-palaces, grottoes, a pyramid. The guide was sentimental and long-winded but we still managed to enjoy our respectful perusal of this extremely old and seventh largest cemetery in the world.

Finally it was lunch time—had been for some time—and this we partook in a paladar, the Paladar Aries, near the University of Havana. In an old house cut up into small dining rooms, a little private enterprise took place in the way of feeding us a decent lunch wedged into a tiny room with two other tables of guests and two mariachis who spoiled conversation until (I hope graciously) I said, *'bastante'* (con dinero, of course).

The last stop was the 'dollar store'. The only way people can buy something is with dollars; i.e. they get their food coupons but if they need anything else, a broom, a brassiere, some sneakers, curtains or any of the other myriad things one needs to keep oneself or ones household running, they go to a dollar store. This one was a mishmash of boutiques, shops and kiosks all contained in a single interior space that led the shopper every upward on a ramp, with noise reverberating like Bedlam, lines to get into the stores and lines to pay. But we were committed to buying Sergio's daughter's day care school some supplies and this we did (everything is dirt cheap so it was less noble than it sounds). As the group's banker I made the purchases with a hundred-dollar bill that was closely scrutinized, the serial number and my passport number duly recorded by the clerk. I mused on this Communist country using the currency of the great Satan to the North as its official currency. When we burst back onto the street we left Sergio to take the stuff back to the school, and headed for home full of our day.

Tuesday 25 March 2003

As I lay in the dim light of early morning waiting for my limbs to wake up, I pondered the commendable, vast project of restoring Havana. It will take more than one generation to do it. As the ancient buildings are chosen and prepared for renovation, the people crammed into them are being moved to housing projects out on the edge of town. As the buildings are finished, they become hotels, galleries, museums and other types of public buildings; their former tenants do not return. In the semi-darkness I hoped the old city wouldn't become Disneyfied, bereft of actual people living their lives, full only of tourists, a Potemkin Habana Vieja with no laundry flapping, stoop sweeping, children in school uniforms, dogs lying in the middle of the street, life going on. And I thought of the people moved from their fallen-down but lively neighborhoods to the sterile landscape of the projects and if they would suffer some spiritual drop in temperature even as they relished their new plumbing.

Dogs. We have gotten to know some of the mangy critters of our hotel district. They're all skinny but friendly, and argue with each other over every crumb that hits the street. Tito, a particularly mangy but eager little fellow, had eggs and sausage for breakfast this morning thanks to some soft-hearted blockade runners from the USA.

Sergio wanted to go with us again today and the price was right, so he appeared at 9:30 and we took a taxi across the ship channel—through a tunnel under it—to Morro Castle, the larger of the two forts that guarded the mouth of the harbor in olden days. Havana was fairly easy to defend from the sea because of the narrow entrance of its harbor, although in 500 years of history this didn't always prevent it from defeat. We loved Morro Castle, high above the restless crashing swells, built with the coral rock with its fossil shell imprints which is a geologist's dream. The great cannons were still in place and a lighthouse loomed over all. We dillydallied, fresh and excited by the handsome fort.

Because we didn't want that part of the excursion to end, we went on that side of the harbor up further to see the giant Jesus statue that looks down beatifically on the city. Only a stone Jesus could remain benign from a vantage such as his over the wicked city below.

We tunneled back to the city proper and went across town to a farmers' market that Sergio said the poor people used. I liked it; I like markets with their arrays of fruit and vegetables, the haggling, the smells and the most elemental kind of commerce, probably the first commerce. We walked all through it and bought bananas and other fruit. The bananas were pretty elemental looking themselves, not slick and yellow, but were lovely and sweet inside their ugly skins.

Our taxi driver, who had had us for two and a half hours, took us to a paladar on the ocean in Miramar. There we settled up with him ($26) and went into a lovely house with one of those lipless swimming pools that dropped off into the sea. We ate upstairs with doors open to the balcony and the Atlantic Ocean below, and for a total of $80 had a feast of lobster, rice and beans, drinks, beer and flan for four. At lunch Sergio told us he was trying to defect, and it cast us into pondering the terrible choices people are forced to make.

Back at the hotel we traded addresses with him and pledged to help him however we could. He's young and bright and strong, and somehow I think we'll see him again. I hope he makes it.

We napped, did e-mail, wrote postcards, then Elliott and I hit the street to forage while Carrie had a massage. It was fun to be loose on the street, and we interacted as we joined the waves of humanity having rush hour on foot. We found a store with the kind of provisions we needed (picnic) and the usual (water). This should not have been the accomplishment it was but you can't just think of what you want and go out and get it. You have to find it.

On the way back to the hotel with our groceries, various people spoke to us. One nicely dressed man asked us where we were from. I quickly said 'Texas' rather than 'Washington, D. C.', not wanting to provoke anyone. In the naivest way, almost plaintively, he asked, 'Why don't more Americans come here?' I responded that it was illegal. His question touched me and made me wonder what Cubans know about our political situation.

We had sunset on the terrace of the Hotel Nacional, the famous old hotel that has hosted movie stars, mafiosi and royalty for decades. Next to us was a Jack Sprat couple, prompting us to tell whispery sex stories of fat people we had known. The Nacional was much larger and more lively than our hotel, a Washington comparison being the Shoreham v. the Jefferson. We got a kick out of seeing the famous site but were happy to repair to our far nicer little palace.

Wednesday 26 March 2003

This morning Carrie and I fed bologna to the smallest canine denizen of our plaza so far, a baby Chihuahua who was cuter from afar as he doodlebugged around chasing pigeons than he was up close, rheumy-eyed and caked with mud. Heartbreak is everywhere in this heartbreakingly beautiful, humbled city. Elliott, unashamedly liberal, rails at every injustice. Carrie and I feel the same but are grimly realistic.

Without our mother hen Sergio we set out to finish up Havana, starting first at El Templete right across from our room (Carrie confessed at the end of the day that the guard had been flirting with her every morning when she went out on the balcony in her pajamas at 6:30 a.m.). A lovely woman explained in Spanish the neoclassical building and its internal mural while Carrie translated for Elliott, then we made a ritual tourneau on the grounds around the giant tree under which it is said Havana was founded.

A taxi took us first to the opera house, the Teatro Nacional, where we hoped to buy tickets to a performance of something, anything, that night. Nothing was scheduled so we paid for a tour instead and had the first serendipitous happening of the our day's excursion. The old theatre was dark and dirty but magnificent, wtih a splendid staircase of unusual grandeur. On the top landing, with the tinny sound of a piano being played somewhere echoing like a remembered tune in the dark cavernous halls, we went first into the set design studio where they, like the rest of Cuba, were stuck in the 1950's. They proudly showed us their painted canvas backdrops of a type we haven't seen on American stages for quite some time. Next we were allowed into the edge of a studio where ballet dancers were going through their exercises, and against the ombre light we photographed their lithe forms and wavy arms. The last studio held four thin, dramatic flamenco dancers hard at work. We hung admiringly in the doorway, their stomps reverberating, and we knew we were witness to the persistence of art even under trying circumstances.

Ballet dancers, Teatro Nacional

A different form of persistence was found at Finca Vigia, Hemingway's home for twenty years from 1939-1960. He had spent much of the '30's in Cuba living at the Hotel Ambos Mundos, about two blocks from our hotel. Then he bought this house outside of town and spent the last two decades of his life there surrounded by 70 cats, 11 servants, family, dogs, houseguests and rum bottles. The house is eerily intact. One can't enter it per se, but we hung in the doors and windows as our guide pointed out things. There were books everywhere, his typewriter, shoes, bottles of Schweppes, 33 and 78 records, stuffed animal heads, tile floors, polished wood furniture and the usual household detritus. Mary Hemingway gave the house to Fidel Castro after Hemingway shot himself in 1961, and the Cubans have done their best to keep it together with their meager resources. They're proud of the museum and the association, partly because Hemingway contributed to the Revolutionary cause (he met Castro once, at a fishing tournament, and told Castro he was a lousy fisherman) and are trying to do right by it within the confines of their ability. The whole thing needs a bell jar put over it but at this rate will go the way of all things instead.

I had found a listing for the Paladar Gringo Viejo in Lonely Planet that described it as having 'invariably brilliant' food. We had the taximan drop us there and we did indeed have a brilliant lunch, stuffed squid, oxtails, chocolate ice cream, everything so tasty we ate too much and practically licked our plates. It was a tiny little place—they all are—but somehow deeply sophisticated. At the end we insisted on meeting and thanking the cook for the food.

Over drinks we discussed the gut wrenching poverty and neglect of everyone and everything in Havana—the polite desperate beggars, the mangy street dogs, the falling down buildings, the hopeless population—and how we come bang up against that membrane between our intense sympathy and the impossibility of following through and doing anything about it for want of belief that it would make a dent, and what keeps us on this side of the membrane with our hearts always in a state of breaking, instead of plowing on out to the other side of the membrane, throwing over everything and working for others, i.e. taking in the dogs, paying off the pensioners, anything to assuage the sympathy. And what keeps us on this side of the membrane is self-control because we could so easily pass through on a flood of tears, a few of which we actually shed as we talked, crying and laughing at the same time at our helpless female love.

Home for rest period, then walking around at the end of the day photographing old cars and perusing the stalls of booksellers in our plaza until that proved too heartbreaking, too, because we had to tell them we couldn't take their books back to our country. The treasures of a lot of people's libraries were out there for the taking, and the longing that books always cause in me coupled with the circumstances under which these were offered finally drove me back into the hotel when I couldn't take it anymore. Carrie and I had earlier gone into a shop and while I was trying something on the shopkeeper told her he didn't care if we bought anything, he was just glad to see Americans. When Elliott came back to the hotel room later she solemnly reported the baby dog had died, and we shared our relief that one less thing was suffering.

Thursday 27 March 2003
Hotel Maria La Gorda, Maria La Gorda

We left Heartbreak City in a rented Mitsubishi we picked up down the street at the Hotel Ambos Mundos. The bellman wheeled our stuff on his cart up and down curbs and over cobblestones from our beautiful Hotel Santa Isabel, which we hated to leave, and helped us load the trunk. With me navigating, Carrie driving and Elliott sitting in the middle of the back seat, we set off across Havana heading West. We stopped on the far West end of town to see Marina Hemingway, said to be full of American yachts and expatriates. We couldn't confirm that but were impressed by how attractive the marina was, wtih houses along the canals and boats at the docks. It looked more like Rockport, Texas than Havana, Cuba.

Using directions given by various people in the Marina Hotel regarding how to get down to the *autopista*, the divided highway that went where we were going, we only got lost and had to ask directions two more times until we reached the autopista and sailed right past it because it was unmarked. Cuba isn't big into signage. Once on it we made good time because there was so little competition for the pavement. Cubans in general are not allowed to own cars even if they can afford to buy one. Instead they stand in the middle of the traffic lanes in town and ask motorists for rides or, out in the country, stand out on the highway and try to get picked up. Therefore the two lanes on our side of the autopista really worked out to one and a half because the people on the sides of the road looking for rides took up a certain amount of space on the edges.

After an hour and a half on this open road we came to the city of Pinar del Rio where we stopped and had lunch in the Hotel Pinar del Rio in a driving-straight-down tropical rain. We ate smoked chicken and rice and fed the hotel cats, and all the men in the hotel were helpful and attentive.

Pinar del Rio was a delightful looking city with block after block of columned, colonaded buildings painted bright pastel colors. We knew nothing about it but were charmed, which was just as well since we got lost either two or three times, I can't remember now, trying to find our way out of it.

Once on the proper road, now two-lane, we still had 150 km. to go to our destination, Maria La Gorda. We had been bowled over all day by the beautiful countryside which at times looked like Southeast Asia. As we drove West, the mountainous spine of the island rose always on our right, and the lush agriculture alternated among fruit trees, palm trees, tobacco, rice paddies and sugar cane. Oxen pulled carts, goats and pigs grazed tethered near the road, the sky was patchy with rain then sunlight, there were no billboards and only the occasional revolutionary saying painted on something; when we had to pass a vehicle it was as likely pulled by beasts of burden as the internal combustion machine, and even the dogs looked a little better.

We didn't get lost anymore but as we neared the coast in a low forest that grew over the road, all of a sudden the blacktop was covered with red and black land crabs, thousands of them, and we began to squish them. They made a sickening crackly sound when run over and we slowed to a crawl and drove carefully honking for quite a way, wincing with every crush and crackle. Elliott even got out and tried to shoo them off the road ahead of us. Vultures were all over the road having cracked crab for dinner, and even a pig was eating them. It was crazy, and gross, and made us kind of hysterical.

Finally we hit the sea, turned at the last intersection and drove 14 more kilometres to Maria La Gorda, a dive resort out on a finger of land where the Gulf of Mexico meets the Caribbean, said to be the most remote hotel on the island of Cuba. We checked in, got settled, had a drink and dinner and eyed the wind level to see if there would be diving tomorrow.

Friday 28 March 2003

The wind laid in the night so Carrie and I, the scuba divers of our trio, were up early to put ourselves together for a dive trip. They put us in the slow group because we had neglected to bring our PADI cards and logbooks and they had to determine how advanced we were. In spite of there being over 20 people on the boat, the dive masters were well organized and we made a shallow dive on an obviously healthy reef. With the reefs of the world in extremis, this was heartening.

We are on a long wide bay with simply nothing on it but this hotel, which is a series of small buildings strung along a beach shaded with stately coco palms. This afternoon two fellows came by, knocked down some coconuts, whacked off their tops, poured rum in them and handed them out to whoever was around. We were sitting on our porch reading after an abortive trip to see the other arm of this bay, a UNESCO natural heritage site. It took a few more crab mortalities to drive to the ecological station to pay our entrance fee and pick up a guide only to discover it was too late in the day to make the trip.

The three of us have been living in the same room together for a week now and while we have made our domestic adjustments and had our fun, today we got downright silly and laughed at things for several hours. Lying on our beds laughing and trying to take a nap, we agreed it felt wonderful to laugh lightheartedly. This has not happened as a matter of course in recent months as the entire country had a nervous breakdown waiting for George Bush to bomb Iraq. We had to go to Cuba to get away from the anxiety of being American, and it has worked.

Saturday 29 March 2003

Carrie and I had a pretty wall dive in and out of tunnels this morning. We had graduated from the baby pool group, thankfully. As the boat motored to our dive site, we were struck once again by the pristine nature of this paradisical bay. There is utterly no one here but us, clear to the horizon in all directions.

As I had to yesterday, I went to the hotel doctor after we returned from the dive to get some alcohol for my ears. The doctor had a little two-room suite; he sat at a desk in the front room, and in the back room next to a bed he did his clinical work from a metal table with six little bottles of medicine on it. As I walked away from his quiet office thinking of him stuck out here at land's end, it occurred to me that Cuba and Cubans seem lonesome like someone who lives on the edge of a big lively neighborhood they can't enter. They would be resentful, resigned and finally sad to be excluded from the larger life they can see but not touch. We've made a terrible mistake by these people, excluding them long after our point was made.

Later I asked the doctor if he would please fix the hotel cats who lounge around the dining hall door. He was perplexed that I would care and wondered why I would want such a thing in any case. I said, because it was *humano*. He remained puzzled.

Elliott and I went snorkeling this afternoon even though we are all in an advanced state of lethargy. As she said, we're close to the "ain't worth shootin'" stage. It was a lovely snorkel with lots of fish including an eel, a flounder and a school of something being driven in one direction by a big barracuda and in another by us. As soon as we felt we'd given the snorkeling its due we came home and went back to reading our books. We're all reading Cuba books: Carrie just finished *Our Man in Havana*, I just finished a book of short stories by Cuban women writers called *Cubana*, and Elliott is reading *Driving Through Cuba* which has among other things a bad story about driving through crabs. We are not out of crab danger yet; crabs loom in our future. We're resigned to killing them but not to getting a flat tire from them.

Sunday 30 March 2003
Playa Larga

As we reluctantly dragged ourselves away from Maria La Gorda this morning, an older Italian couple asked us to take them to Santino, an hour up the road, to catch a bus because their car had broken down, it was Sunday and the car rental office at the hotel was closed. Thus we took on our first hitchhikers in a country simply covered up with them. We sympathize with them but have been up to now going too fast to do anything about it. Elliott gets mad at the country for not having a better transportation system; she's the kind of liberal who takes things personally. She's been a 'little old lady in tennis shoes' for as long as I've known her and chronologically still doesn't qualify as old. In all fairness to Elliott's anger, this is the first communist country I've been in that has such a poor transportation system. That is one thing communists usually provide.

It was Sunday morning and half the world was on the road on foot, on bicycles and in oxcarts. We saw an old gentleman who had decked the heads of his ox team with hibiscus; another tilted ox cart revealed a colorful birthday cake on the floor of it. We took out a few crabs, giving ourselves the heebie-jeebies as we smushed them.

Backtracking on the autopista to the outskirts of Havana, despite the almost complete absence of signage we managed to find a ring road that took us to another autopista, the one we needed to take us to Bahia de Giron, the Bay of Pigs, where we would break our trip and spend the night en route to Trinidad.

After we successfully manoeuvered our way through Havana and were underway, we finally stopped to have a picnic lunch in an open-air pavilion beside the highway. The proprietress sold us drinks and gave us plates on which our tuna fish, hard-boiled eggs and crackers were soon embellished with countless flies. We made short work of it, even Elliott whom we usually have to sit and watch take five or six times as long as Carrie and me to eat.

We flew down the autopista on which, as on the other one, there was no traffic. None. We got to our cutoff so fast your trusty navigator was almost caught unawares. We stopped for gas at the intersection and picked up two hitchhikers unrelated to each other, a man and a woman, and 35 km. later we were in Playa Larga. The man got out and the woman went on to show us where our hotel was.

Our luck had run out. The Hotel Playa Larga was tacky and shabby. We didn't carry on until we got the young Cuban woman safely home, not wanting to seem ungracious. It did, however, take us about an hour to calm down and resign ourselves to this place where we have a yard full of land crabs, a cinderblock bungalow full of mosquitos, a resident cockroach in the bathroom and, just as we had all gingerly settled down after dinner with our books and writing utensils, a tree frog who cut loose like a Banshee. I got up on the toilet and tried to catch him but he eluded me. I have draped a mosquito net over myself to go to bed; I look like an aging bride. Things have gotten quiet again except for the rainy cold front blowing outside.

The Bay of Pigs is a long narrow finger of water that comes up from the Caribbean. It is unattractive here at its head, although some Canadian scuba divers told us that down toward the sea it's beautiful with good diving. Up at this end I wouldn't dip my pinky in it. We are wondering how our travel agent in Havana could have put us here, but we won't know until her office reopens tomorrow. I had remarked somewhere on the outskirts of Havana that I had grown used to the shabbiness of Cuba. However, that only applied to where other people had to live and was a comment made from the vantage point of one who had not herself been subjected to same. Tonight I'm having an empathy recharge in this nasty hotel.

Monday 31 March 2003
Hotel Trinidad del Mar, Playa Ancon, Trinidad

Our creepy bunglow had two bedrooms. Carrie and I were in one in beds next to each other; on the other side of the bathroom full of night creatures lay Elliott. At 2:15 a.m. after hours of restlessness and insomnia I got up out of boredom and peed, then got out my sleep mask and earplugs, put them on hoping to zone out, got all tucked back in with my covers and pillows, squinched my eyes shut and started to drift.

At that point Carrie, who was aware I'd been up and moving around, reached over and touched me. I screamed and thrashed the covers off, thinking some small mammal had gotten on the bed. It took her a minute or two to get me calmed down, then we lay in the dark laughing, thinking Elliott couldn't hear us. This morning she disabused us of that idea but said she had declined to come in and join the merriment in the hopes we'd shut up. I never did sleep and along with the rest of the cohort couldn't disembark fast enough this morning and get back on the road.

It was chilly as we left. We crunched a few more crabs, now as hard-hearted about the stupid things as everyone else. We took a hitchhiker couple out to the autopista on the same road we'd taken the afternoon before. Refreshed (so to speak), we noticed this little road had monuments on both sides to Cubans glorified as martyrs who had died in the Bay of Pigs invasion.

Once back on the autopista we headed further East, driving 140 kph on rough pavement with sometimes not another car as far as the eye could see. With no billboards (they have nothing to sell and no one to buy it) and no traffic, the countryside was all ours. Vendors would materialise in the middle of nowhere selling garlands of onions or blocks of cheese. We finally stopped and bought some cheese and a block of guava paste just to see what they tasted like. Our exit, unmarked of course, cast us onto a narrow country road that went through a series of towns until it came to Cienfuegos, which we skirted using excellent directions from a man in a filling station (full service, clean bathrooms). Even with my powers of dead reckoning, Carrie's championship driving and Lonely Planet, it was inevitably confusing to reach and have to turn at a series of intersections. At one crucial intersection in the middle of nowhere we picked up two hitchhikers who helped us navigate, and gave away bars of soap we had brought along for the purpose to all the other people waiting for rides, much to their delight. ("Three American women in a rent car gave me a bar of soap at an intersection, mi esposa!"—"Sure!")

Thus began one of the most enchanting and remote drives of the trip. It took us over mountains and down to the sea while encountering basically nary another soul. When hitchhikers ask us if we like Cuba we all exclaim, yes, it is so beautiful, and when they ask us what we like best we say la gente, the people.

The road finally hugged the coast as it approached Trinidad. We dropped our last hitchhiker, Esteban, and rolled into our fancy resort hotel out on the beach from town just in time to eat a famished lunch. It turned out Cuba had switched to daylight savings time over the weekend and we'd continued to be on the old time. We skinned into the lunch buffet with minutes to spare and discovered they had vegetables. We hadn't seen any for a week and a half and we ate silently and intently of them until we were full.

After our unpleasant previous night we felt we deserved our handsome new digs. There was just one hitch: it was cold. The great open air lobby pavilion was a tunnel of strong north wind; the desk clerks shivered in their miniskirts. Obviously this was not a normal phenomenon. It put a crimp in our desire to go in the water, which was just as well because in our suite after lunch there was enacted a version of a madcap 1930's comedy as maids, porters and engineers came in and out fixing things and providing our eccentric necessities. The maids alone were a cheerful frenetic pair who hugged and kissed us, showed us how to fold towels into fantastical animal shapes and could've been on some slapdash Latin television version of "I Love Lucy". Naturally the tips flowed from our fingers.

Elliott and I walked on the beach in the wind for an hour, then we all got cleaned up, went into the bar where we made some friends, and ate again (vegetables). Carrie and I, who are on the same schedule, slept together in a kingsize bed; Elliott, nocturnal, had the parlor. Carrie had a flock of no-see-'em bites on her legs. Trying to think what might neutralize the irritation, I gave her oil of clove to put on them, and now sleeping with her is like sleeping next to a Christmas ham.

Me, Elliott and Carrie, Hotel Trinidad del Mar bar

Tuesday 1 April 2003

We did nothing all day except sit by the pool in the cool wind, reading and talking. We ate three times. Elliott had a salsa lesson in the morning and a scuba lesson in the pool in the afternoon, and that was the extent of our production. We are in a self-contained resort that we might have made better use of had it not been slightly cold; as it was we wallowed in our lazy inability to make a plan due to the weather.

Wednesday 2 April 2003
Casas de Campesino
Outside Trinidad on a river

We left our resort this morning with the car packed and drove into Trinidad, our real reason for being in this province and on this part of the Caribbean coast. Trinidad is a UNESCO World Heritage site. It is a 16th century town which later acquired a shameful history as a slave trading port. We saw little of this aspect in the museums but you could say that all of Cuba is a slave museum because its people are now predominantly of African descent. The Cuban Negroes are grateful to Fidel for his even-handed treatment of them and indeed may have acquired themselves a country since most white Cubans are now in the U.S. The Blacks fear life after Castro when the oligarchs will return to try to reclaim their island.

Whatever happens, it's going to be a big mess.

Trinidad was a tiny little colonial city we managed to cover between breakfast and lunch. We started at the Plaza Mayor with Elliott looking like an Englishwoman briskly guiding her big doofus charges (Carrie and me), reading from the guidebook and keeping us on message, her glasses at the end of her nose, one hand or the other waving in the air and lips hopelessly unable to wrap themselves around the Spanish names.

[She wanted to buy a lock for her luggage, of which there was certainly not one in the whole empty country. She kept asking shopkeepers and street vendors, "Loco?" I'm sure they agreed.]

We walked into, around and out of the museums in the great homes around the Plaza, buildings with gorgeous frescoes, 20-foot ceilings, louvered doors, windows and screens, huge rooms full of Romanian crystal, Limoges china, English porcelains, Italian marble, European and Latin antiques, and nice docents. We climbed one tower and one hill to photograph the red tile roofs with the line of blue sea out beyond. The streets were actually cobbled with smooth river stones, artfully canted to drain.

Lunch in a paladar, sitting in the family's garden—food not so good but a lovely old lumbering Black hostess. Our time was running out because after lunch we had to put Elliott on a bus back to Havana. Her award ticket from Delta back to Washington had to be used a day before we were leaving, so she had reconciled herself to parting a day early. Still it was wrenching because I of course have loved her for a long time and now Carrie loved her, too, and we had watched her go off in the night so many times to satisfy her nocturnal ramblings and here we were watching her go off again, so far this time, with no Spanish on top of it. I have to remind myself that she's fearless and not the small fey (albeit highly intelligent) person she appears.

I got her settled at the bus station with some simpatico employees to shepherd her, then Carrie and I drove a few kilometres west of town and checked into an attractive "recreation area" with cabins on a river. Our cabin is new, clean and everything works. We have read by the pool and admired its concrete sculptures, and now we're clean and contemplating our last evening on the road. Tomorrow we, too, return to Havana in order to fly home.

Thursday 3 April 2003
Hotel Riviera, Havana

Last night as we had dinner on a breeze-cooled thatched pavilion, the skinniest dog we'd seen so far in Cuba came over for a handout. She was a pelt stretched over a skeleton but with a sweet pretty face. Naturally half our dinner went over the side. I thought, this dog is a metaphor for Cuba and a symbol of our trip to Cuba: a hungry, tottering creature with liquid eyes and a resigned, gracious, un-pushy way about her who can't help but look longingly at our robust health and wealth, and we, frustrated and humane, can't look away as painful as it is yet can't change things, either, except temporarily and ephemerally.

As we prepared for bed last night I told Carrie I wondered if some thread would emerge from these unconnected daily ruminations. She said the thread for her that bound the trip had been the three of us together and the fact we'd brought everyone we'd ever known along with us; that we had sat over breakfast, lunch and dinner tables and rolled along the highway absorbing Cuba and telling related stories by way of synthesizing what we were experiencing. It's true: we've told sad, terrible and screamingly funny stories that have served both to entertain and to connect us to the present. We have talked of loved ones and seen the country through their eyes. The thread of life is the thread of my thoughts, all the crazy unrelated ingredients that get tossed into the mix and somehow make into a whole. It is a testimonial to the breaching of borders and why it should not be illegal.

We blew up the autopista toward Havana, collecting hitchhikers as we went. Instead of self-navigating, we followed tourist buses, first one and then another, which went through the little towns en route to the main highway as fast as cyclones. We were more polite, slowing down for la gente as they made their way along the sides of the road on foot, bicycle, horse and wagon. It would have been morally difficult not to share our car with some of them.

At noon we were in Havana, and found our way from memory back to the Hotel Ambos Mundos to turn in our car. One of the car men took us to our new hotel, Meyer Lansky's monument to Miami/Las Vegas Mafia chic, the Hotel Riviera. We were skeptical until we walked into the dated but imposing lobby and were flooded with cultural memories of an old glamourous time. Our room on the 9th floor looked down on the Malecon and out to the Florida Straits, and there was something touching about its spacious dimensions and modern furniture that made us slyly nostalgic.

We took a taxi back to the paladar we had enjoyed so much, Gringo Viejo, and the taxi was a '55 Chevy. We laughed to think of all the funky, beachy places we'd stayed and how good it felt to be back in the city, grownups again starring in an old movie. Later I swam in the hotel pool, 30 meters long and 12 feet deep; they don't make them like that anymore. It had a three-story diving platform and cold salty water and it took a minute to get over the shock of the chill before I could luxuriate in the sheer quantity of the water. We're going to bed early in order to be picked up at 5:00 tomorrow morning.

The Malecon, the broad thoroughfare that spans much of Havana along the water, is a theme that recurs in literature and guidebooks about Cuba. It has a wide sidewalk on the ocean side and a low wall separating its pedestrians from the rollers crashing on the rocks and jetty-like infrastructure below. It is a lovers' lane and can be a festival scene, but we have witnessed little activity on it. As we drove along it today on the way to the Hotel Riviera I studied once again the decayed and abandoned buildings on its cityside and thought, this must be what Beirut looks like. Does the architectural destruction wrought by his revolution give Castro any despair? It is terribly painful to the visitor.

Well, dear reader, as this narrative draws to a close you may be left to tie up the threads, detect the theme, question motive and draw lessons from the experiences in a way I cannot help you with. It was a serious trip with a lot of self-indulgent fun laced through it. We were in a constant state of cerebration about Cuba whether we were scuba diving or studying antiquities. We worried over the poverty, the dogs, the cats, the buildings, the horses, oxen, chickens, goats and pigs. We loved the gentle destroyed people and were amazed by the beauty of the countryside and its coasts. We have loved Cuba with embrace, sorrowed after its past and feared for its future. Part of our fear is what we could do to it given the opportunity, a fear that appropriately parallels the fear we feel for all the old good parts of our own country, now so squandered. It has been strangely appropriate to be here during the Iraqi war, not wishing for defeat but not wanting anything to embolden our already arrogant Administration. Our thoughts of Cuba are all wrapped up in our thoughts of our own country and we wish with all our aching love that, as Rodney King said, 'we could all just get together.'

NORWAY, GREENLAND AND ICELAND
INTRODUCTION

In the summer of 2002 my mother and I took a trip with three other friends to Denmark and Norway. It was a lovely cruise but it left us wanting more of that part of the world.

Mother started watching her mail for a trip that would satisfy that curiosity and would also satisfy her desire for such a destination far from any war zone. When we learned our San Antonio friend Lynda Billa-Burke and her husband Jimmy Burke had gone to Greenland, we invited her to give us a synopsis. Based on that, we began to make the plan.

We used a travel company in Seattle called Expedition Trips which puts travelers on small-ship cruises. We picked a Russian ship called the Polar Pioneer, leased by an Australian tour company, and chose the dates and itinerary that suited us: late summer, to Greenland and Iceland. As it turned out we were part of only a handful of the fifty passengers on the ship who were not Australian, which added a dimension to our perception of the voyage.

The trip was not easy for two reasons. One, we were bored part of the time and two, we had some scary and some ill-timed travel experiences. These were not the fault of anyone but the travel fates and our own inconstant minds. I think it would be safe to say we had on balance a good time but in the pantheon of our travels it was not our favorite trip.

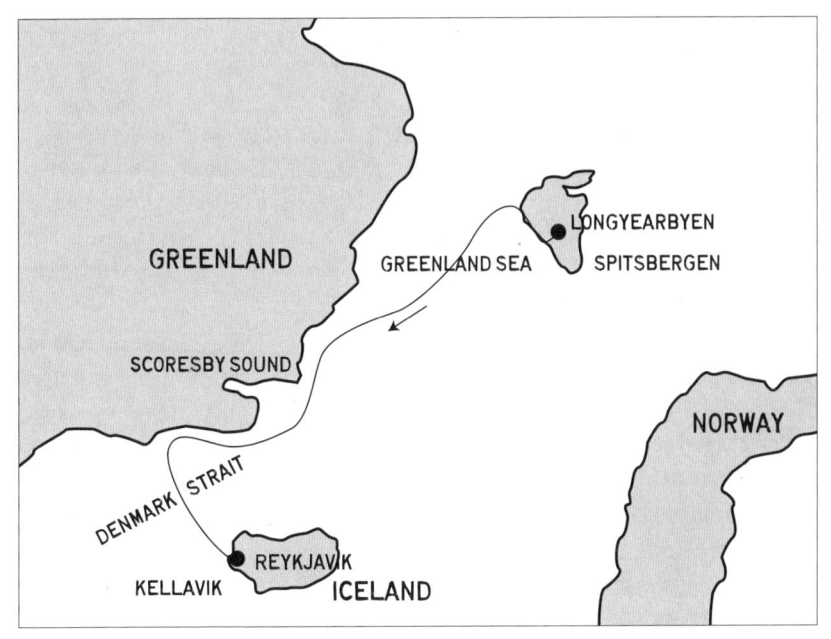

THE JOURNAL
Friday 22 August 2003
Svalbard

Mother and I left so many issues stewing on both the front and back burners of our lives, it felt almost illegal to leave the country. We'd spent the summer at the mercy of our own relentless albeit self-concocted schedule and it resembled a bit running away from home, i.e. bad girl fun, to get on an airplane and fly away. And so we did, four long days ago, from Washington to Oslo.

In Oslo, feeling crummy from the trans-Atlantic flight, we checked into the Grand Hotel where we indulged ourselves eating good food, partaking of the beautiful city, lolling about our suite and of course sleeping. On the second night we sat down and talked about everything that was going on in our lives by way of a verbal exorcism that gave us permission to stop thinking about home and concentrate on the adventure ahead.

On our one full day in Oslo we went to Holmenkollen to climb to the top of the famous ski jump. Problem was, Mother had a hitch in her giddyup and couldn't walk, so this was not a good choice of activity. The concierge had urged us to take the subway out to the park of the ski jump and its museum, neglecting to mention it was a fifteen minute walk uphill from the station to our destination. So we hitchhiked, up and back. The man who took us up even got us onto the grounds with his own passes, and the one who took us down took us all the way to our next stop, Vigeland Park, the famous sculpture garden we had visited last year and wanted to see again.

At the ski jump I climbed to the top (my thigh muscles are still telling me about it) while Mother waited below in the museum. From the top it was clear that one would have to be certifiably crazy to ski off such a contraption. At the sculpture garden we made a desultory pass through the front half of it before breaking down and flagging a real live taxi instead of some hapless but thoughtful male motorist to take us back to the hotel, where we ate both days in their Grand Cafe, panelled, chandeliered, tapestried but open to the sidewalk. The swells had been meeting there since the 19th century. We people-watched and felt fortunate to be in such a civilized place in such a civilized city in such a civilized country.

Yesterday morning the idyll ended at 5:00 a.m. when we got up to start the next leg of our adventure and the real reason for our trip, to fly to Longyearben on Spitsbergen Island in the Svalbard archipelago, an international possession like Antarctica, administered by Norway. It lies above the Arctic Cirlce out in the ocean above Norway and east of Greenland, and we were to meet our ship there for an eco-cruise.

Our Braathens Airlines (SAS) plane left Oslo at 9:20 a.m., landed in Tromso in the far north of Norway around 11:00 a.m.—that was an experience in itself, as the pilot had to weave past mountain tops to position himself to land on a strip plastered narrowly between the fjord and the mountainside, then upon landing throw on the brakes and quickly make a 180 degree turn because the landing strip was so short. We deplaned then re-planed and took off for Longyearben.

I was innocently reading my book, as usual, when after about an hour and a half I looked out the window. It took me a minute to process what I was seeing: Black mountain peaks sticking out of thick white clouds with no ground in sight, and us heading down toward them. I grabbed Mother and she grabbed me. The captain came on and said the fog was very thick in Longyearben but he was going to attempt a landing. I silently sent telepathic messages to everyone I loved, trying to make peace in case I was going to meet my maker, and into the clouds we plunged with these black mountains on either side. I thought of Ron Brown, Mickey Leland and all the other unfortunate souls who bought the farm in weather-related plane crashes, and tried to keep my breathing steady. There wasn't a sound in the cabin.

Then suddenly the pilot pulled up and we weren't landing after all. It was a relief of sorts but scary in its own right. He announced we would circle for thirty minutes, then head back to Tromso if we couldn't land. Thirty minutes later we were heading back to Tromso where we had another exciting landing with the plane having to make a tight spiral this time to get into position. In spite of the snafu we were content to be on terra firma back in the Tromso terminal. At 4:30p.m. they announced we'd leave again for Longyearben at 1:00 a.m., and took us in buses into town to an SAS hotel. Mother and I weren't inclined to lie around on the lobby floor for eight hours so we got a room at a nice little hotel next door and I got on the phone.

Incredibly, when I reached our ship's agent in Longyearben to find out what to do, fully expecting them to sail without us, they said they'd wait for us. I said we'd be there around 3:30 a.m.

After a little walk around downtown Tromso in the gathering cold, a little supper at our hotel and a little rest on the bed in our room, we got up and went over to the other hotel where we boarded buses and returned to the airport. It was midnight. At 1:45 a.m. we finally took off. At 3:15 a.m. as the plane approached Longyearben, there were the same evil looking mountain tops and the same deep fluffy clouds, only this time with a random patch you could see through. I made my peace with the world again and we descended into the marshmallows, this time tinged with the peach of the Arctic dawn. The plane shook and rumbled as they do descending. We couldn't see anything. I thought, the next thing I'm going to feel is my limbs being torn from my torso. I tried to think if SAS had ever had a crash.

Then there was the ground and within seconds of being able to see the ground we landed, safely. The ceiling couldn't have been more than 100 feet. [Come to find out they have to make visual landings at Longyearben. I was so glad not to know that until after the fact.]

The little airport with its metal walls and concrete floor was in chaos. Crowds of people were waiting for a flight, more were lined up at ticket counters, and we added to the biomass. Once we had the bags we stood out on the cold wet driveway waiting for a taxi to appear. The taximan drove us a short distance to a waterfront and pointed to our ship, resting offshore, then got out to offload our bags. We were wondering how we were going to get from here to there when two men came out of a shed and greeted us: Henrik, our expedition leader, and Andre from the crew. Henrik, tall and handsome, hugged us, picked up the bags as if they weighed nothing and led us to a Zodiac. In minutes we were climbing the gangplank of the Polar Pioneer. Onboard Sue, the assistant expedition leader, hugged us and took us to our room. I was in bed ten minutes later; it was 4:30 a.m. It had taken us 24 hours bed-to-bed to get from Oslo to Longyearben.

The hugs meant a lot because we had been concerned everyone would be mad at us for holding up the ship. As it was, starting at breakfast when we first saw them, everyone could not have been kinder. Their concern had been for us. In our stupor after only two hours of sleep, this was soothing.

The ship sailed immediately upon our embarkation, heading west out Isfjord, the huge fjord that divides Spitsbergen in the middle. Mid-morning we stopped up in an arm of it called Skansbutka and went ashore to walk on a rubble beach where there was an old wooden boat, and an abandoned gypsum mine and a hunters' shack. It was an uninspired outing to my mind, but it put us on our feet and in the fresh air. It would have taken a celestial chorus to inspire us at that point, as tired as we were. At all other times of day I was on my bed with my eyes closed trying to relieve the tightness of fatigue around my head.

Heading continually West out Isfjord, mid-afternoon we stopped in another inlet on the north side of the fjord and went ashore to climb a hill of squishy tundra below Alkhornet.

It took some doing merely to ascend the dirt embankment from the rocky beach to the tundra. On this outing we saw a few reindeer (caribou) and a colony of kittiwakes high on a cliffside above a talus slope we did not attempt to climb. Mother didn't make it to the top of the hill; I took her and another older lady back down toward the beach. Sharpshooters were watching everywhere for polar bears.

I began to rally and back onboard, began to write. We went in the evening to the captain's cocktail party, not one of those flossy affairs on an ocean liner but just all 50 of us crammed into the bar to hear Henrik's rundown of the day and our Russian captain say a few words of greeting. I had already met him in the hall ; he is our next door neighbor. We have the biggest room on the ship, about which we are not complaining. We have four big portholes—windows, really, that look out on the bow and port side, a long writing desk, gobs of storage space, a well-engineered bathroom, a sleeping nook for me with a platform bed and a curtain across the door to block Mother's late night light, one and a half walls of built-in daybed where Mother sleeps, and a big open floor for our calisthentics and our psychology.

Dinner was good. I had eaten piddly little meals catch-as-catch-can for two days and real, hot food tasted divine. We were given an extra hour as we crossed into a new time zone—we were now in open sea heading across the North Atlantic toward Greenland—and when I went to bed, finally, in night clothes and under the covers for the first time in 2 nights—it was to sleep until I woke up.

Saturday 23 August 2003
At sea

Ten hours and fifteen minutes. That's how long I slept. I felt like a real live human bean when I woke up.

We were at sea, steaming West-Southwest in calm seas, and we would be at sea all day and part of tomorrow. I went to the bird lecture and began to focus on the fulmars, guillemots (of which we have seen little auks, murres and puffins), terns and gulls (kittiwakes) we have seen as well as brands predicted to be seen. I got queasy in the lecture room because the slide screen was wavering and it was dark and close, so I put on my sea bands and part of a patch and lay down when I got back to the room. Mother had done her hair and also took a nap before lunch. Then we had another nap after lunch before the whale lecture (she slept through that, too). This enforced idleness may do wonders for our usually abused sleep quotient although our figures are sure to suffer without any exercise.

The ship has been slowly picking its way through ice floes all afternoon. We went up to the bridge and spent some time watching the helmsman subtly steer between the larger floes that bobbed everywhere in the hypnotic glassy sea. We bumped some and were glad this was an "ice rated" ship. Henrik showed us on the chart where we were and admitted he was "watching the clock" because the ice was slowing us down. Even the Russian captain came onto the bridge and said to me, What is this? The North Pole?, and shrugged. He had on slacks and a sport shirt.

Now at the end of the afternoon it has gotten foggy on top of everything else. We've had some hard bumps against ice; they elevate the pulse and are gone. Maybe at this rate I'll get all my reading done, if I can stay awake.

Sunday 24 August 2003
In the Greenland Sea

Mother and I watched a video of "Amadeus" after dinner last night and it gave me negative thoughts as I went to sleep, thus a night of tossing and turning probably exacerbated by being too full of sleep anyway. I volunteered to write the ship's log today so I must try to be particularly perceptive. I may simply use the ship's log entry for this daily journal entry—why write the day twice? The log entry follows:

Henrik's voice aroused us at 7:40 this morning to announce breakfast and tabular icebergs on the port side. We were still steaming West-Southwest toward Greenland, slightly off schedule after slowly having had to traverse an afternoon of ice floes yesterday. There was a noticeable but not uncomfortable swell for the first time since leaving Spitsbergen.

Gary [Miller, our PhD. lecturer] celebrated his 50th birthday by giving us a morning lecture on what he academically or perhaps tongue-in-cheekily called the megafauna of Greenland: Polar bears, Arctic foxes and musk oxen. He is a clear lecturer with good slides and keeps almost everyone awake in the warm dark gently rocking lecture room.

Suddenly Greenland loomed before us, appearing around noon. We'd been at sea suspended time out of mind in our ship capsule for 36 hours and here was something to draw us to the future. It looked dramatic, bare brown mountains rising out of the water with icebergs in the foreground—nothing unprepossessing about it.

Mother and Greenland

Still we had to have lunch (who would miss it?)—Thai soup and other goodies today—before heading back to the bow or to the bridge to watch the unfolding scenery. The ship entered Gail Hamkis Bay, a wide open mouth of water off which was our first destination, Youngsund (sund is sound), where we were to pick up a park ranger, Kunuk, who will go as far as Scoresbysund. Kunuk is a member of the Sirius Patrol, a military company that polices some incredible swath of national park in coastal Eastern Greenland by dogsled all winter and by plane, foot and boat in summer. Before we could effect that, an orange Zodiak came zooming up alongside us with three men and a movie camera in it. One of them hollered up to Henrik and had a conversation with him in Danish. He came up the gangplank looking dashing in a dry suit—it was Goren, a Swedish adventurer who was doing underwater filming for a BBC documentary. He sat in the dining room and told stories, and was given cigarettes. He said he and his crew had been reduced to smoking tobacco rolled in fax paper.

Kunuk the park ranger came out with two men in another orange Zodiak (they also wear orange survival suits that save them if they go overboard, and keep them warm as well). They all visited onboard for awhile, giving the rest of us time to revel in the scenery and windless, manageably cold air. The sun came out, adding to the beauty of the fjord (Youngsund) by putting down layers of light on the mountains and valleys that dropped to the sea.

Perhaps the most dramatic moment came when Kunuk's compadres left and we proceeded out Youngsund, slowly slaloming between icebergs that tried to block us from the larger Gail Hamkis Bay. Brushing past them in their extreme beauty and authority was an exercise in aesthetics as well as respect.

We ran for another couple of hours, still in the Bay, to Dead Man's Cove where we would have our afternoon excursion which in this case started around 7:00 p.m. Al [the kayak master] took off with two kayakers, Eric and John, and they looked awfully small to those of us who waited eagerly on the bow for our turn to board a Zodiak and go ashore for the first time in two days. The water was slightly rough but not too much of a roller coaster as we skied into a real live sand beach. Up the slope were five musk oxen, certainly the first musk ox your scribe had ever seen and probably the first for most. They are prehistoric looking and immensely furry with German helmet-shaped horns down the sides of their faces. We were warned not to get too close to them.

There was a shabby looking wooden shack near the beach; some rusty barrels and spent shells that were the remains of a World War II Danish gun emplacement; a rocky stream bed; and perhaps most important of all, archeological holes in the ground indicating where some East Greenland Eskimos camped until apparently scared away by their first white men who demonstrated to them how firearms worked. When the white men awoke the next morning, the Eskimos were gone and no one has seen them since. That was in 1823. There was something ineffably sad about the holes, after hearing this story, but ruins frequently make one thoughtful or wistful even as they connect one in a positive way to a past one cannot otherwise possess.

Dinner was wonderful—lamb and smashed potato cakes—and dessert was a birthday cake for Gary decorated with a frosting polar bear and sparklers. Henrik announced after dinner (at ten p.m.) that the Zodiaks were going out for one last excursion, this time to Eskimo Point. Those who thought it was a good idea went.

Monday 25 August 2003
East coast of Greenland

One is struck by the monumental scale of Greenland on this coast. Distances are deceptive on water in any case, but what looks like a fjord and is called a fjord on the charts may be seven miles wide. If we have to skirt two large islands separated by fjords, it may take hours. The scenery unfurls and unfurls and still there is more of it. Where we are it consists of bare brown mountains, azure water and icebergs.

When we're walking on the mountains—foothills, really—they are not brown underfoot. They are well covered with tundra, spongy soil held by plants and flowers that don't grow over 3" tall if that. The flowers alone are heartbreaking little creations that cling to their big brown inhospitable hillsides in defiance of the harsh. The rocks are beautiful, scoured by eons of ice; I want to take home pocketsful. We are not supposed to pick up even a single rock, which is kind of funny when you consider you could fill the hold of a supertanker with rocks from just one beach and they wouldn't be missed, there are so many of them.

Because of the distances the ship has to cover between stopping places, we spend a lot of time simply contemplating scenery when we are not eating or sleeping. After an inert period we put on our gumboots and rain suits, parkas, hats and gloves and get in the Zodiacs for an excursion. These excursions seem to happen in slow motion, 50 people milling first on the beach, then slowly fanning out and with little announcement following Henrik or Gary up a mountainside or down a beach. We are not supposed to walk by ourselves because of bears, yet we're not necessarily led, either.

This morning at Mosquito Bay I climbed a mountain with the fit group, stopping before the steeper summit in honor of my knees which like to ascend but not descend. Mother stayed near the beach at a Sirius patrol hut that was our landmark. One of the pleasures of a walk on the tundra is the flowers. Another is the softness, a phenomenon people who work out can appreciate.

We spent the next few hours "repositioning" the ship, i.e. moving to another spot which, after a pre-lunch nap, lunch and a post-lunch nap, turned out to be Cape Humboldt at the narrow entrance of a fjord two islands below Kaiser Franz Josef Fjord. There Henrik, Kunuk and Gary, the gunbearers, determined there were no bears, so I left Mother at the Sirius hut (some wag asked Henrik if we were going to stop at every hut in East Greenland) and walked hard for over an hour. When I got back to the ship I had to peel off three layers wet from the exertion and from being overdressed.

The Sirius huts are provisioned for the park rangers and probably whoever needs them. They are unlocked and have staples, dried fish, firewood, a stove and beds. They are small, orderly but plain. Because Greenlanders live communally and don't own property, there is little concern for theft.

Tuesday 26 August 2003 — Kaiser Franz Josef Fjord

We awoke to scenery I instantly dubbed "Lake Powell with Icebergs." We were surrounded by fancifully colored striated cliffs and mountainsides with icebergs in their own fanciful shapes bobbing at their bases. The sun was out, the water was glassy and the temperature a perfect cool-to-cold.

Shortly after breakfast we were lightered over to a small rocky beach on Flower Bay whence we walked ever upward on what would have been an Alpine meadow if it hadn't been Arctic tundra. There were some rocks to clamber over but mostly it was the easier tundra, uphill though it was. The terminus of the walk was a rocky promontory that looked down on a lake, Lake Noa. We shucked off layers of clothing, took pictures and admired the gorgeous scenery.

Then I was ready to go back down. Yet no one else was. Ten, fifteen minutes went by. There's something wrong with me, I thought, that 50 other people are content to lollygag around looking at the same scenery when it doesn't change and nothing happens. I am congenitally unable to stand staring at the same item in a museum or the same mountain or even see the same movie twice. I always think to myself, I get it, let's go.

Some of the Russian crew had come up and when they started back down Henrik told me to go with them. I retraced the flower-carpeted walk back down, thinking about the flowers and wondering what this place would look like covered with ice and snow.

From late morning to late afternoon we were underway hemmed in by deeply dramatic scenery. The incredibly beautiful sedimentary striped mountains had been faulted every which was so no two patterns repeated; below them their iceberg outriders carved themselves into fantastical designs of shining turquoise. The water was mirror-like as we went from Kaiser Franz Josef Fjord into Antarctic (really) Fjord, then Kempe ("large") Fjord and Narwhal Sound, at the end of which we stopped at Cape Harry for a shore excursion. That trip ashore started so late we didn't have dinner until 9:00 p.m., but it was worth getting hungry for: beef Wellington. We're eating well and hoping our figures will survive the indulgence. Slogging up mountainsides twice a day helps.

Wednesday 27 August 2003

We didn't want to get up this morning and considered staying in bed all day in our nighties.

We were stopped at the dead end of Alpefjord. Straight ahead a glacier came to the water's edge, and high above were some rugged-peaked snow covered alps. We could feel the cold through the walls.

A long morning excursion by Zodiac was announced; bundle up, we were told. We scored Henrik as our Zodiac pilot, and Ian and Brenda, our next door neighbors and new friends, in our boat, and set off to cover the distance between the ship and the glacier (called Sefstrom Glacier). Distances being wildly further than one first perceives and scale making a mockery of perception, we motored through aquamarine colored water made milky by glacier runoff. At the terminus of the glacier we were amazed at the high cliff face of it; it had looked from afar like it ramped right down into the water.

The water was full of brash ice, icebergs and bergy bits we dodged as we skirted the glacier face. Also unseen from the ship was a continuation of the fjord around the right side of the glacier; we motored along, marveling at the marbled ice designs and reveling in the glorious day.

Ahead of us Sue, driving one of the Zodiacs, drove it up on the sloping side of an iceberg. Her passengers hopped off and onto the berg. Henrik eased into position to disgorge us so we could have the same iceberg experience; all of us went onto the ice except Mother, who remained in the Zodiac.

The iceberg was slippery so I basically leaned on an upright piece of ice and didn't move. I hate to walk on ice. In fact I was wondering why I even got out on the damn thing when there was a crack and a large piece of it broke off, causing it to start to capsize. The passengers of the first Zodiac, which was just positioned to pick them up, panicked and started screaming and sliding, throwing themselves head first into the boat or getting very wet as the edge of the ice went under.

I grabbed Kunuk, our Eskimo, and headed for high ground around to one side of the iceberg where Henrik had nosed in to catch us. Ian was trying to calm the panicked (of which I was not one). Finally we were all aboard our boats, some in a boat they had not necessarily started out in. It had been a case of the panic being more dangerous than the incident itself, and I'm sure Henrik and Sue made a mental note they'd not try that type of landing again.

Once it was clear we'd all survived, the laughing and storytelling began with everyone trying to sort out what had happened to whom and in what sequence. It was thereinafter referred to in mock-grave tones as "The Incident".

The excursion continued to very nearly the actual dead end of the fjord. We all pulled up on a moraine beach and walked around for a few minutes, then re-embarked for the trip home.

On the trip out I had been facing the glacier. On the trip home I faced the steep brown mountains that bounded the other side of the fjord. I thought of those old mountains and how they'd seen it all, yet stood like sentinels up at the top of the world, unconscious of their power, waiting out geologic time as we little ants scurried around importantly at their base, no bigger in the grand scheme of things than a grain of sand on their beaches and to last less long than the beat of a bird's wing. Yet for all my unimportance I was glad to be there to celebrate them in my hyperconsciousness for what it was worth, to do honor to their mute grandeur, to anthropomorphize them if you will by even attempting a comparison.

Back aboard ship we settled in for a late lunch and a 24-hour voyage out of Alpefjord, then out King Oscar Fjord to the sea once more, to turn south for a run down to Scoresbysund (Scoresby Sound). Mid-afternoon we had a group photo on the bow and some hot rum punch to sooth the nerves if they were still jangled from "The Incident". A video followed on glaciers, then drinks in the bar and dinner with Ian and Brenda et.al. We are ready for bed after ricocheting around our stateroom; the seas are rough and we are rolling.

Thursday 28 August 2003

It stayed rough. Mother took to her bed last night with unusual haste, feeling none too well. I had to switch ends of the bed to keep my head higher than my feet as the bow dipped and rose. I willed my stomach to stay calm. Just before waking the water smoothed out; we had entered the influence of Scoresby Sound.

Scoresbysund is the largest fjord system in the world. We entered its big main channel and motored inland on it until 11:00 a.m., when we stopped for a shore excursion to a point of glacially scarred bedrock interspersed with tundra on which there were tent circles of rocks left by paleo-Eskimos a couple of thousand years ago. There was also a hunters' shack surrounded by the usual detritus—old lumber, animal bones, tin cans, even a pantyliner. After climbing the rocks and walking around the tiny bay to the hunters' shack I got a ride home in the Zodiac so I didn't have to stand around looking at the same junk for another hour. I think I'm a bad person not to be interested in what others find so interesting.

The trip back out to the ship in the Zodiac was excruciatingly beautiful. The great fjord, many miles wide, had become a lake of glass mirroring the sky. Off in the distance turquoise icebergs floated, and at the horizon the water became the sky. One could've gone right off the negative edge and into another dimension, given the right drugs.

We spent some time on the bow in the afternoon, reading, visiting and soaking up scenery. We were finally seeing a glimpse of the great Greenland ice cap as it oozed over mountaintops and down glacial valleys. It had been too far inland to see when we were in the fjords further north.

The fjord we were in doglegged right and further transit in that direction was suddenly not going to happen thanks to a field of icebergs. We disembarked and Zodiak'd over to a kelp-covered beach from which we climbed the solid rock center of a small peninsula. The bedrock was so thoroughly etched and carved that tundra had grown up in the cracks, enabling us practically to climb tundra stairs to the top.

Me on the bow

Dinner was late again but great: rack of lamb, roasted potatoes and cauliflower. We'd had taco salad for lunch. I was personally nearing the end of my rope in terms of tiredness, so when Henrik announced a sunset (10:00 p.m.) Zodiak cruise amongst the icebergs I was unmoved. Mother went, however; she hadn't moved all day and was wide awake.

Friday 29 August 2003
Scoresbysund

I woke with a sore throat and malaise and didn't do any hikes all day. I just ate and read. I'm reading Jane Smiley's book *The Greenlanders*, having finished Gretl Ehrlich's *This Cold Heaven: Seven Seasons in Greenland*, an exquisitely written, amazing book I have passed along to Brenda.

Right after lunch Henrik announced a long walk from Harefjord, where the ship lay, over a low saddle of land to Rypefjord on the other side. Those of us who didn't walk spent some of those hours on the bridge as the ship chugged out of Harefjord and into Rypefjord to pick up the walkers on the other side. As we waited for them, others went ashore. Finally the original group came over the horizon, looking about as big as ants in the field glasses. I thought of Lewis and Clark and how their company would split up in the wilderness and meet one, two or three days later right where they'd planned.

The lazy day of inaction (for me) was redeemed in the end by a party on the fantail of the ship. The cooks moved dinner outside: grilled meats and a buffet table of salads. Music was playing and it didn't take long to get past the food and into the dancing. About half the passengers and several of the crew danced wildly for a coupie of hours out in the cold air surrounded by scenery and sunset. This included yours truly and of course the queen of dance, Mother, although she was not so enamored of the disco beat or some of the music. Brenda managed to get almost every male wallflower out on the dicey wet metal "dance floor"; Ian danced Mother and me and all the cute Russian housekeepers. Everyone danced en masse, laughing and cutting up. Many of these people had already made two hikes in the course of the day; all we'd done was sit around. It felt wonderful to dance, and made me forget I was sick.

Saturday 30 August 2003
Scoresbysund

I awoke with full-fledged bronchitis, richly deserved.

The morning activity was not hiking but a Zodiac ride among icebergs in Osfjord. This was something we could all do. We got decked out in our warmest duds since we would be out two hours and instead of our usual sun there was a lowering sky, making it damp. Nikolai, the chief mate, ran our Zodiac. Our group was inordinately interested in every little detail of the icebergs, which were huge, as big as office buildings, and even wanted to see one twice, on the way out and the way in. I was cold and got restless with all the idling, and was glad finally to return to the ship. Then I couldn't get warm. Mother had to get a hot water bottle from the infirmary and wrap me up with it under layers of covers. I finally thawed out in time for lunch.

After lunch we were motoring through a maze of icebergs toward Kap Sud, South Cape, where we would make a landing to see some ancient Eskimo bones and outlines. Mother went down for a nap, then I, and we slept through the announcement and the landing. When we woke up we made light of our sloth and watched a movie, "True Grit". When it was over we were still in Greenland, surrounded by icebergs.

Sunday 31 August 2003

We had motored back out Scoresbysund heading toward the open sea all night, and breakfast found us nosing in toward land and Ittoqqortoormiit, or Scoresby Town, the only habitation we'd seen on this immense fjord. From the ship the town was cute, with little brightly colored Monopoly houses built up a hill from a rocky beach. After an orientation we motored over in a cold damp drizzle and began picking our way around the town. The houses were painted either red, blue, yellow or green. Many had rocky yards full of sled dogs. Puppies played and rolled everywhere. There were wooden sleds, drying racks for meat and skins, dog s--t, not terribly much trash, children with lollipops in their mouths, and general detritus everywhere, We went to the church, hospital, old people's home, women's handicrafts shop, post office and grocery store in the company of a handsome 30 year-old Danish man whose father was the harbormaster and majordomo of the town. This guide was a humble lad who had just spent a month and a half kayaking by himself back in Scoresbysund. To understand the dimensions of his aloneness, it would be like beinq left on the face of the moon for a month and a half. He had a wise calmness about him; I tried to think of any Americans I knew who might have been inclined to or able to do the same, and couldn't come up with a single name.

Of all the days we've bundled up to go ashore, this was the coldest, oddly, the one day we were in a town. I had to lie down with the hot water bottle on my chest when we got home. But I leapt up when it was announced that some passengers were going to take the "polar plunge," i.e. jump into the 4-degree Centigrade water. About six did it while the rest of us hung on the rail and screamed in sympathy.

With that the ship weighed anchor and we headed out to sea, leaving the peaceful influence of Scoresbysund and entering the rough and rolling precincts of the Denmark Strait between Greenland and Iceland. We will be at sea all day tomorrow as well; the following morning we dock in Keflavik, the harbor town of Reykjavik, where we will end our cruise.

(Later.) The dining room was strangely unpopulated at dinner. We were in a force 8 gale and fully half the passengers forewent eating. Ian, Brenda, Mother and I laughed and ate, then had to practically crawl up the stairs to keep from getting knocked silly. Mother and I went on up to the bridge where the height of the waves was even more evident; Mother went back down the stairs on her bum.

Now we are snug in our stateroom as water crashes over the bow and against our windows (just below the bridge). It is difficult to move around; I even fell out or the bathroom and wound up sprawled on the floor, to Mother's great surprise. We have laughed ourselves hysterical trying to relay our stuff and each other around the room. We've had to put towels in the windowsills to keep the sea water out because I didn't have the portholes screwed shut tightly enough. Sleep is probably out of the questions unless we can tie ourselves in our beds somehow.

Monday 1 September 2003
Denmark Strait

It was a long uncomfortable night. I banked myself with pillows to keep from falling out of bed. Sometime in the night I either got used to the pitching or the waves got lower because I finally slept.

Nikolai, the chief mate, had told me yesterday the Denmark Strait was equal to the Drake Passage between South America and Antarctica in roughness, something else I was glad I hadn't known until it was too late. This morning the captain told me the water will get rougher in the course of the day and be the worst at night. [I quickly did my packing when I heard that and didn't leave it for tonight; we are leaving the ship tomorrow morning.] Being on the ship in such high seas is like being handicapped: you have to plan your every move. The crew estimates the seas at "5 or 6 metres." What few people showed up at lunch couldn't talk about anything but vomiting and remedies for it. If we don't coldcock ourselves before dinner, I am going to try to find a better mealtime topic.

(Later.) We had a farewell cocktail party in the bar, following which Henrik took to his bed. The captain was sick and didn't make it. Our Brenda lasted five minutes and went back to her lair. Mother, Ian and I had a farewell dinner together with Sue, and now we are bouncing off the walls getting ready for bed. Our e.t.a. in Keflavik is 5:30 a.m. so we know at 5:30 a.m., at least, the boat will stop rocking. Mother says now all we need to make the trip complete is for one of those Icelandic volcanoes to act up.

Tuesday 2 September 2003 — Reykjavik

At 5:30 a.m. we were still offshore, rolling. Relief didn't come until around 7:00, by which time we had already negotiated the shower (you pressed your butt to the wall, legs akimbo, and soaped as fast as you could before a big wave cracked against the side of the ship and sent you flying out the shower curtain). At 7:00 there were lights on the shore; I willed us to hurry to them. Then breakfast happened, bags were put out, we docked and left the ship, hugged the crew and thanked them, all piled on a bus and headed for town, into Reykjavik.

First we dropped several people at the international airport at Keflavik. We admired two sculptures there, one signifying a rainbow and the other the beak of a bird breaking out of its shell. The trip into the city was a lesson in vulcanism. There was nary a tree, but the moonscape landscape was redeemed by green ground cover. The guide on our bus said Keflavik had a population of 7,000 and the whole country has a population of 288,000. That is mighty small.

After a nice ride through the countryside, including past a golf course in the lava where the concept of a rough would have had to be redefined, we came to Reykjavik and to the hotel where we were being dumped. There we were faced with saying goodbye to Ian and Brenda. They helped with our bags and waited in the cold wind with us for our taxi to come, and then we hugged and hugged. They had made our trip, and I hope we see them again.

Mother and I taxied to the Hotel Holt and checked in, then tried to decide what we wanted to do. We came within a hair's breadth of taking a city tour at noon but concluded we were too hungry to do it without lunch so we had a very good lunch in the hotel dining room that was filled with well dressed locals. The Fodor's said it was one of the best restaurants in the city and within the confines of our ability to know, we agreed.

Then we hit the streets and walked for about three hours, window shopping and trying to get a feel for the place. The scale of the city is so small we had to remind ourselves we were in a world capital. About the time we decided to head back to the hotel it began to rain hard, and we laughed all the way back huddled under a single umbrella. I was in my jammies by 4:30 p.m. Between not sleeping in the gale of the last two nights and being sick on top of it, I was pretty near the end of my resources. All will be well, however, after a night of sleep in a bed that doesn't move.

Wednesday 3 September 2003
Reykjavik

And sleep we did, about ten hours' worth. We're still rocking from the boat, however, gingerly tap-tap-tapping the floor to get our footing whenever we get up.

Yesterday afternoon when we were browsing along the main shopping street, we ran into two ladies from our cruise. I told them we had earlier seen the tour company bus loading the new passengers to take them to the ship—it is returning to Greenland—and this woman exclaimed, Oh, the poor things! That was exactly what I had thought: those poor schmucks don't know that in about six hours when they get out into the Denmark Strait they're going to wish they'd made other plans.

At breakfast a couple came in, and when he spoke to the waitress it sounded Texan. As we left I asked if he were from Texas and sure enough, they were from Houston. We told them a little about our trip and the last few days at sea. I began to see how the story was going to shape up as we synthesize the experiences of the last twelve days. The story will get regularized and institutionalized, then told enough not to vary more than a word or two. Everyone does this; it is almost a search for meaning. It made me think what my own response to questions about the trip would be. Here are some of them:

I would not recommend the trip except to serious hikers, outdoorspeople and nature lovers (all of the above, not just one or two or the above).

Since probably 20-25% of the trip fell into the category of "hours of boredom punctuated by moments or terror," I would not recommend the trip to anyone bored with finding meaning in a microcosm. This trip was definitely not macro like, say, Iran, which had 5000 years of ruins and a history as a crossroads or civilization. In Greenland we were at the end of the Earth, not in the middle of it.

As much as we enjoyed the other ship passengers, it is better to take someone with you around whom your life revolves instead of missing that person(s) as you bounce around some very lonesome scenery, lost in the cosmos. Feeling like less than a pinpoint can be liberating when you're hiding with the right person but can leave you a little hollow when you wish the phone would ring and there ain't no.

(Later.) Iceland redeemed itself today, and really had only our fatigue going against it if anything yesterday in any case. A guide-driver picked us up this morning in a Mercedes-Benz and took us out from the city to see the sights of "The Golden Circle," a day trip we could've done by bus but wanted to do at our own pace. Svenbirn (we called him "Swain") drove first east then north out of Reykjavik to Pingvellir, a spot important for two reasons. One, it was the site of the first Parliament of Iceland in 930 C.B. which became the world's oldest continually functioning parliament, and two, it is the geologic meeting place of the North American and Eurasian continents. There in front of our eyes was the rift between the plates, a rift that is widening about one-half inch a year. It is the only place one can see the rift on land.

We drove further east and further north through glorious landscape with vistas some 100 km. out, no wires, no advertisements and no other cars, to Gulfross, Golden Falls, 105' high and made of glacier melt water. Down the road from that we saw Geysir, a series of hot springs and mud pots that gave rise to our word "geyser".

Iceland is basically lava, in some places older and broken down into soil but in many places still young enough to be just rocks. We saw widely separated farm houses, hay baled for the winter, sheep, Icelandic ponies and a few cows. Otherwise the countryside with its mountains, lakes and pastures seemed uninhabited. There was a patchy grey sky with the sun coming down off in the distance in Jacob's ladders throwing color patterns on the rolling land.

We drove south toward the ocean, then turned right and drove west back toward Reykjavik. Before we got to the city we veered off southwest and went to the famous Blue Lagoon, a hot mineral water bathing place in the lava rocks. A geothermal plant let some overflow run into the lava assuming it would sink and filter back into the Earth, but the minerals closed up the lava holes and the lava held the water. After people started using it for a swimming hole the local governments built a facility around it and now it is one of the most popular places in the whole country. We ate a good late lunch there, then came back to the city. Swain showed us a few more city sights before dropping us off. We're going to bed early in order to get up at 3:00 tomorrow morning to start flying home.

Postscript. Iceland lost some of its charm at the airport at 6:00 a.m. There were no porters and no carts and several hundred too many people for the terminal. I put Mother in a line and began to ferry our six bags over, under and around the masses of people jammed in huge revolving doors and mobbed to get to airline counters. It was a stressful way to start a long day of travel already made irrational by our use of award tickets that required us to get back to London to use the return portion. There we missed our connection and spent three extra hours in Heathrow, so by the time we got back to Dulles, home to my apartment in Washington and into bed, it had been another 24-hour bed-to-bed day.

Our travel problems subsequently made my feelings about the trip rather ambivalent, a result of profound exhaustion. The ratio of travel problems to fascination in the trip itself was out of whack. If we had been more stimulated by the subject matter we could have been more gracious about the snafus. We suffered boredom, inactivity and discomfort but we also had a great time with new friends and were properly awed by the Arctic scenery we had gone to such lengths to see. I was sorry not to see more animals and compared the trip unfavorably to Antarctica, which was covered up with animals. Tundra was just not enough for me, without animals. The ice was gorgeous—in fact, there may be few things more beautiful than an iceberg. But the 410th one was not as fascinating as the first 409.

What I learned about myself on this trip is I'm more interested in the built environment. If I can't have animals, I want ruins. I'm glad I've seen Svalbard, the East coast of Greenland and Reykjavik but I can safely say I won't be driven to return, or to recommend the trip to anyone else without certain caveats. My memories of our experience are more positive than negative for all that and understandably so, because it would be out of character for me to be too fussy about an experience that enabled me to see another part of the world I crave. For that I'm grateful but for now, also, temporarily satisfied.

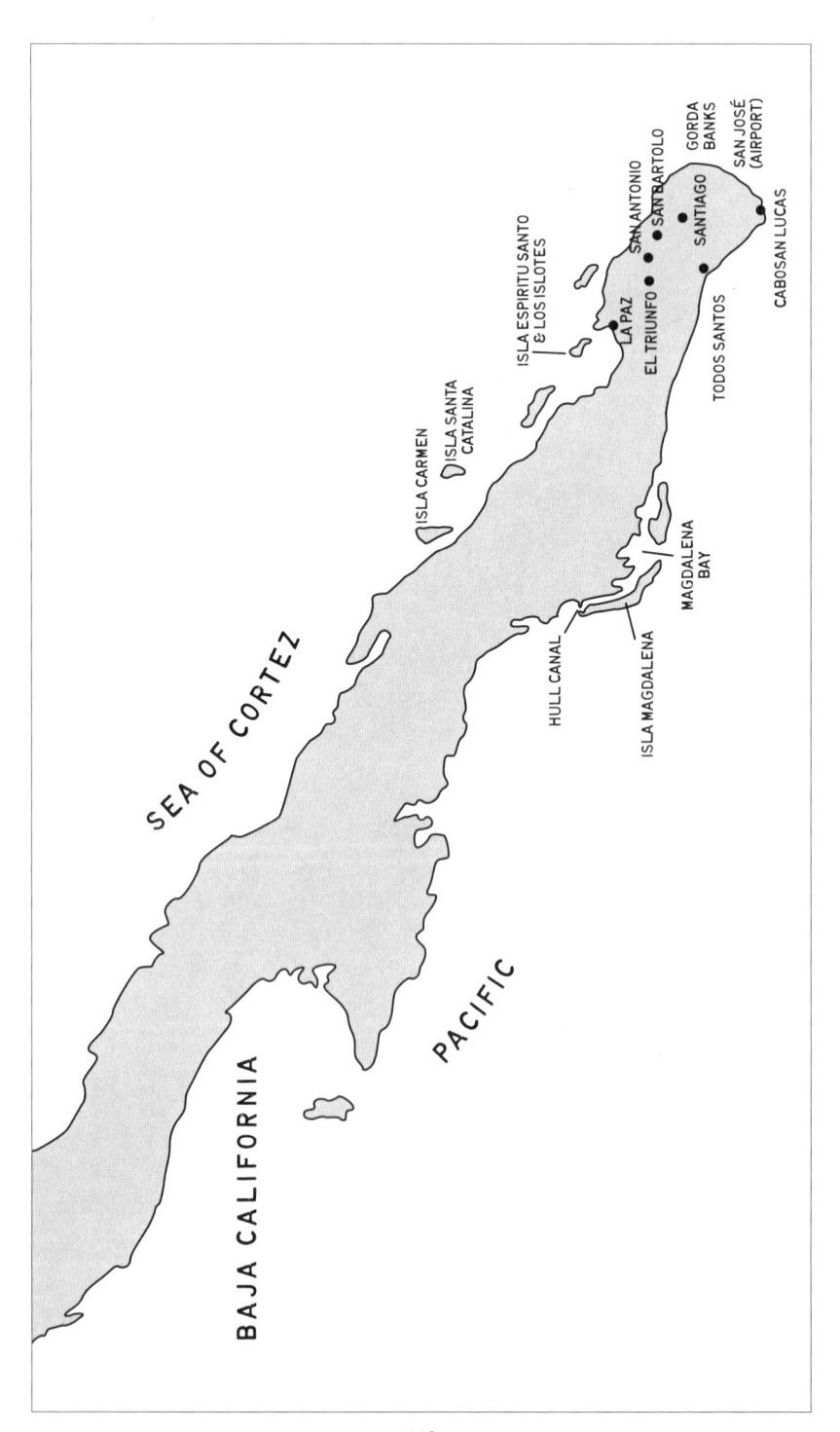

WHALE-WATCHING
A TRIP TO BAJA CALIFORNIA

Sunday morning 8 February 2004
In the Sea of Cortez

At 6:45 this morning on the port side of the ship there were a few sparkles left on the water from the full moon still hanging over the mountains. Just across the wake on the starboard side Regina Nature was preparing for her Morning Show by trying on every color in her wardrobe, choosing then discarding pinks, reds, oranges, greens and yellows before strutting her Sun out on stage. The water was calm and the soul began to go peaceful.

We are on the M.V. Sea Bird, a mate of the M.V. Sea Lion on which I traveled the Sea of Cortez with Elliott Jones ten years ago. On this trip my roommate is Mother. Fortuitously we have the same Smithsonian tour leader, Larry Hobbs, whose voice on the p.a. system has already described a pod of dolphins and four fin whales blowing off the bow.

We boarded the ship in La Paz last night, tired from a long day of travel from Los Angeles via Cabo San Lucas, thence a bus journey up the Pacific Coast to Todos Santos and across the Peninsula to La Paz. I suppose this was done to distract us while the ship was cleaned up and reprovisioned from the last group, but for us it was a roundabout bother.

We slept like the dead on our hard narrow bunks and redemption came even before breakfast. All morning the marine mammals in this rich soup of a gulf entertained us until we cranked up and started the run over to Isla Santa Catalina. We were about 100 miles north of La Paz, but with all the zig-zagging to watch fin whales, blue whales, bottlenosed and common dolphins, I wasn't sure where we were.

In the afternoon at Santa Catalina Island we had the first snorkel of the trip around some rocks. It was murky and the water was so cold I hyperventilated the first two or three minutes and thought I'd have a heart attack before I began to warm up. We didn't last long in the water.

[Our trip started on Thursday morning, February 5th when we flew from San Antonio to Los Angeles. Mother had received a big honor the night before and had had virtually no sleep. I had had fever and a sore throat and didn't feel too hot. Thus when we checked into our hotel at LAX mid-day Thursday, Mother hunkered down and didn't re-emerge until Friday noon. In an effort to stay awake myself, I went to the movies at a nearby mall ("The Last Samurai") before throwing in the towel and taking to my bed. Friday morning we were much improved.

We had lunch wtih my old sweetheart Peter Falk at some place in Beverly Hills called The Farm. Mother had never met Peter but she was charmed, as was he. In fact I was somewhat extraneous to the process as they laughed and talked and flirted on their side of the booth. This of course is the story of my life: I line 'em up and she picks 'em off.

After lunch our Port Aransas friends Lynn and Tony Amos's son Michael, his Israeli-born wife Tallia and their children picked us up and drove us downtown to see the new Disney Hall, a Frank Gehry concoction. We weren't allowed in the concert hall so we clambered instead around the outside of the building on the irregular and hidden staircases of the facade, marveling at the vertiginous walls and silky, slinky surfaces.

Late in the day Michael and Tallia left us across the street from The Ivy, where we were due for dinner. We were early so we went into the local shops and could have done some damage had I not quickly lost interest.

Dinner was with three old San Antonio friends who now live in L.A.: Joe Kaplan, in the architectural lighting business; Barbara King, now editor of the Home section of the L.A. Times; and Matthew Ferguson, youngest son of late friends Howard and Joanne, now in advertisement production. None of them had more than a passing idea of the others but they meshed serendipitously, charming each other and us, too. Joe took Mother and me back to our airport hotel afterward.

Saturday morning we were at the American terminal at 8:00 a.m. for a 10:00 a.m. flight that finally left at 11:00 a.m., getting into Los Cabos at 2:20 p.m. We lost an hour, as the Peninsula is on Mountain Time. It did put us one hour closer to Texas time which is of no use to us since we have no way to communicate with anyone in Texas. We are where we should be on vacation: in the "middle of nowhere".]

Monday 9 February 2004
The Sea of Cortez

We arrived at Los Islotes after running all night. Los Islotes are ocher-brown rock islands in a cluster, steep-walled and covered with guano. They were originally pyroclastic material that over tens of millions of years has been compressed, striated, pocked and taken over by the birds and sea lions. Within moments of closing the distance to them, we could hear the barking of the sea lions, or at least we who were awake and on deck being me on a stationary bike, Karen our neighbor who is going to veterinary school, and a couple of others. I had waked feeling lousy but sea lions can bring a smile to the saddest face. Mine wasn't sad; it just had a sore throat behind it.

As soon as breakast was over we piled into Zodiacs to putter over to the rocks and commune with the pinnipeds. The youngsters obliged us by swimming over to the Zodiac, flipping around and acting silly, and looking at us quizzically with their little doggie faces. As much as I hated to, I forwent snorkeling with the little darlings in an effort not to worsen my health. Mother suited up and buddied with Karen, and had some sea lion-encounter adventures including one large specimen who jumped over her and a little one who wiggled up between her and the Zodiac, bumping her arm and looking up at her from upside down. I was a jealous wreck on hearing these tales, but didn't miss going into the icy water.

Late morning we left Los Islotes and motored down to the southernmost point of Isla Espiritu Santo. The ship lay at anchor and the Zodiacs ferried people all afternoon over to the beach for kayaking and nature walks. I took the 4:00 p.m. botany walk for the hell of it and not out of consuming interest, and when that was over I beachcombed until a shore supper was announced. Mother, timing herself, arrived just in time to eat. Before an overcast and desultory sunset the view from the beach of distant islands and the mainland softened and took on that unfocused blue-grey of the end of the day when all the world becomes one color. Later there was a bonfire and s'mores, but for all the camaraderie we still took the first Zodiac back because we were cold.

Mother has just finished reading *Life of Pi* which I had been talking about for months and finally insisted she read. I watched her out of the corner of my eye to judge her reaction(s), then relaxed when she got so bound up in it she didn't want to do anything else. She finished it tonight. I'm two-thirds of the way through *Bone by Bone* by Peter Matthiessen.

Tuesday 10 February 2004
Coming around the southern tip of Baja California

Even Mother got up in the dark this morning so she wouldn't miss any humpback whales as we motored south toward the tip of Baja California and the end of the Gulf of California, the name the Mexicans prefer for p.c. reasons to the Sea of Cortez. We were heading for Gorda Banks, a place of upwelling and rich nutrients and therefore a place the humpbacks like. Sure enough they entertained us all morning, they and the Thornton's Devilfish, small manta rays that antically flipped and flew out of the water in one of those animal behaviours people speculate about but are in the end unexplainable. My theory is they do it because they can.

We fiddled around and floated in circles while sating ourselves on whale frolics. There were also dolphins, the aforementioned mantas and even off in the distance a sailfish who came out of the water in a flying arc. Finally we had to go in to lunch, served just as we came around the bottom of the Peninsula and steered into the harbor at Cabo San Lucas.

We settled at the end of a dock full of yachts, then were allowed to peel off and go snorkeling, bird watching or shopping. Mother and I went shopping. Cabo appeared to be one long beer and margarita event in a setting of T-shirts and silver jewelry. I'm beyond appreciating these things, although being from South Texas I certainly logged some lost time in Mexican honky-tonks in my youth.

One convenience store had the New York Times so I bought two days' worth back to the ship which made me very popular. I'm always torn on vacation between wanting to read the paper and not wanting to read it, but the paper usually wins.

We made an exquisite exit from the Cabo San Lucas harbor, lingering for some time in neutral at the beautiful upthrust rocks at land's end, admiring some 70 frigate birds soaring above or perched on the sheer cliff sides; also masses of cormorants, pelicans and a small group of sea lions. Margaritas were passed around on the bow and as the end of the day took on its wordless colorless mantle we celebrated vespers with obeisance to the elemental moment.

Wednesday 11 February 2004
Bahia de Magdalena, Pacific coast of Baja California

From 6:30 last night until 8:00 this morning the ship made its way up the Pacific coast of Baja against gentle winds, heading for Magdalena Bay where we would find the grey whales and their calves. At 8:00 a.m. we passed through La Entrada, the entrance to the Bay between two offshore islands, Isla Santa Margarita and Isla Magdalena. Once inside the Bay we hooked a left and anchored on the leeward side of Isla Magdalena. When the Zodiacs were ready we were ferried over to the beach and split into groups to walk across the sand dunes to the Pacfic beach side.

Mother and me, Isla Magdalena

Mother and I chose the birder group whose walk was projected to be the longest but easiest. With Brian the Bird Man as our leader we fiddled our way down the lee beach looking at every little thing. I walked a zigzag pattern from the water's edge to the dunes in order not to get too far ahead when everyone had to stop and oh and ah over a pen shell or a Willett for ten minutes. Finally Mother and I and another couple sheared off and started across the dunes to the Pacific side.

I had promised Mother that birding would not be a forced march as she is not crazy about walking (she'll dance ten miles). That turned out to be woefully unprophetic. As we slogged across the soft sand of the interior dunes, thinking that from the next rise surely we would see the Pacific, I had thoughts of *The Sheltering Sky*, of Balboa, the Trail of Tears, the Silk Road and all the barren places people have had to traverse to get where they were going. I was enjoying every step of the way but I had to think of Mother.

Finally we tumbled down the last dune wall and onto the beach, stunningly scattered with large sand dollars. We walked along the beach until we came to Larry's backpack (he was jogging). From that marker we re-entered the dunes and began the trek back across the island toward the Zodiacs and the ship beyond. Larry and his friend Taylor caught up with us and we laughed most of the way back.

Lunch was served and as soon as we were finished some of us hit our beds to rest from our hike. The ship with a pilot at the helm entered the Hull Canal, a beautiful narrow finger of channel off the north end of the Bay bound by mangroves with bare pink dunes behind them. We would live in this channel for the next two days because it was the most prolific for grey whales. The birding wasn't too shabby, either, with mangroves full of nesting cormorants, pelicans, great blue herons and gulls. We have these species at home so we didn't have to get all giddy over each bird. We already loved these birds.

Hull Canal was Whale Soup, as one lady on the bow exclaimed. Larry kept count and during the cocktail hour wrap-up announced that in the four hours we had threaded our way up the Hull Canal, we'd seen 49 cow-and-calf pairs and 18 individuals—116 whales, an altogether overwhelming and heartening statistic. Some lounged at the surface, a few breached and "spy-hopped", and as far as the eye could see the geysers of their breath broke the surface. One came out of the water so close to the ship that I screamed. I said afterward, I've always wondered what I'd do if I got close to a whale and now I know: I'll scream.

Years ago I read a quote by Ross Perot that said, great institutions are always on razor's edge of danger. When one thinks that the international fishery decimated the whales before substitutes for their oil were found, and how fragile in spite of being widespread the current good will toward whales now is, and when one thinks what it takes to grow a whale and keep it moving through a long life notwithstanding any external threat or lack thereof, it is obvious or should be that each and every one of these animals is a miracle.

There's something poignant about whales, too, having to do with their size. They seem so lonesome, their world so uncertain. I think of them with the same kind of empathy I feel toward refugees, internally displaced aboriginals, fish in fish bowls—all the creatures who have lost their worlds and are condemned to finish up somewhere else. Hell, for all I know I may be one of them, on the very edge of extinction myself. If so, I will have put one foot in front of the other until fate shows its hand, and may actually feel invulnerable until that moment. I hope the whales enjoy their present healthy numbers and the TLC of their millions of fans because it is hard to think it can last. All afternoon I kept thinking, I am so lucky to see these huge animals. Carpe diem, whales, and I shall do the same.

Thursday 12 February 2004
Hull Canal, Bahia de Magdalena

I got three inches from a whale this morning and only yelped when it exhaled. I did not scream.

The captain was in charge of our panga and the local guide, Modesto, was driving. The water was glassy, the sky clear, the sun sparkling, the air cool. Whales were all around in pairs of mother and baby. We idled over to one pair and stayed with them quite a while, the mother lying huge and casual while the baby rolled around, stuck his face out, wiggled his tail and generally acted cute. Other pairs were nearby; the other Zodiaks were scattered around. After half an hour or so the whales had rounded up all the Zodiacs and were all around us, blowing, rolling, fluking and flapping.

The captain and I were on our knees leaning over the side of the boat splashing water with our hands when a massive head as large as an automobile rose slowly out of the water right next to the Zodiac and let us touch it. My fingers missed it by three inches but the captain was able to pet it. Everyone was pretty overwhelmed, and people in the other boats took pictures of it.

Why would a wild animal let a human touch it? Maybe because we look so inconsequential. I think they were as curious about us as we about them, the difference being they could afford a little nobless oblige, having the upper hand and being superior to us. They were large and in their element; we were small and out of ours. Of course that's not the reason (!) but the reason is a mystery and so can be speculated upon.

Mystery aside, the gift, the life gift of being in this beautiful narrow channel surrounded by whales and their babies, the gift of being among the whales causes all other considerations to recede in consequence. Ones perspective clicks back into adjustment and the order of things is straightened out. Like many gifts these will be squandered but if memory serves, the essence will prevail.

At lunch Larry's friend Taylor said she thought animals went about their behaviors and we merely stumbled on them, that they were not directed. I think Larry, who has a spiritual nature, agreed more with me that something esoteric happened between us and "them". It is the kind of belief one could have without doing too much violence to scientific inquiry, and indeed could drive it to some extent.

We cruised again in Zodiacs after lunch with whales all around. The wind had picked up and there was a chop so the conditions were not ideal but we still managed to commune and even have one leviathan swim under our boat. The channel is only 30 feet deep and the whales are 40 feet long and 8 feet high so they are sailing their bulk through some pretty meagre water.

Mother declined to go over to the beach after the Zodiac cruise but I went with a small group and wound up walking alone with William, a funny, erudite, communicative naturalist on the staff, across the island (all this time we have been anchored in the lee of Isla Magdalena, at the northernmost end) to the Pacific side, around the point and back down the leeward beach. The dunes were gorgeous and the sensation of being surrounded by them, unable to see back to the horizon in any direction, made one understand the life perspective of a sand crab.

William talked and pointed things out (the angle of repose of sand dunes, Venus clams, coyote tracks, tiny sea urchins—polymath chatter, and excellent at that) until at the end of the day I thanked him and told him I loved to beachcomb and it had been especially nice to do it with a scholar. He said he had enjoyed it because it was nice to teach and have someone actually listen. It was cold and the sun had started down when the pangas came to pick up the beach people.

Friday 13 February 2004

In that quiet period between first light and dawn as I sat on the exercise bicycle on the top deck, the whales entertained me by rising and falling. I imagined that if I were a World War II submarine spotter I would be running around like a chicken with its head cut off, shouting and pointing. Instead I was in a state of peaceful co-existence with my submarines.

Henry Hudson wrote that when he sailed into what is now New York Harbor, the fish were so thick he could have walked on them to land. I pictured myself using my whales as stepping stones to land, there were so many of them. If one could shovel sights into ones eyes the way we have shoveled food into our mouths on this trip, I was shoveling in the dawn of whales.

We were in the second wave to go out in the Zodiacs. The first wave came back energized from having seen sexual behavior, and sure enough we were also treated to some frisky "finorkytoodling" (Larry's made-up word for whale sex), and even got to see "Pink Floyd", the gargantuan male member. They have sex orgy-style, more than two at a time, and flukes and fins were all over the place, roiling up the water and titillating the tourists. It was great fun.

We were also surrounded by mothers and babies, the great long backs and blows mimicked by the little backs and blows next to them, with sometimes little faces out of the water and one resting its head on mama's back. I think it is the baby animals that really get our anthropomorphic juices flowing.

We left our idyllic anchorage at 10:30 a.m. and said goodbye to a day and a half in what must surely have been one of the most peaceful places on the planet.

Lunch was on the deck, a treat allowed by the windless sunny day and mirrorlike water. The afternoon activity, which took place in defiance of Morpheus, was a lovely Zodiac ride into the trackless mangroves of our same Isla Magdalena, this time back near the south end that we had reached by backtracking down the Hull Canal. For an obscure waterway that most people in their right minds would never have heard of, this was an enchanting channel that at times today made me feel like we were on the African Queen, or traveling the Mekong River.

The mangrove trip was fun, with William the naturalist talking about how mangroves defy the rule that salt kills living things, and a couple of showy bird happenings—one a flock of 23 white ibis scared up from a sand spit, and another an osprey that flew with us a way, following our same channel. Mother helped William identify the various other birds we saw.

We had a sad job to do back onboard: pack. The 62 passengers, the naturalists and the crew had had some memorable shared experiences and I would guess the passengers if not the others were loathe to go back to the civilized world, whatever that is.

Saturday 14 February 2004
La Paz

We had anchored offshore from San Carlos, a little port in Magdalena Bay, all night and this morning we motored over to its dock, parked and disembarked with fond farewells and thanks to the good people who had cared for us. Larry and Taylor came with us so we had them for another day. We boarded buses and were driven east across the Peninsula to La Paz. There at noon we checked into the Hotel Los Arcos, where our rooms were so commodious the bathrooms alone were bigger than our cabins on the ship.

Our cabins were so small two people couldn't move around in them at the same time. If one wanted to move the other had to get in the bathroom, get on the bed or leave.

At Los Arcos we had a huge buffet lunch in the fresh air of the arcaded patio. In the afternoon I left Mother to her devices and went with a group to the Serpentarium, a nonprofit attempt to educate the Mexicans to the benefits of snakes, lizards, tortoises, turtles and related monsters. Being a lizard lover, I was enthralled, but it was a sad place in the end because so many of these fascinating creatures are threatened with extinction by us stupid humans in our hellbent determination to own the earth, even if it's dead.

We had a farewell dinner in the hotel and scored Bruce and Mara Mayor—Mara is the director of the Smithsonian Associates and Bruce and I had deep conversations over breakfast every morning—and Larry and Taylor for our table companions. They were four special friends among the many people we enjoyed dining with and talking to in our eight days together.

Sunday 15 February 2004
In the air

We left La Paz and drove south on an old scenic road to the Los Cabos airport where we suddenly had to say goodbye to Larry and Taylor. Most of the rest of us got on the same flight back to LAX and there we finished melting away to our individual destinations.

Mother's and mine was Beverly Hills, to Mary Davis's house where we spent the night. We were such good houseguests we only stayed 16 hours but we managed to have a good visit with this old friend and widow of our late beloved Stuart Davis. She had friends in for dinner, cooked and served by her Chinese houseman Jack (a treasure I'm sure people have tried to steal from her), and Mother and I each had our own huge luxurious guest room. At 8:30 this morning a car service took us back to LAX. With any luck we'll land safely in San Antonio in an hour or so.

EPILOGUE

Captain Kalbach of the M.V. Sea Bird was a hands-on captain who sometimes helped us in and out of the Zodiacs, let us poke around the bridge and stopped the boat to whale-watch however long we wanted him to. The couple of times he spoke to us as a group one knew we had a New Age old hippie for a captain, one who spoke in spiritual terms about the trip, the sea and the animals.

On our last night aboard he reminded us to take some of the peace and communion we'd enjoyed back with us to our busy lives, to stop every once in a while and think about the whales. He didn't realize how important his words were to some of us, and how intensely remembered they will be. Fair winds Captain Kalbach. Fair winds all of us.

THE WOLVES AND WILDLIFE OF YELLOWSTONE
JANUARY – FEBRUARY 2005
INTRODUCTION

Mother and I, both hot house flowers in spite of the lady-like athletics to which we're addicted, responded to a brochure from Natural Habitat Adventures to see the wolves of Yellowstone. It appealed to the terrible tenderness we feel for animals. It did not occur to Mother, anyway, that there might be any discomforts associated with such a journey and indeed it turned out to be a lovely luxurious trip within the confines of our chosen locale. But the altitude, the ice and snow and the cold took some adjustment. Mother, being one to look helplessly around with a beautiful smile on her face when she needs assistance, thrived in spite of a lack of regard for altitude, ice, snow and cold. At 86 she deserves someone at her elbow, and she got it. We had a wonderful time in the spectacular scenery seeing the animals, cocooning with our van mates and listening raptly to our guide. It was an unusually beautiful trip.

"If all the beasts were gone, men would die from a great loneliness of spirit, for whatever happens to the beasts also happens to the men. All things are connected. Whatever befalls the Earth befalls the sons of the Earth."—Chief Seattle

THE JOURNAL
Early morning
Monday 31 January 2005
Alpine Motel, Cooke City, Montana

Our Yellowstone adventure started inauspiciously on Saturday with flight delays and lost luggage, but we bore up through the preliminaries of finally arriving in Bozeman, Montana, having dinner with our guides and another late-arriving couple and being fitted for boots and parkas that we would wear until our bags appeared. A short fitful night was followed by a brighter morning.

Our guides were Scott and Jared, both wildlife biologists, and they were backed up by Nick who did arriving passengers and luggage. It was Nick who waited the next day (yesterday) for our bags to weave their way to Bozeman. When he caught up with us after lunch in the Park we were awfully glad to see those duffles. In the meantime Scott had taken me to Wal-Mart after breakfast to buy some essentials in the event the bags waited another day to manifest.

We are thirteen guests. Six of us got in our van with Scott, and seven in the other, and we began to drive south toward Yellowstone National Park. We drove down Paradise Valley, past Livingston to Gardiner, the little town at the north entrance to the park. It was at Gardiner that, for the reintroduction of the wolves into Yellowstone in 1995, they emptied the schools so the children could line the road to welcome the wolves as they went by on their way into the Park.

We were watching for pronghorn deer, mule deer and anything else that moved as we slowly descended Paradise Valley. Eagles were first, bald eagles in trees and aloft, our national symbol, magnificent rapacious scavengers and fishermen. Also ravens and magpies and ducks (mallards, common mergansers, Barrow's goldeneyes and common goldeneyes) in the streams. Just outside of Gardiner we came on pronghorns, then mule deer and bison, all grazing by the road as peacefully as cows. We were on a gravel road parallel to the highway, and the bison walked right by our stopped vehicle looking huge and primitive, glancing up at us with their whale-like one-eye-on-each-side-of-the-head eye. Bison have an elemental historic profile that has "America" written all over it; they are apparently crabby and not to be messed with.

We drove through the [Teddy] Roosevelt Arch and into the hallowed precincts of our first national park, Yellowstone, founded in 1872 and thought to be the first national park on Earth. It was cold and there was snow on the ground but it was patchy because there had uncharacteristically not been any snowfall for two weeks. The weather was milder than average, above freezing.

We were continually on the lookout for animals but mainly we were heading for lunch at Mammoth Hot Springs, the first major installation south of the north entrance. We had lunch in the dining room of the hotel complex there and with the exception of one other table had the hall to ourselves. It was great to be in such a popular place when no one else was around, and that held for the entire day of quiet, uninterrupted game viewing in scenery unmarred by other tourists.

We turned east to run parallel to the north boundary of the Park, heading to the Lamar Valley but going slowly and savouring the magnificent elk and herds of bison, always on the lookout for wolves. At a crowded parking area covered with snow and the SUV's of other wolf watchers (not tourists like us, more the local cognoscenti) we stood for a long time watching through our telescopes a family of wolves from the Slough Creek pack under a tree at least a half mile up a mountain. It was fun to watch them lie down, get up, jump on each other, walk off and come back as aimlessly as dogs, or humans for that matter. Some were black and some were grey. They live in multi-generational packs run by an alpha male and an alpha female. The naturalists all know these wolves and call them by their individual names or numbers and by their pack names. Many of the wolves are collared. Some 25 packs have grown from the handful of Canadian wolves first released ten years ago.

When it began to get dark we started on into Cooke City, Montana, just a few miles east of the northeast Park boundary, and came on a moose just off the road picking her way moose-style, one foot at a time off the ground, through the snow. They are lone animals and so have to walk carefully because no one makes a trail for them.

Cooke City was a snowbound Old West town with little stirring on the main street. We checked into the Alpine Motel and Mother and I, suddenly very tired, opted out of dinner. We were both asleep at 8:00 p.m.

Monday night 31 January 2005
Alpine Motel, Cooke City, Montana

We were supposed to be up, dressed, fed and in the vans by 6:45 this morning in order to see the animals stirring at the start of the day or coming in from their night of hunting. The other van got off on the money but our van, thanks to a certain octagenarian, ran five minutes late. As a result we were the only van to spot and watch a mountain fox (cousin to the red fox) mousing across a snowy meadow for several minutes, and after a few more bends in the road a wolf, right by the road. We stopped and got out the telescopes and had him to ourselves for a good long while as we followed his peregrinations. Scott was beside himself that we'd seen one so close, since usually you can barely tell them from rocks in a high powered telescope. Scott said this one was probably a disbursing loner from the Agate or Slough Creek pack.

After our wolf disappeared we drove on to a large congeries of vehicles and telescopes that were all focused on an elk carcass being finished off by the alpha male and female of the Agate pack as the ravens flapped around waiting their turn. Ravens are the vultures here. We spent an hour there standing in the cold and getting in and out of the van to warm up. The day started out around seven degrees but it warmed up into the 30's during the day.

We began slowly to make our way back to Cooke City, stopping at turnouts for Scott to scan the hillsides with his practiced eye, and right away he spotted bighorn sheep on a ridge at the very crest of the mountain of the moment. We piled out to watch the sheep through the telescopes when who should appear but a black wolf pup near the same spot as our wolf of this morning. We visually followed him for awhile, being serenaded intermittently by howling.

Howling is so interesting. Apparently wolves howl to find each other or to warn others off, among other things. Each howl has its own distinctive timbre and sonority. This wolf stopped, threw his head back and howled. That was followed by howling from behind the mountain. It has a lost tone, howling, and is evocative and poignant. To us. To them it's probably just their internet, not to be anthropomorphized into anything poetic. Still it's not every animal whose method of communication takes the listener atavistically on a stirring mental journey into childhood fears.

Lunch in Cooke City was at a deli with good soups and sandwiches. We had time to walk back to our motel and brush our teeth before going three miles down the road to the home of Dan and Cindy Hartman, wildlife photographers. Dan gave us a delightful slide show of his pictures, adding by his commentary to the fun of seeing the animals in his photographs. He was one of those outdoorsmen, like our Scott, who lives to be outside in nature every day and so winds up seeing phenomena the casual observer would miss, and developing a wisdom about animals that blurs the line between his species and theirs. They are remarkable people, naturalists, and it's marvelous to be around them and soak up their knowledge before going back to city life and ones own far less noble mores.

We headed back toward the Park for a late afternoon foray and didn't get four houses down the road before stopping to watch two wolves of the Druid Peak pack who had initially chased an elk up the mountainside above the town. Soon the usual cars stopped and telescopes appeared. We decided if someone stopped his car on the side of the road and set up a telescope peering at absolutely nothing, others would soon stop and join him. Fortunately the traffic consists of about one vehicle every half hour, so it never gets out of hand.

We stood and peered until the two wolves bedded down. Then rather than stand any longer in the cold watching them lying there, we got Scott to drive us the three miles back to our motel where we are in for the night. We'll picnic on fruit, cheese and crackers and go to bed early to meet the relentless pre-dawn departure schedule.

5:30 a.m.
Tuesday 1 February 2005
Cooke City

It is clear the joint would have started jumping when the apes rose onto their hind legs and began to use their front paws as hands. They were uniquely configured to do so; it wasn't going to be an ungulate, a fish or a bird. In addition the ape cranium lent itself to a growing brain to go with its hands (whereas that famous ungulate, the horse, still has a brain the size of a fist). Part of my profound sympathy for animals has to do with their drawbacks compared to the smarts and agility of homo sapiens. No matter how wonderfully adapted they are to their environments, animals still cannot thumb through a book or put a man on the moon. They still sleep all night in the snow instead of on a Serta Perfect Sleeper. They're still helplessly in their spot on the food chain. As one who loves animals with a passion that in degree may exceed my pinko love of all mankind, I could weep for a century over their travails at the hand of Man. Their travails at the hand of Nature go without saying.

End of the day
Tuesday 1 February 2005
Old Faithful Snow Lodge

Gorgeous is the best way to describe this day. Deeply cold in the morning, 35 degrees by the end of the day, bright windless sunny blue skies and the Earth sparkling in the snow. We started before first light, saying goodbye to Cooke City, Montana and our Alpine Motel, all of which we had loved. We entered the Park once more through the now-familiar Northeast entrance and backtracked along the Lamar Valley looking for animals.

It turned out to be our only morning without wolves but we were on a bit of a schedule and before when we spotted a wolf it became something of a production, so it was just as well. Instead we stopped at several turnouts and viewed bighorn sheep on their mountain peak, coyotes piddling along a ridge just off the road, and elk and bison galore. They call it "the little Serengeti" and it is. Everywhere the crisp white snow was crisscrossed with animal tracks; one frozen river bottom looked so churned up with hoofprints it must have been an elk freeway.

Mother and me

At the end of the morning we were back at Mammoth Hot Springs to have lunch in the deserted dining hall (this time there were three other tables of tourists besides ours). We sat with some people from the other van—we are so bonded with our own van mates that we wind up eating together, too—and had an interesting conversation about history and related subjects.

Mother and I wandered over to the museum run by the Park Service and enjoyed a cursory look-see at the ethnographic displays and especially the Thomas Moran sketches and watercolors and W. H. Parker photographs done by these artists who accompanied the early expeditions that doped out Yellowstone.

We reported back to the hotel to our new conveyances, two snow coaches. They looked like our vans only with tracks for tires. We even got to keep our van mates and Scott and our exact same seats. What creatures of habit we are. These amazing muscular trucks proceeded to take us south to Old Faithful, 51 miles over snow roads that are closed to regular automobile traffic. Fifty-one miles took us over four hours because we stopped to see things.

The drive was outstanding through snow fields undisturbed by animal tracks, making them look particularly bright and crispy in the afternoon light. After snow fields came mountains, gorges, rushing rivers, a couple of waterfalls and, dotting the landscape, steam columns from the hot springs, fumaroles, geysers and mud holes that make Yellowstone unique. We spotted bald eagles and a golden eagle, trumpeter swans and more ducks, bison and elk.

We walked around Upper Geyser Basin and marveled at the ways our Earth shows us what's inside it. Like seeing ones own guts, it was not pretty. At 6:00 we pulled into the Old Faithful Snow Lodge, a welcome sight after a fairly rough ride in the snow coaches.

The Old Faithful Snow Lodge is new and good looking. It is reachable this time of year only by snow vehicles and so is somewhat secluded. It is in the same compound with the Old Faithful Inn which is closed in the winter because snow gets in the rooms (!). We were glad to be in a fancy hotel with telephones in the rooms after two nights in Cooke City in a motel where one had to stand out in a snowbank to call out on a pay phone.

Mother and I went to dinner for once and it was a mistake because we were so tired by the time the food finally came we couldn't eat. I took three bites and slipped away to prepare for and then fall into bed.

Wednesday 2 February 2005
Hatchet Motel, Moran, Wyoming

What looked like fog out the dining room windows at breakfast this morning turned out to be moisture hanging in the air from Old Faithful and the surrounding geysers. It was so cold when we all walked out to see Old Faithful erupt that when we talked, our breath caused frost to form on our hair and collars. Some of the group hiked around the far side of the big geyser to see the other neighborhood geysers; Mother, Scott and I walked about half way around, then returned to sit on icy benches to await the eruption scheduled for 8:53. Scott has been so sweet to Mother, who walks on the snow and ice like a geisha, always hanging onto someone; he takes care of her like a precious grandson.

Old Faithful blew but it was hard to see the water because of the steam that billowed out of the hole and formed as the hot water hit the cold air. Still, we had seen it, so we hobbled back to the hotel to thaw out. The weather has been so beautiful one can deceptively step out in only a sweater until the authority of the low temperatures quickly asserts itself and drives you back into your fur coat or parka.

Back in the snow coaches we made our way south on rough washboard roads, stopping at three calendar-perfect waterfalls and a couple of other vistas to stretch and take pictures. Around noon we passed through the South entrance of the Park and said goodbye to Yellowstone, burned now in memory and added to the list of beloved places to worry about.

Yellowstone and Grand Teton National Park are joined by a narrow waist of land called the John D. Rockefeller, Jr. Memorial Parkway. He bought up a lot of the land that created Grand Teton National Park and donated it to the feds to found the park (the mountains section in 1929, the rest in the early 1950's), so they named the federal land between the parks after him. There is a big tourist facility in this buffer zone called Flagg Ranch. It was closed for the winter but they had opened a room for us to use for a brown bag lunch.

There we also said goodbye to the snow coaches and our cute drivers and got blissfully back in vans, now that we had returned to the land of pavement. The snow coaches were rough and we weren't sad to get out of them. Naturally we all transferred to our exact same spots we'd been in all week, made our nests with satisfaction and set out to enter Grand Teton.

The Tetons send everyone into a swoon because they rise sharply with no foothills, making them pointy and dramatic. They really are pretty, especially framing Jackson Lake. We made one lake stop, two moose stops and a bison carcass stop with coyote and golden eagle as we turned east into Buffalo Valley. We drove out of the Park proper and landed a short distance away at the Hatchet Motel, a rustic log "resort" where we are lodged in a row of pine-panelled rooms with lodge pole pine beams.

I started out to go snow shoeing with some of the group but found it uncomfortable and cold and turned around and came back. At least I now know what snow shoes feel like. Mother and I are in for the night with our usual picnic and reading materials.

"Leaving Cheyenne"
Friday 4 February 2005
Wyoming Inn, Jackson, Wyoming

Yesterday, our last day of the trip, started out below zero in brilliant dry clear air. We left our funky Hatchet Motel (pine log rooms with marble bathrooms) before breakfast to watch sunrise on the Tetons. It was worth getting up to see the great white mountains wreathed in pink with aspens glowing in the valleys. We were energized, and understood further the plethora of art based on this part of our country.

Back at the Hatchet Motel we had an excellent breakfast served in their conference center-style dining building which was so handsome we had to walk around remarking on each design aspect as we waited to be served. Then it was on the road again, looking for moose as we made our way south through the Park toward Jackson.

Close to noon, with Jackson in view up ahead, we stopped at the National Museum of Wildlife Art, an organic architectural gem looking more like a rock formation than an institution built into the side of a mountain looking out over one of the immense valleys of the National Elk Refuge. This would be our base for a few hours. Upon entering the museum we watched a slide show about the Elk Refuge, then went right away down the hill in a specially designated bus, crossed the highway and were debouched to board a large horse-drawn sleigh to go out and look at the elk up close.

The horse-drawn sleigh was not as romantic as it sounded. It was a long red wooden wagon with benches along the side so you had to turn in your seat to look forward or outward no matter what direction it was going. It was pulled by two Belgians; the teamster was a young woman. We stopped first under a bare-branched tree and looked up at two bald eagles casually and fearlessly peering down at us. Then we sleighed over to be close to groups of bucks, most lying down chewing their cud, their staggering antlers testimony to their good health.

The Elk Refuge was founded in 1912 to ensure there would be a safe terminus when the elk migration from higher elevations arrived. It covers 25,000 acres with some 5000 elk on it at present. It is managed by U. S. Fish and Wildlife which husbands the land and the creatures, feeding them if the snow gets too deep and improving the grasses during the summer months. It was a unique sight for us flatlanders to look down the endless broad valley with the Tetons towering over it and see the thousands of elk.

We had lunch back in the cafe of the museum, then toured the galleries. We were impressed by the exhibits and collections, and were delighted to learn that the next day a retrospective of our friend Kent Ullberg's sculpture would open.

Scott took us into Jackson to our hotel, the Wyoming Inn, which was quite a bit fancier than we'd been used to. Released, we fell on the bed and slept until we had to dress and go to the farewell dinner.

In a restaurant called the Off-Broadway Grill we gathered in a (fortunately) private room and proceeded to have a good dinner with much hilarity as well as serious talk about what we'd seen and how our guides' lives worked. In our van we'd had such a special experience with our Scott, who added a spiritual dimension to his solid science and swept us along in his enthusiasm. I think Mother wanted to put him in her pocket and take him home, but he belongs out in the hugeness of nature, which he embraces like a lover and then gives back to his students with his beautiful careful descriptions. Our van mates were all widely traveled but agreed he was one of the best guides if not the best any of us had ever had.

Back at the hotel in the lobby there were hugs all around and promises to write. We had a short night, a cold morning start, a de-iced prop plane ride to Denver, a Wolfgang Puck lunch in the Denver airport, then a bumpy ride home to San Antonio, both of us subdued after our week in the wilderness. "Fate ordains that dearest friends must part", and so we left our Scott and our new van mate friends and the spectacular scenery and the precious animals, the animals who had the world to themselves for so long and now exist at the mercy of our legal constructs, and turned our backs but not our hearts to return pensively to our lower horizons. It was a beautiful, beautiful trip in every way and made us think with love, as these things do, of our precious endangered country, so strong, so tattered.

"TO THE SHORES OF TRIPOLI"
LIBYA
MARCH 2005

INTRODUCTION

In the fall of 2004 my dear friend Elliott Jones and I were kicking around ideas of where to take a trip together in the spring of 2005. She mentioned her friend and neighbor Dugan Romano was signed up for a trip to Libya. "Let's go there!" I enthused. Libya had only been open to Americans since the lifting of the embargo in February 2004.

Dugan was traveling with a company called Distant Horizons with whom she had had a successful trip before. Elliott and I enrolled in her same group, leaving the United States on March 3rd, 2005. We would travel to Tripoli via two days in London. We started our reading.

In retrospect I think how innocent we were as we prepared for this new land. We were not concerned about going to a terrorist dictatorship; rather we were more concerned that we wouldn't be grounded enough in the classic period we were going to study. As it turned out, it was our own group of 24 people—too many in any justification—that caused us the most problems. Several of our group were too decrepit to be on the trip, and this made for even longer days as we waited for everyone to muster, gather, catch up and complain. Those of us still ambulatory were mystified why someone infirm would want to take such a hard trip, and why the travel company would allow it. I'm sure the mystery will be solved in about 20 years when I, too, bored and infirm, inflict myself on some hapless group of travelers going to the latest new country.

We saw Libya with very little competition for the sites. Libya has 1200 miles of Mediterranean coastline with virtually nothing on it but the most extensive Greek and Roman ruins outside of Greece and Rome. Twenty years from now it, too, will have changed, and as I gasp for air and lean on my cane I can regale the young with whom I'm traveling about how crude it was back in "ought-five".

The story of our trip, which started in London and proceeded on to Tripoli, follows.

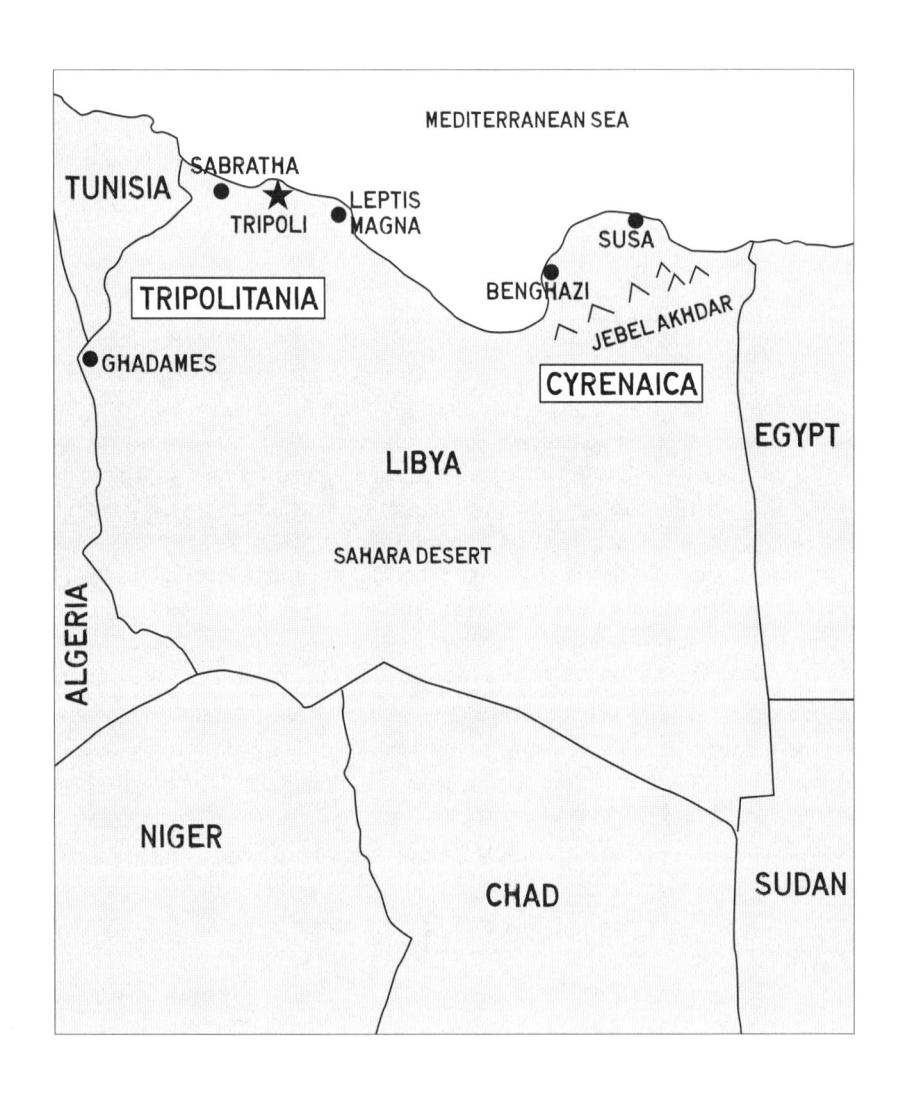

THE JOURNAL

Sunday night 6 March 2005
Corinthia Bab Africa Hotel, Tripoli

The day started on an ambivalent note, and also started early. We left our London hotel, where we had been decompressing for two nights and a day, at 6:30 a.m. to go to Heathrow for a 9:20 flight to Tripoli. Susan Pollack, our group leader, announced calmly that there might be a problem with our visas in Tripoli. She would confer with British Air and talk to Tripoli before we would check in. This put us all in a pensive mood.

We hung together in clusters across from the British Air counter. Susan came back from the phones to say it was probably going to be all right. We checked in. Thus we flew the three hours to Tripoli still not knowing if Immigration would let us into the country upon our arrival.

They did. There was more clustering and more waiting and then they processed us as cheerfully as you please. We blew out to the bus with Bashir, our national guide, in the lead, most of us hoping we would now fade into the Libyan woodwork.

Bashir was a tall, thin, elegant older man who exuded good nature and reassurance. None of us had been really nervous; we just didn't want the hassle of a travel foul-up. Once under way we promptly put the day behind us and began to concentrate. It was two hours later than London time; all of Libya, like all of China, was on the same time zone.

Before going to the hotel we took the ring road from the south side of Tripoli, where the airport was, to the west side of the city to see some tombs at Janzur that had been excavated in a neighborhood of houses. There was a tiny, dusty museum of artifacts, and one could go down some stairs and look in a lovely preserved tomb with frescoes. The disrepair and apparent lack of attention to this place were disturbing, but we did our best to give it its due in the five minutes it took to see it.

We drove another twenty minutes or so through the central city to our hotel. Elliott and I agreed that Tripoli was a sorry looking place. There is no height to it; everything is one, two or three stories tall. It is shabby, and it is built on sand. It looks down-and-out, which is pretty indefensible considering the obscene amounts of oil money this country of (now) 5.5 million people has reaped since 1959, the year their oil was found.

The city sits right on the Mediterranean, which adds a dash of glamour. Our hotel, tall and hysterically fancy compared to everything else except a half dozen office buildings around its skirts, was a welcome sight notwithstanding the jarring juxtaposition. We're in a huge smashing room with marble floors, a living area and a bathroom as large as our hotel room in London. It is overdone in the Arab way, but not too garish. Out our window on the 8th floor we can see the sea, and a tantalizing slice of the old walled medina part of the city.

Backtracking: There are 24 of us guests in the group plus Susan and Ken Perkins, our scholar, so we are a big group. Half of us flew from Washington overnight on Thursday the 3rd, and everyone arrived at London Heathrow the morning of Friday the 4th. I didn't feel too bad, considering the position in which I had "slept" all night on the plane. Then again I didn't feel too perky, either. As soon as we got settled in our hotel Elliott and I went around the corner to a chain restaurant with a frankly American menu and stilled our famished stomachs. We walked around trying to move our limbs and stay awake until it got late enough to give up and go home to our beds—Elliott for a nap as she had plans with an old English beau that night.

Saturday morning we attended a lecture and slide show about Libya given in a conference room of the hotel by a retired curator. Our appetite whetted for the treasures to come, we then walked a block down the street to the British Museum to see their Libya-related antiquities.

The British Museum has a new atrium entrance that is a real knockout. It was full of a colorful, multinational crowd. We spent the morning admiring all the purloined Libyan sculpture, and had a little discussion at one point about the efficacy of Western museums' keeping these unique objects. Our guide said the abiding rationale was, they were safe and available to the world in the museum, which you could not say about them if they were still on sites in Libya. She also addressed a nagging question about Greek statues, to wit why do the men have juvenile genitalia? She said, "We've all been baptised and had our inoculations so let's just talk about GENITALIA." Then she told us that some Lord Somebody had tired of skirting the issue and taken to referring to them as "dainty dicks." That brought the house down.

She was thorough and veddy British, our guide, and spent a long time on each object while I tried to find ways to stay comfortable standing on the stone floors. She pronounced things so perfectly that sometimes we would crack up at the back of the crowd: "We'll meet at two empty PLINTHS (spit flying)", or: "In this bas-relief you have the LUPINE figure in the center, in other words the she-wolf who suckled Romulus and Remus..." (saliva sucking), or: "The statue of Apollo, being AURAROELEPHANTINE, in other words made of gold and ivory..." Maybe it's not funny in the telling but we were tickled at the time. Elliott adored her and wished she were going to be our guide in Libya. I said if she were I'd blow my brains out.

We did adore the Museum, simply a treasure beyond measure, and wished we could have pored over it for days. We had a good lunch on the top floor in the chic Court Cafe and, since that was the first meal at which we had all gathered, began to focus on each other and start to make friends. After lunch we poked around in the shops, but the dollar is so weak (I got 45 pounds for 100 dollars) it's like a blow to the solar plexus every time you calculate the price of the simplest object. It kept us on the straight and narrow.

It had gotten late in the afternoon so I went home, tended to some domestic chores and had another early night in order to get up at 4:30 this morning to start the main event, getting to and journeying in Libya.

Monday 7 March 2005
Tripoli

As I sag onto the couch to resume this narrative I realize how tired my body is from our day in Tripoli. Everything hurts, and sadly not from exercise. We followed the Director of the Jamahiriya or National Museum around for three hours on stone floors this morning, listening to him walk us through Libya from prehistory (99% of human life on Earth, as he pointed out at length because he was a Neolithic scholar not a classical one) through the Garamantes (early desert people), the Phoenicians, the Greeks, the Romans, the Vandals and the Arabs. The museum was full of treasures, particularly Greek and Roman since culture flowered most effusively under them—everywhere. Many of the artifacts and statuary we saw came from the great ruined cities we will see in the next ten days, removed to the museum for safekeeping.

It was fascinating but by the time it was over we were perching or leaning on everything from curbs to columns to PLINTHS to keep ourselves erect.

Lunch was at the Al Mahary Hotel, also considered fancy but not as fancy as ours. There was a huge buffet and a view of the waterfront; we rested, ate and enjoyed ourselves. Bashir showed me his driver's license: he's 51! He looks 75.

Tripoli looked a little better today, a little more attractive and not so shabby. Libya is shaking off a long bad dream as it rejoins the world community. The museum director referred to "our previous isolation", and our national guide, Bashir, has made references such as "now that our Lockerbie period is over". They are good men and proud of the long history of their country but, like many of us, are better than their government.

We spent two more hours on foot, first at the Marcus Aurelius Arch, the only Roman thing left in Tripoli. Around 1 C.E. Tripoli was known as Oea and was part of Tripolis, Three Cities, being Oea, Sabratha and Leptis Magna; their area was Tripolitania. Tripoli is now a modern city and the others are ruins.

From the Arch we walked into the medina. We went into a mosque, where I began to get restless. We had a pretty young woman guide with us but no one could understand her. Finally we moseyed into the souk, the market, and walked around looking in the stalls. Of all the souks I've been in, this was the quietest and least lively. None of us was brokenhearted to head for the street and the bus.

George Bush beats the drum for "freedom" and although he is a pathological liar with a terminal case of bullshit, he's right about freedom. Living free, free from fear and free to do what you want, is the best way to germinate creativity, resourcefulness and innovation. Living in a distributive state like Libya under a dictator like Gaddafi could really suck the life out of you.

Tuesday 8 March 2005
Tripoli

In an effort to keep us occupied until we headed west of the city to see Sabratha, we were taken to a School of Arts and Crafts. My antennae should have warned me away but did not. In a good looking quadrangular building we went from area to area looking at leather goods, furniture and furnishings—student art that was pretty horrible. Also, it was very cold. Then we sat down in a classroom and had a lecture on Islam by our scholar, Ken, who is a professor of modern Middle Eastern history. I got bored because I already knew everything he was telling us, so I went down the street to buy some postcards. It was fun to be out on the sidewalk by myself.

We got sprung from the marking-time activity and headed to Sabratha, 80 km. west of Tripoli. There is so much sprawl the traveler can't tell where Tripoli leaves off and the next small town begins. There was some agriculture but mostly it was little machine shops, tire stores and household goods kiosks. We stopped for lunch in the modern town of Sabratha and had a nice lunch in a place also serving another busload of tourists. I thought, here we sit cheerily tucking into lunch in a restaurant on the side of the road in a terrorist nation, and don't even have the sense god gave a snail to be worried.

It was bright but cold and windy when we left the bus in the car park and entered the ancient city of Sabratha. The first impression was the marvelous sensation of seeing these ruins with the Mediterranean, covered with whitecaps but turquoise and clear, crashing at their feet. Every vista, every perspective was photogenically enhanced by the blue water beyond.

The ruins were extensive; we walked around them almost four hours, freezing the entire time. Our guide was garrulous but his English was hard to understand and he had a bit of the showman to him which made him seem as much a carny barker as an expert on antiquities. He was full of silly stories that he broadcast as true. I caught only a fraction of what he said.

Sabratha started out as a Phoenician outpost around 700 B.C.E., then the Greeks had some influence but the Romans really took the place in hand and made something grand of it until an earthquake destroyed it in 365 C.E. It returned to the sand after that, not to be dug up until the 20th century. The extent of the work done by Italian archeologists in particular during the Italian colonial period (1911-1943), and the others who have followed, is exceeded only by the extent of the ruins themselves.

We drove the 80 km. back to the city and I, as usual, didn't waste time going to dinner. Between my domestic chores and this journal, there just isn't time at night to have another interminable meal.

Wednesday 9 March 2005
Tripoli

Every morning when we left our hotel the wind would hit us and we would spend the rest of the day cold. We left Tripoli for the day early this morning to drive two hours east to Leptis Magna, the principal ruined city of Libya. We were all hopped up to see it in spite of the fact it was cold and rainy. At Leptis we picked up our guide, less showoffy than the one yesterday but just as hard to understand, and went first to the amphitheatre and hippodrome, somewhat away from the rest of the site. Again we were right on the sea, and it was "fresh" as Bashir kept saying, i.e. eye-watering cold.

The amphitheatre, where people were killed by lions, was deep and intact but held bad vibes when one thought of all the lions killed in the wild animal trade during Roman times, not to mention Christians and other criminals. Beyond the amphitheatre, between it and the sea, was the hippodrome where chariot races and other bigger sports than mere killing went on. [I know I know, I'm not supposed to be superimposing my hyper-21st century political correctness on these long-gone cultures but really, one doesn't have to approve of them.]

A black sheet of rain was rapidly advancing across the water toward us and we barely made it to the bus before it hailed. The weather gods were not smiling on us. We retreated down the way to the museum on the site where much of the Leptis Magna statuary resides, again to keep it safe. We blew through that because we still had so much ground to cover, having not yet entered the site proper.

Leptis Magna is so huge it makes Ephesus look like Podunk. Leptis Magna was Rome's second grandest city after Rome itself. Leptis, Sabratha, Carthage, Alexandria and other famous North African cities were destroyed in the 365 C.E. earthquake. Some of them held on, some went under. Since Rome moved to Byzantium around that time, the whole Mediterranean balance of power was out of whack. The remains of Leptis sank into the sand.

And what a lot of city to disappear! Our mouths fell open and would have stayed that way if it hadn't been for the eye-stinging, nose-running cold wind battering at us, and some rain, too. It was serendipitous to find ourselves witness to the imaginary splendor of an historic Roman city fancy enough to compete with the great capitals of Europe, but our awe was tempered by serious discomfort.

We started at the Arch of Septimius Severus, the only Roman emperor from Leptis Magna. He came back for a visit and the city outdid itself building this magnificent four-sided arch in his honor. Then we began to 'walk the streets', stone-paved, set at right angles to each other in a grid and aligned north-south and east-west; this compulsive straightener appreciated that.

We saw all the things I had admired in the books I'd read before coming on the trip: Hadrian's Baths, the Forum, the Basilica, the theatre. It was a world of columns, some erect, some on the ground, and a world of capitals and carvings and tons and tons of stone, purposely cut stone straggled around but much of it laid out on or near where it started. To think of ancient people without electric- or gas-powered motors moving this universe of stone into place, not to mention making it beautiful, was to be seriously humbled.

We were amused over and over again at the phalluses carved into cornerstones, paving stones and keystones. The phallus was used as the evil eye to keep harm at bay. They were subtle, not obvious—just everywhere. I remembered the great phalluses painted on the houses of Bhutan. Can you imagine how happy it would make your neighbors in the U.S. if you displayed a giant phallus on your house?

We staggered back to the bus and sank into its warmth but alas, our ordeal was not over. We drove another ten or fifteen minutes to a farm where we had to slog through the mud to a leaky makeshift tent and sit in the cold with water dripping on us, holding our umbrellas over the tables, while three tall black Libyan boys played traditional music and a lukewarm lunch was served to us. It was 4:00 p.m. We laughed and smiled and put on a good face for our hosts (and each other) but it was pretty miserable.

One of the musicians played a bagpipe-style instrument made of a goat's head with ibex horns. Through a bamboo straw the player blew down into its neck to inflate it. Out its nostrils came two flute-like reeds with finger holes to control the tune, and at the end of these two cow horns emitted the sound. It was unlike any other musical instrument I had ever seen.

Before we could head back to the city, now muddy to our knees and thoroughly disheveled, we made a last stop at Villa Sileen, a 2000-year-old beach house dug out of the sand. It is under restoration and all locked up but we managed to weasel our way in through the good offices of Bashir and our policeman, Ahmed. Every floor of the villa and its outside decks was mosaic, finely done mosaics of tiny tiles enabling the artist to refine the pictures almost to painting quality.

Villa Sileen was the coldest of all the cold places we went all day.

Ahmed the policeman who travels with us declared himself to me today and now makes moony eyes at me. At Villa Sileen he presented me with a silver bracelet he had made at one of the kiosks in the car park at Leptis. It even had my name engraved on it. I don't know how this happened.

We finally got back to Tripoli at 8:00 p.m. — a 12 hour day.

Thursday 10 March 2005
Funduq Winzrik, Ghadames

Against our will we said goodbye to the Corinthia Bab Africa Hotel (bab means "gateway"), which had been our gorgeous home for four nights, and headed south into the desert toward Ghadames. It was still cold, though bright and sunny. We managed to turn an 11-hour day into a 12-hour one, but the journey into the Sahara was fascinating and I had no complaint.

The first stop was Qasr Haj, an 800-year-old fortified granary built by a trusted man of the town for people to store wheat and olive oil. It was round, big enough inside for a horse show, with its three stories of compartments open to the interior. It was mud and rubble construction (everything is) with some gypsum trim. Everything was a few bubbles off plumb giving it a friendly old inviting air. It was used until only recently.

The lunch stop was at a hotel in Nalut, a sizeable town on the top of a mountain reached by a modern switchback road built up the side of it by the Germans. We had the usual interminable meal of soup and bread, salad (eggplant with chili powder this time) and roasted chicken with rice and french fries. The soup is always the same, a reddish color with orzo or vermicelli in it. I thought it was tasteless. The bread was terrific.

After lunch we walked over to the old town (all these towns have an old part in ruins and a new part where everyone lives now with running water and electricity) and within the jumble of the rubble found intact an olive press, a mosque and another troglodyte granary that was surpassing strange. In this one the storage units were built several stories high and both inside the walls and in the middle, so there was one narrow path around the interior. The mud walls, the palm trunk beams sticking out, the gypsum doorways, the rotting rope pulleys and the little wooden platforms outside the mouths of the storage rooms all combined to create a weird, organic place that must have been a beehive of activity at times but which had passed into the ages with its amphorae and its architecture intact.

Ahmed the policeman walked me around these ruins, talking the whole time. He only spoke Arabic and Italian, neither of which I speak, but I could understand him. At one point when we were alone he told me he was forty years old and I was sixty. He must have mined the passport list. I shrugged and said I couldn't help it. It didn't deter him. He also admitted he had eleven children.

Next stop was a filling station where the owner gave us all little unfired pots to thank us for stopping by.

Then there was a long spell of quiet driving as the landscape went from sand with scrub brush to sand and rocks only as we got deeper into the desert. We saw camels. The pavement was narrow and in some places had blowing sand over it. The driver had to be careful.

Forty km. outside of Ghadames there was a bad engine noise and we stopped. Ali the driver, Ahmed the policeman and Bashir got out and went to the back. It was a broken fan belt. Like the law of the sea, everyone who came along stopped (2 vehicles) and didn't leave us until it was certain we were fixed. It was 8:00 when we arrived at our hotel in Ghadames.

The hotel was shabby, to put it generously. I actually had a hot shower and managed to get organized and ready for bed before the electricity went off. We dug out flashlights, then said to hell with it and went to sleep.

Friday 11 March 2005
Ghadames

I set the alarm for earlier than usual because Elliott thought she might get up and wash her hair. Instead we used the extra time to huddle in our beds waiting for our little space heater to warm a room so frigid I hesitate to guess what the temperature was— under 50 degrees F. I'm sure. Finally I braved it first and got up. I had to put my clothes on under my nightgown. Breakfast followed (in our coats) and some good-natured banter about how low we had fallen.

Ghadames was a fabled oasis and caravan stop for the trans-Saharan as well as the north-south trade in ivory, gold and slaves for the Levant and the rest of the Mediterranean world. The old part, which we toured all morning, felt as old as time and deeply exotic. Its restoration is in the hands of the United Nations Development Project (UNDP) and is being done locally by the very people and their descendents who only recently moved (or were moved) out of it and into modern houses. Their old houses belong to the world now.

There is not a free-standing structure in the old town; everything is organically melded into everything else. The passageways are covered, with only openings to the sky every few doorways. The walls are thick and ceilings are low. It is meant to keep heat out in the summer and heat in during the winter. We were not allowed to straggle because it is a labyrinth from which one might not emerge. We quickly got the picture and behaved. Our local guide, Mahmud, spoke good English for a change so we didn't get restless. He had earlier taken us through the Ghadames Museum. It didn't require an advanced degree to appreciate the simple displays but once inside the walls of the old city it would have taken Theseus to find the way out. I couldn't have told you where I was at any given time without GPS. They must have lost some children from time to time.

Towards lunchtime we walked out into the light between mud walls separating animal enclosures from the palm gardens that begirt the old town. This had more of a Biblical feel than the houses, which could have been Biblical or from Mars.

Lunch was in a restored house, now a restaurant. We sat on cushions on the floor and had the usual faintly red soup with tiny pastas in it, salad (which I never eat) and vegetable couscous with camel meat. Unfortunately the camel meat was good. I love camels so I only ate it for the experience, but I can see why they're raised for food. It was a treat.

At the end of lunch we had a brief talk by the man who runs the UNDP restoration project. I asked him if the World Monuments Fund or any foundations were helping and he wistfully said, "no." Libya has not exactly been on anyone's radar screen for awhile, but maybe now they'll get some help. Tourism is paying the bills for the present.

After a brief rest back at the hotel (!)—we never have any down time it seems— Ken gave a lecture which I skipped because I was nerve-wrackingly behind on this journal. I took advantage of the almost two hours of rest-and-lecture to write.

At 5:30 p.m. we boarded Land Rovers and drove out to the Grand Erg Oriental, a sand sea that spills over from Algeria into this western border region and abuts the city limits of Ghadames. At the base of the "star" dunes (so-called for the shape they assume when blown by winds from all directions) a Touareg encampment was set up for our entertainment. Touaregs are tall, slender nomadic desert people who live in Libya, Niger, Algeria and Mauritania. They wrap themselves in bright beautiful fabrics. They had a fierce reputation in days of yore and made a living protecting caravans.

Today's Touaregs were attractive but tame. They were cooking bread in the sand which they served to us hot after they had dug it out and dusted it off, and was it ever good, chewy and salty and delicious. Some young men danced with swords and subse-

Touareg and camel outside Ghadames

quently with us while a covey of women banged a drum and ululated. There were two colorful men on camels which we were encouraged to ride. And there were some darling girls selling beaded jewelry and other bright things. I learned all their names and showed them my silk long underwear, which made them giggle.

Toward sunset we climbed the dunes. From the top we could see Algeria and Tunisia to the west. We watched the sun set, then I begged Bashir to get one of the drivers to take me on a wild dune ride. This young man took me down the steepest highest dune in the neighborhood, probably at about an 85 degree angle, with me grinning and screaming the whole way. Then we went back up, or tried to and wound up at the bottom again to get up some speed. At the top we got stuck and had to dig ourselves out before we could descend to where the other vehicles were. It was great adrenaline-producing fun and I'm here to tell the tale and not banged up in a rollover.

Me and Elliott on top of "star" dunes at the corner of Tunisia, Algeria and Libya

And home, too, in our shabby room, clean and organized for the night. Elliott is writing her postcards. One has little of a domestic nature to do when traveling, no cat to feed or household matters to address, but on the other hand when one has ones entire life, at least for the next two weeks, in a bag on ones back (so to speak), that bag must be addressed before one can successfully press on.

Saturday 12 March 2005
Hotel Tibesti, Benghazi

A rocket ship dropped out of the sky, landed on a sandy runway, picked us up and flew us away from the past to the present, from the Sahara back to Tripoli. Our two days in the desert were sadly over.

In Tripoli some walked around the main square (Green Square—everything in Libya is "green", the flag, Gaddafi's Green Book—ironic because it's the least green country in any respect except greenbacks), some of us went with Susan back to the Corinthia Hotel to retrieve checked luggage. I went with Susan and wanted to fall on my knees and kiss the lobby floor of the Corinthia after the elegance-challenged caravanserai of the last two nights (where, in its defense, we were mostly comfortable when we weren't freezing to death or groping in the dark).

We all rejoined in Green Square and walked two blocks to a nice restaurant called Gambieri where we had a good though not memorable fish lunch and conversation. Back to the bus, back to Wheelus Air Force Base, a huge formerly American air base where we had landed in our chartered jet this morning, to board a scheduled Boraq Airlines flight to Benghazi (Boraq was the name of the horse that carried Mohammed to heaven to confer with Abraham, Isaac and Jesus; they gave him their blessings).

The day had gone so smoothly. Now we sat on the plane on the tarmac getting hotter and hotter. Rumor had it we were waiting for a VIP; this made us democrats growl. Other rumor held it was mechanical trouble. Finally they transferred us to a plane parked about four planes down from ours and we took off for Benghazi. We rolled into our hotel at 8:45 p.m. It is really tiring not ever to have down time; we're starting to feel haggard.

Sunday 13 March 2005
Benghazi

Benghazi is the second-biggest city in Libya. It is a port in the Eastern part of the country, which is called Cyrenaica. We are in Cyrenaica to see some of the five Greek cities of antiquity (the Pentapolis, as opposed to Tripolitania, the three Roman cities of the West coast).

We were bedeviled by bus problems. After the late arrival of our plane last night there was no bus waiting to pick us up. We went to the hotel in two vans, with the bags in a lorry. The hotel was a modern highrise but it was cold and the heat in our room didn't work. This morning the same bus that didn't pick us up last night didn't pick us up this morning. We stood around 45 minutes until the back-up bus arrived. It was not as nice as our other buses. Our bus is our home, so we depend on it to be the clean safe cozy efficient machine that is our lifeline and beacon. This one was adequate but the driver was not great. However, we were under way, and that was important. We kept reminding ourselves that if we wanted to be in on the birth of nascent tourism in a Third World country, we had to take our lumps.

Benghazi struck us as more snazzy that Tripoli, wealthier and more cosmopolitan. It is a port so it has the usual water and palm trees. We bombed Benghazi in 1986 at the same time we bombed Tripoli; I wonder how many countries I've been in that the U.S. has bombed. Yet people's faces light up when we say we're from "America."

Before leaving the city we went to a Commonwealth cemetery, one of the many Allied cemeteries in North Africa. The British really take their war graves maintenance seriously. I was surprised at how small it was; I guess I was expecting Normandy or Arlington. We walked around reading the tombstones. Elliott copied down a little poem on one of them: "But now he is dead./Can I bring him back again?/I shall go to him./He shall not return to me." Walking around by myself I got upset and cried thinking of our own poor cannon fodder in the current war and what a terrible terrible waste war is and how awful it is to go around starting them. If only the effect of my crying in North Africa had the same effect on our Administration as the proverbial butterfly flapping its wings in the Amazon did to cause great outbreaks of weather in faraway places. But I'm as helpless as an insect with a shoe bearing down on it. Actually that powerlessness made me even more empathetic toward the people of Libya.

Leaving Benghazi was not snazzy but miles and miles of dreadful, shabby concrete buildings with the rebar sticking out of them, everything an incomprehensible jumble of poor-country mess and covered with trash, as is most of the country. There is apparently no trash management outside the central cities. All other trash is thrown on the ground or dumped in bags beside the road. It looks like a futurist film maker's idea of environmental meltdown: the world as a giant trashcan.

Finally we left the city exurbs behind and found ourselves in some very pretty landscape. We were driving East with the Mediterranean on our left. On our right was the low mountain range, the Jebel Akdar, and Libya was at last green. Farms with fields and animals were on both sides of the road, and down at water's edge palm trees and white beaches. The eye could rest momentarily.

It took two tries to find the little road to Ptolemais (also known as Tolmeita), our goal. This was the prettiest drive of all, right by the water with green on all sides. As usual we arrived at an unprepossessing looking entrance with a dirt yard full of cats. They would later help us finish our lunches. The entrance building housed the statuary and artifacts found in the excavations. We had a good guide who walked us through it.

[This might be the best place to insert a disclaimer regarding my understanding of these sites, my writing about them and, consequently, the reader's understanding of them. I do not parade as a scholar because I cannot. I'm not. I have enough historical knowledge and sensibility to understand what I am seeing, but I would encourage anyone who wants deeper study of the area and the era not to depend on me but rather to peruse the contless books on the history of Libya, its art and architecture. That is not the purpose of this journal.]

In another concrete building off the dirt yard we had lunch of grilled chicken and couscous at one long table. The cats waited and were rewarded. They needed to have a spay-and-neuter clinic day at this place. Muslims like cats because "they clean themselves," and dislike dogs for the opposite reason. You never see dogs.

Then we set off on foot in a high wind, though not cold for a change, to walk ten minutes up the foothill behind us to enter the site of Ptolemais. This was the loveliest site so far. Instead of being right on the water it looked down from lush green heights at the sea below. The influence on this city was more Greek than Roman. We saw the Odeon, a music theatre, the Agora or marketplace under which lay a cistern of large extent, the Palace of Columns, the house of the governor and the Byzantine Wall which many did not trek through rocks and nettles to reach. The site needs a lot more archeological attention, as all these places do.

We finally finished up there at 5:00 p.m. Back on the bus it was announced we were returning to Benghazi (this was a change of plans). Bashir told me it was to get rid of our bus and driver and await the arrival of our former fancy bus that took us to Ghadames, and Ali, the champion driver. We were disappointed to return to Benghazi, but like good cattle we went where we were herded.

Monday 14 March 2005
Cyrene Resort, Shahat

The bellman who carried our bags down this morning saw me in the hall and said, didn't I see you yesterday? These poor guys had to schleppe our luggage up and down and in and out of the hotel twice in two days, since we were supposed to be at Apollonia (Susa) and not back in Benghazi. But there at breakfast was our trusty Ali, a welcome sight. We got off at 8:00 a.m. to backtrack out of Benghazi heading East again.

This time we went up into the Jebel Akdar, the Green Mountains. It was beautiful: vivid green grasses, dark green conifers and wildflowers galore, framed by red escarpments. There was little trash. We were in a 'rich' part of Libya and it showed. This was the area that bred Omar Mukhtar, the hero of Libya who fought the Italian colonialists with guerrilla tactics for the twenty years from 1911 to 1932. A movie called "Lion of the Desert" starring Anthony Quinn was made about Omar Mokhtar; we individually rented it before leaving the U.S. and all agreed it was good, and because it was fairly accurate helped us to understand the Italian colonial period of Libyan history.

The first stop was at Qasr Libya, two Byzantine churches found in the 1950's by workers digging for a dam. Fifty mosaics were moved out of the floor of one church and into a museum building. We met our guide of yesterday there, Abdul Rhim Shariff, and admired the mosaics which were mostly about animals with some having human figures and one showing the famous lighthouse in Alexandria that went bye-bye in the earthquake of 365 C.E. The mosaics were charming and even though their tessere were not as tiny as those we saw at Villa Sileen, they still managed to evoke a whimsical world of wildlife that was at least partially accurate.

We then drove through more scenery to Al Baydah, a sizeable town where we had the best lunch of the trip so far in what could have passed for a bus stop cafe. Turns out the chef had cooked at the Sheraton in Cairo. He had to have been in semi-retirement in Al Baydah but he had an appreciative audience today.

From Al Baydah we descended the mountain (these mountains are not tall, 2500-3000 feet), drove past Cyrene, the major site of Cyrenaica which we will see tomorrow, and on down to the sea to Apollonia, the ruins of the port that served Cyrene. This spot was even prettier than Ptolemais yesterday. Unlike the Roman ruins at Leptis and Sabratha that were right on the beach, the old Greek and Byzantine stones and columns of Apollonia were on cliffs above the water. We could have been on a Greek island if we hadn't had the continent of Africa right behind us.

Abdul Rhim walked us and talked us through the buildings—outlines of buildings, really, only partially put back together—and we pondered the art, architecture, religion and daily doings of lives that are lost now in the mists of time. With respect for the connection we contemplated their churches and graves, where they sang and danced, and tried to think how they lived. The last stop was the theatre, carved into a great cliff with the sea at the bottom. It was spectacular.

We continued East on the beautiful coast road with the breathtaking views to Atrun, the remains of a Byzantine basilica of white marble with mosaics. In the ruins of Atrun we saw new ruins caused by the poor job done recently by a famous French archeologist named Andre Laronde who did his repairs on the cheap and they all fell down, or apart. Last was Ras al-Hillal, a church we reached by walking down a dirt road. We were just about basilica'd out at that point and the sun was setting so we headed for our hotel.

The Cyrene Resort was one of those places erected by well-meaning people to take advantage of a new influx of tourists. It was incredibly tacky but had a staff of darling, smiling young men who tried to help us. I'm always touched by these places and the sweet friendly proud faces who try hard to please. We were all so frazzled we were like firecrackers set to go off. Nothing was right. The dining room was built back into a cave and was cold. Knowing that tomorrow is always another day, I hunkered down to do laundry and eat a banana and try not to think what came next.

Tuesday 15 March 2005
Al Manara Hotel, Susa

We were subdued this morning, our last day of touring. We were tired and burnt out but calm and ready to see the rest. Every day had its gifts and this one would, too. We left the tacky Cyrene Resort to move once more; we were tired of moving.

Abdul Rhim Shariff was with us again. He was a scholarly man, cute and funny, but talked a lot. We liked him but after standing on the stones for ten or fifteen minutes in the same place listening to his thorough, logical explanations you could have tipped any one of us over with the tap of a finger.

It was our day to explore Cyrene, the original Greek settlement, then city, founded in the 5th century B.C.E. Yesterday we had tramped around Apollonia, its port on the cliffs of the Mediterranean; today we started at the top of the mountain where the Apollo oracle at Delphi had told the Greeks to find the spot where "there was a hole in the heavens". This sent them to the beautiful Jebel Akdar in what would become Cyrenaica in what would become Libya. We were witness today, March 15, 2005, to their ancient life of 2500 years ago, and their awesome architecture.

As the words tumbled out of Abdul Rhim's mouth I tried to stay focused. I have a general idea of classical history but this trip has been a Ph.D. in my shortcomings in that area. I always come away from my trips wanting to know more, then life intervenes and I'm on to the next thing. So without any scholarly ado, here is what we saw:

The Temple of Zeus, the biggest Greek temple in North Africa, bigger even than the Parthenon—huge columns;

The museum (i.e. a big concrete room full of unbelievable treasures, as all the site museums have been) with most of the statuary and sarcophagi from the site;

The Agora zone, the highest point of the city with the most Roman influence, including the Gymnasium, the Portico of Hermes and Hercules, the Greek Odeon (music theatre), the house of Jason Magnus, a high priest—a huge house paved with mosaics);

[I will stop here to say we have sated ourselves on mosaics but ones brow wrinkles to watch the group mosey across 2000-year-old mosaics that probably by rights ought to have a guard rail around them. Fortunately for the time being there are so few tourists we only saw one other group all day and so had one of the major wonders of the world to ourselves.]

Lunch, long and slow, at a restaurant at the entrance to the lower city, the Sanctuary of Apollo;

From the roadside we descended down into the beautiful ruined lower city, built into the mountainside with a sheer drop to the coastal plain a few thousand feet below, and admired the Fountain of Apollo (a spring), the Temple of Apollo (they had carried a statue of Apollo with them from Greece and had to throw up a temple for it right fast, probably before they started growing food or building houses);

The Theatre, the Amphitheatre and Trajan's Baths.

At Trajan's Baths the last lecture was given to a seriously bedraggled bunch of tourists who were all laid out in various postures of late afternoon fatigue as we all lolled on rocks and tried to keep concentrating.

Back to the bus, one quick stop to look up close at some tombs of the extensive necropolis that covered the hills surrounding the site—the cave mouths adorned with architecture and of course full of trash—then a slow picking our way down the mountainside in low gear to the town of Susa and the last hotel on this road trip, Al Manara, which looks out over the ruins of Apollonia to one side and the Mediterranean directly in front. There were some skiffs in the water that caused me to have a pang of homesickness for my own coast, but it has been too cold to consider being either in or on the water, so I got quickly over my pang. Abdul Rhim told us today we were lucky with the weather—today it was not cold for only the second time this trip—because he said it is usually cold and rainy in Cyrene. We laughed like that was nothing; we'd been cold for two weeks.

Wednesday 16 March 2005
Corinthia Bab Africa Hotel, Tripoli

Labraq, a pissant little airport near the Cyrenaican sites we had been visiting, had a scheduled flight to Tripoli for us this morning. "Scheduled" did not mean "on time"; we waited in our hotel lobby for two hours reading and schmoozing until we were sure the Libyan Airlines flight was in the air and coming our way. Then we jumped up and drove half an hour to Labraq, an airfield with ten miles of concrete block wall around it apparently built for the late King Idris. King Idris was out of the country when Gaddafi pulled off his coup in 1969 and was invited not to come back.

We breezed through the airport, the ladies only stopping to be felt up or patted down by a hideous fat scowling woman who looked ready to commit sadism. They let our group on the plane first, which I'm sure made us popular. An hour and a half later we landed safely in Tripoli. It was 2:30 and we were hungry.

We went straight to an elegant downtown restaurant, Konez Bahar, for the usual long lunch. Ken said he didn't normally push back from the lunch table at 5:00. There was to be a dinner tonight which I would skip in any case but for once everyone else was wondering how they were going to eat it, too.

After "lunch" Ahmed the policemen took Elliott in a taxi back to the airport to fly to Malta. I was sad to see her go, and sadder still to be subsequently back in the gorgeous Corinthia Bab Africa Hotel with no roommate. Part of the glory of being once more in a fine hotel was tempered by loneliness. I miss Elliott, my cat, my boyfriend, my mother, my pillows—when asked what would be the first thing he would eat when he got home, Ted, one of our group, said "my pillow". We are ready to go home.

Thursday 17 March 2005
Heathrow Hilton, London

This morning in Tripoli I took off by myself and went into the souk to buy a couple of presents. It felt livelier and more normal this time, and certainly was more fun to amble through by myself with no grave time constraint. I communed with various shopkeepers, even engaging in a long political discussion with one. We have tried to impress on everyone we talk to that the American people and their government are two different things, that at least half of all Americans disagree with their government on most major matters. The Libyans are like everyone else in the Middle East in that they get their news from Al Jazeera and other colorful sources, and might not know that America is full of good people who care about the world and don't just want to war with it.

We had lunch in the hotel and went to the airport to start the lengthy check-in process. Susan had left us to take on a new group and Bashir was on his own. He was thin, nervous and smoked constantly and so was not as organized and calm as Susan. We all liked him but his dynamic personality did not stand him in good stead when it came to plodding details like getting 24 people on an airplane. We finally made it to the exit lounge where we said goodbye to him and Ahmed, my policeman, who pretended to weep tears by making circular motions with his fist over his eye for the last three days everytime he caught my eye. He got a big tip.

Later, safely back in London for an overnight, a few of us gathered in the brasserie of the Heathrow Hilton and had alcohol for the first time in two weeks. I also had red meat and chocolate.

EPILOGUE

It was a hard trip, a memorable trip, a beautiful trip but not the best trip. We had five one-night stands at the end of the trip that exhausted us. I wouldn't travel with Distant Horizons again because they lied about the size of the group and didn't screen the guests properly. That's not a good way to breed repeat customers.

Those caveats aside, it's the ruins that stick in my mind's eye, the vast extent and majesty of the ruins. I also loved the Sahara Desert and would like to see more of it; it has a strange drawing power that has affected Western people from their earliest exposure. The long unspoiled Libyan coastline will someday become the purview of the developers, the same fate that has befallen most of the beautiful places on Earth. In our dotage we will dine out on tales of how it used to be, but it is small consolation we saw it before it was ruined.

On a more personal note, I noticed on this trip my level of curiosity was not as high as it used to be. I hope it is a function of having been so many places and seen so many things, and not of losing interest in life. Maybe it was a consequence of the cold, discomfort and lack of down time to think about, assimilate and synthesize the huge quantity of stuff we saw. I think my coming away from such an interesting trip with such ambivalent feelings is the result of my visceral response to the logistical problems, not an intellectual response to what we saw. What we saw I can recommend unconditionally, and will never forget. Now like other countries that have occupied a discommensurate place in our imaginations, Libya will join that list of those we will be watching with hope and optimism to grow into the 21st century in a humane and progressive way, inshallah. The people certainly deserve it, and the world is ready for it.

ENGLAND AND SCOTLAND
AUGUST 2005

INTRODUCTION

In Santa Fe with Mother and friends for the opera in the summer of 2004, a plan was hatched to go somewhere else for the opera the following summer. That somewhere turned out to be Glyndebourne, the summer opera festival in England south of London in Sussex. Tickets to Glyndebourne are notoriously difficult to obtain but our beloved, trusty Rudy Avelar at the Houston Grand Opera easily got us some. Subsequently at Glyndebourne, everyone on our row wanted to know how we had gotten tickets. The man next to Mother had been on the list for twelve years to get a subscription!

As long as we were in Great Britain, Mother wanted to go to Scotland and find the McAllister Lands. We had both been to Scotland before and although it is my practice not to go back to places I have already been, the prospect of driving around Scotland under new and different circumstances was irresistible.

My two pals Elliott Jones and DeJuana Jones (not related), both opera-goers and globe-trotters, signed on for the two-part trip. If one does not see much of Elliott in this journal it is because she did more than we did, especially when the sun went down. She was otherwise her usual excellent traveling buddy self.

THE JOURNAL

Friday 12 August 2005
The Grand Hotel, Eastbourne
East Sussex, England

It's difficult to nap when there's an air show going on outside the window. When we checked into this hotel mid-day the desk clerk said proudly, we've given you sea view rooms. Great, I said, only to discover what a left-handed gift it was when the sonic booms started and the fly-by's roared past the tall windows. This beautiful old hotel is not air conditioned and it is summer, so the windows are open to all the wild noise of a large and serious air show going on over hundreds of thousands of people on the beach across the street and on their boats offshore. It's colorful but not restful. I gave up on my nap although Mother is across the room obliviously sawing it off. She sleeps the sleep of the innocent.

Yesterday we landed in London late morning after the usual uncomfortable trans-Atlantic flight, and Mother went immediately to bed. DeJuana had arrived after midnight and was in our room at the Stafford Hotel. She and I set out to walk to the National Gallery for an afternoon of museum inhalation but I was overwhelmed by the sheer extent of the collection and the endless rooms and on shaky legs went back home for food and rest. Later DeJuana and I had an early supper in the bar and I personally was sound asleep at 7:00 p.m. and slept eleven hours.

This morning we left the Stafford and taxied to Victoria Station to catch our train down here to Eastbourne in East Sussex on the English Channel near the bottom right hand side of England. With the demise of porters, one of the drawbacks of modern life, we had consolidated suitcases and now wheeled and hauled our own bags through the station and onto the train. Without wheels we'd still be at home, or actually not, since there would be porters. We didn't just throw a dart at a map and choose this charming city; we are here because there were hotel rooms available and it is somewhat close to Glyndebourne, where we will attend the opera tonight. We were delighted at the fin-de-siecle wedding cake appearance of this grand hotel and haven't been too inconvenienced by the roar of the jets.

Saturday 13 August 2005
The Grand Hotel, Eastbourne

The fourth member of our traveling group, Elliott, materialized in the nick of time yesterday afternoon from her independent travels and managed to get cleaned up and spiffed up in time to meet us in the lobby at 4:00 p.m. to be picked up by our driver to go to Glyndebourne. The driver, John, was a competent well-spoken fellow who whisked us the 20 or so miles to Glyndebourne through "Old English" countryside that caused memories of a lifetime of English literature to come to life, and indeed we were in Virginia Wolff-land.

The approach to Glyndebourne was past tended fields of hay, cows and sheep. The driveway to the opera house was the entrance to the Christie family estate on which it sits. Three generations of Christies have run Glyndebourne since the founder, John Christie, started it in 1932, although the hall itself has grown considerably in eight decades. Yet it is still small by American standards – only 1200 seats – and intimate in the European fashion. It is red brick on the outside and polished wood on the inside with a state-of-the-art stage.

We strolled the grounds and got the lay of the land before the performance. We were as interested in the people in their black tie finery as we were in the location. There is a tradition of Londoners getting on the train in the middle of the day in their formal clothes to come down to operas at this famous summer festival. "Flight", on the bill that night, was a contemporary opera about a man trapped in an airport that I abused by sleeping through part of the first act (remember that interrupted nap?), but by the end of the second act, when we dined in one of the onsite restaurants during the "long interval", we could talk of nothing else. The last act cinched it; the audience went nuts and we talked about the story and symbolism all the way back to Eastbourne with our driver John.

This morning DeJuana and I walked for exercise (my first in 3 days; I was happy for it), Mother swam in the heated outdoor pool and Elliott slept in. She then took off for the day to go to Brighton on the train. DeJuana and I walked again for an hour and a half in the middle of the day, savoring the pretty bright, cool weather, the crowds and displays of the air show and the very town itself. We found we could change money at

Elliott, DeJuana, me and Mother in the audience at Glyndebourne

the Post Office for no commission. We walked out on the old Victorian pier with its onion-domed buildings housing various entertainments, the chief of which was fighter jets doing loop-de-loops and flying upside down above us and the audience below on the pebble beach.

Naturally the noisiest airplanes performed when we got back to the hotel to rest. For all the noise there was something touching about the vintage planes and references to the Battle of Britain, part of which had taken place nearby over the white cliffs of Dover.

Sunday 14 August 2005
En route Eastbourne – London

John the driver picked us up again and this time we cut it close to curtain time because it had started to rain and all the air show traffic was leaving town as well. But I had an ace in the hole as we stressed about missing the curtain: the curtain doesn't go up when they say it does. It goes up ten minutes later. We arrived in plenty of time

This night we saw an "Otello" we all agreed was the best we'd ever seen. I think Verdi choruses were intended for larger halls; I was particularly blasted out of my seat (fifth row center, thank you Rudy Avelar of the Houston Grand Opera) but all the singing was superb and the Iago was unusually well acted. We dined in a different restaurant, a carvery called Under Wallop, and ate roast beef and Yorkshire pudding during the long interval. We were ecstatic and voluble in the car on the way home as we dissected the opera.

This morning DeJuana and I walked toward Beachy Head, the white chalk cliffs of Eastbourne that are characteristic of this part of the coast. We had an invigorating time admiring the plethora of flowers while huffing and puffing uphill. After breakfast as we were dressing and packing to leave there was a dog show sideshow down below at the air show. Police dogs jumped onto high platforms and through burning hoops. This was an improvement over the great engines of war (boys and their toys) that had entertained us the two days before.

We are training back to London as I write.

Monday 15 August 2005
En route London — Inverness

Back at our beautiful Stafford Hotel, this time in the "carriage house" (350 year-old converted stables), Elliott, not one to miss a thing, set out in rain gear to go to the London Eye (the Millennium Ferris wheel), the new Tate and other points. DeJuana, Mother and I had a leisurely lunch in the hotel (on Sunday at 2 p.m. there was not a lot of choice of where to eat), then spent the balance of the afternoon at domestic pursuits in order to go to bed early. We admired Elliot her boundless energy and curiosity without necessarily wanting to share in it.

We left the hotel well in advance of our flight this morning because Heathrow had been in chaos for four days due to a wildcat strike and sure enough, even though things were said to be getting back to "normal", it was still pretty hairy. We got in the "Bag Drop" line even though we hadn't gone through the "Self Check-In" line so Elliott and I left the Bag Drop line and went to tackle the Self Check-In line with all our tickets. The machines wouldn't work for our tickets so an expediter took pity on us and said we could check in with the Bag Drop clerk. By this time Mother and DeJuana had inched our luggage (on carts) to the head of the Bag Drop line and minutes later we were free and on our way to the gate. It pays to get to the airport early.

[Later, in Inverness]

We flew directly to Inverness, our entry to the Scottish Highlands. Paul McLean, our guide, met us in Baggage Claim kitted out in a green kilt—the McLean hunting tartan. Our bags were the last ones off the plane – I hate that – so with all kinds of relief we set out in a spacious van to do some sightseeing before going to our hotel. At Culloden Battlefield (one battle, April 16, 1746, but a decisive one that cinched England's dominion over Scotland) we saw where "Bonnie Prince Charlie" and his Jacobites were defeated. The battlefield, some hummocks covered with heather and gorse, had to wait while we had an excellent lunch (macaroni and cheese, and baked potatoes stuffed with salmon in mayonnaise) in the National Trust for Scotland tourist facility on the grounds. We walked around the small battlefield for a few minutes looking at the old gravestones put up to commemorate clan losses. Here we began to get a feel for our guide Paul's clan loyalties and antipathies.

On a little one-lane back road we found the "Clava Cairns", a 5000 year-old pre-Pict burial ground with stone cairns and standing stones still somehow intact under great shade trees. In neither of these places, and no place in England, did we see many tourists to speak off. London was quiet as a tomb, although to say that may be bad luck after their recent Al-Qaeda travails.

In Inverness proper we drove around admiring the pretty little city on the Ness River ("inver" means mouth of), and when it still seemed too early to quit we had Paul drop us back downtown after we checked into our hotel. Our hotel was somewhat funky and when DeJuana saw Mother's reaction to it she quickly volunteered herself and Elliott to take the smallest room. This was helpful.

Downtown we window shopped in desultory fashion until we got a little too far away from the heart of things and, after being passed by a bunch of drunk townies (part of the "lad" culture), turned around and headed for the taxi rank. It was a bit of a wait—rush hour—but we made it safely home.

We're having our usual banana night; Elliott is out pub crawling.

Thursday 16 August 2005
Heathmount Hotel, Inverness

DeJuana and I set out to walk for exercise at 6:30 this morning and I timed us on the outbound leg so we could get back to our hotel for breakfast, toilette and 9:00 departure. We only missed it by a few minutes, but all of us kind of missed it together so there were no recriminations.

This was our day to soak up the Highlands and as it turned out, we went as "high" as we could go, to John O'Groats, the village at land's end on the north point of Scotland named after the Dutch ferry captain who also gave his name to a coin.

On the way we experienced beautiful scenery as we drove up the North Sea coast road: tilled fields, rolls of baled hay, sheep galore, dairy cows including the rare Belted Galloways with snappy white bands around their middles, one small herd of long haired cattle who must be related to yaks (no, let's see: God created all this stuff in six days so there wouldn't have been time to relate cows in Scotland to yaks in the Himalayas), seagulls, migrating geese, a couple of fallow deer and all of them set against the background of the North Sea.

Half way to John O'Groats we stopped to tour Dunrobin Castle, the last "great house" this far north, still inhabited as so many are. I'm not a big lover of touring castles and always try to act cool and bored like I've see this stuff before, but this one caught my fancy and all of our fancies and we enjoyed it. Down in the formal garden that sloped to the sea we watched a falconry demonstration in which the falconer put a hawk, an eagle owl and a falcon through their paces while intermittently feeding them dismembered baby chicks. As the great birds whooshed over our heads we fell in love, and I don't think there was a one of us who wouldn't have paid good money to pet the huge owl.

By the time we got to John O'Groats it was 2:00 and most of us were ready for lunch. In the Sea View Hotel dining room in company with a "rinse and wrinkle" tour as Paul called them (very old English people with blue hair and wrinkles), we had a darned good lunch considering we were in Nowheresville: cullen skink (smoked fish soup), mushroom stroganoff, steak pie—just your usual lunch dishes. As in all foreign cultures we have laughed over signs and the names of things. Today we saw a highway sign that said "Heavy Plant Crossing". With visions of trees moving themselves from one side of the road to the other (they do take their "Macbeth" seriously up here), we learned it only meant "heavy equipment crossing". At John O'Groats there was a sign that indicated how far it was to the Arctic Circle, New York City and other points for which this could have conceivably been a jumping-off point.

There was a long uneventful drive home punctuated with laughter and storytelling but we were ready to disembark when we finally rolled into our hotel (after a quick stop at the Safeway for the usual bananas and sweets) after 6:00. Elliott went out to her pub and the rest of us had a pajama party and ate our fruit supper.

Wednesday 17 August 2005
The Barriemore Hotel, Oban

We left Inverness this morning and had a gorgeous drive all day down Loch Ness and all the succeeding lochs south of it and the canals that bind them into one excruciatingly beautiful waterway. We stopped constantly, which kept us occupied and stretched our legs and backs. Our stops were:

- Urquhart Castle, ruins on a cliff above Loch Ness;
- Fort Augustus, the fort part of which which doesn't exist anymore (so why did we even get out of the car?), to see "Neptune's Staircase", mechanical locks between the lake lochs, and a "Nessie" sculpture made of wire mesh.
- The Well of the Seven Heads monument commemorating a gruesome clan–on–clan revenge crime (everyone gets along now but they all hate some other clan and everyone hates the Campbells);
- Spean Bridge Commando Monument (10 seconds, stay in the car), and a pit stop at a nice souvenir place;
- Glencoe, where a seriously heinous Campbell clan travesty against the MacDonalds happened that still rankles even though it happened in 1692 – a massacre made worse by an abuse of hospitality involved (I know how they felt);
- Rannoch Moor, one of Europe's last true wildernesses, a starkly beautiful drive between hard old mountains and over vast ancient peat bogs;
- Another rest stop to pee and buy chocolate; and
- St. Conan's Kirk (church), on Loch Awe, a 150 year-old folly of architectural styles than nonetheless garnered our praise and respect. It included a recumbent statue of marble and mail of Robert the Bruce and, outside, metal rabbit rain spouts.

We came over a last hilltop and there was Oban below, a picturesque seaside town full of B&B's. We're in one, a handsome Victorian manse where we are in comfortable rooms. We're going out to dinner for the first time since our on-site dinners at Glyndebourne five nights ago.

Thursday 18 August 2005
The Barriemore Hotel, Oban

We had wine, pasta, dessert and indigestion last night. At the time of ingestion it seemed worth it.

I fell in love with Scotland this morning. DeJuana and I didn't walk early because it was raining too hard, so when I got dressed I went out just to get some fresh air. It was still drizzling a little, and standing on the esplanade across the street in the grey mist the view was stunning of glassy water, a ferry going by, islands across the harbor, sailboats and seagulls. Over me was a war monument with the names of the dead (McLean, McPhail, McNaughton) and beyond it, on a hill, some mossy ruins. Scotland respects its ruins and doesn't try to clear them away. I stood for some time in a state of enchantment and felt that giving in, when a place finally enters you like a lover.

Paul fetched us at the usual 9:00 a.m. and we drove to the other end of this small town to queue for the ferry to the Isle of Mull. At 10:00 we sailed and for 40 minutes floated through exquisite scenery made more dramatic by the sky of clouds that hung so low they laved the hillsides. We also got to admire Judi Dench and Maggie Smith who were hanging on the rail next to us. We took their pictures and said nice things to them.

Judi Dench and Maggie Smith on the ferry to the Isle of Mull

As we approached Mull we passed under Duart, the castle keep that is the clan seat of the McLeans, of which our Paul is one. Our first stop on Mull was "his" castle which seemed much more the old, rough, thick walled hard-hearted fortress-type castle of yore than the flossy "castle", Dunrobin, that we saw north of Inverness.

After Duart we drove almost the entire north coast of Mull, stopping in the picture-book town of Toberrary (Mother called it Topiary), the only real town on Mull and a tiny one at that – the whole big island only has 2500 people on it – and had a kind of lousy lunch in a pub. In defiance of how lousy it was we stopped at a chocolate store on the way out of town and bought some candy to assuage our feeling of deprivation but which of course only added to the problem of poor diet.

We drove further west, amusing ourselves with gorgeous scenery and sheep who looked like they had on Argyll socks, finally turning back at Calgary, a village that gave its name to a city in Canada. Calgary, Scotland had a jetty in an inlet from which many of the dispossessed crofters during the "clearances" of the 1830's took ships to North America to escape their sudden precipitous downturn of life plan. We may all have friends whose ancestors left from this quay, and indeed relatives. All over Scotland we saw their sad roofless stone huts which are left standing to remind the people of the clearances.

At that point we turned back and took an even tinier road back across the island to the cluster of buildings at the ferry landing. In one building was a pub where we drank hot chocolate while we waited for the ferry. The ferry ride back didn't have any noticeable movie stars aboard but was equally pleasant and beautiful to the outbound leg.

The sun is back out, Mother and I have walked the esplanade and are now eating fruit on the bed for supper. I'm sure our stomachs are thanking us.

Friday 19 August 2005
Jury's Hotel, Edinburgh
Edinburgh is pronounced "Edinburra".

We left Oban and the West this morning with some regret, we'd had such a pleasant sojourn there. At times in the last few days we have all secretly longed for the city but now that the time had come to go to the big city there was some foot dragging.

We had the usual beautiful drive from one side of the country to the other, west to east, stopping for lunch in Perth in a new restaurant in a 14th century building. I had beef cobbler, which turned out to be stewed beef, and we all had Caesar salads with lots of white anchovies in them.

And then before we could even protest, we were in traffic and having to adjust to the noise and chaos of a city that was in the full middle of its Edinburgh Festival, its Fringe Festival and the Pipefest, some 10,000 pipers in town. We threaded our way through the old streets to Jury's, an unremarkable modern hotel with few amenities (no doorman or bellboys, for instance) but convenient and away from the street noise. I had told our travel agent we didn't want to spend a lot of money on hotels and she took me at my word.

We got settled in, Elliott took off on her own to try to score a ticket to the Military Tattoo in Edinburgh Castle [she succeeded], and at 4:30 DeJuana, Mother and I set off to walk The Royal Mile, accessible a block from our hotel. On this famous street of shops and restaurants we walked and window-shopped and watched the buskers, some of whose agendas were performance art specifically advertising some aspect of one of the Festivals, and others who were out to make a little change. It was noisy and colorful and even though mother was moving very slowly we got a kick out of the scene and some of the crazy talent.

After two hours we landed, unashamed, at a Mexican restaurant called Pancho Villa. We had a margarita and some nachos and soothed our foreign souls. This was not a night for a banana in a dreary hotel room.

Saturday 20 August 2005
Jury's Hotel, Edinburgh

While I waited for Mother to finish getting ready this morning I put my elbows on the window sill, put my chin on my hands and cast myself back 800 years to when the buildings I could see would have begun to rise. They are romantic to us 21st century travelers but life must have been inconceivably difficult for those who lived in and built this city. Slops would have been poured from windows, sheets would have been washed on boards in tubs, loads would have been borne by animals, stone would have been broken by hand, water and fuel would have been carried in. The ghosts must hate us our gaiety and disregard as all the silly teenagers punctured in their various facial parts and with their stomachs hanging out drink and flirt and cling to their ignorance, and we, too, serious ardent grownups, fail to give the past its realistic due. We only love it for what we get from it without walking in its shoes.

By prearrangement we were on our own this weekend. Paul, our driver and guide, was in the hotel but tied up with Pipefest. We walked two blocks – the four of us – and boarded an open-air double-decker tour bus and took the "city tour" to orient ourselves. The air was cool and fresh and for the first time since we arrived in the UK there wasn't a cloud in the sky. We looped around Edinburgh Castle, an immense "kremlin" of buildings dating to the 13th century that seemed to grow organically out of the volcanic hill that predominates over the city; and around Holyroodhouse Palace. These two institutions anchor The Royal Mile at either end, and are number one and number two on the hit parade of sights to see in Edinburgh.

After the full city tour we rode the bus back around to the stop for the Castle and walked up to it and up, up, up into it until we reached the top. This took a lot of stopping, photo ops, bench rests and confusion. Finally we entered the building with the crown jewels of Scotland, called The Honours: the crown, the scepter and the sword that were packed away in 1707 when Scotland joined England, and only found 111 years later and put on display.

Back on the street it was already 12:30 so we returned to Pancho Villa and had a real meal. It took some fortitude to get there through the masses of people and performers on the street, and none of us was too sure how far we'd walked but over lunch we concluded by looking at our map that we were two-thirds of the way down The Royal Mile.

That meant we were only 1/3 mile from Holyroodhouse Palace and it was downhill so we walked there, walked through it and walked back to a bus stop to catch our tour bus for a ride home. It was 4:00.

Then it wouldn't do but we had to have an ice cream cone, so when the bus stopped where it had originally started we hiked back up to the Mile to find an ice cream parlor. At that point it was either go home or carry Mother, so home we went.

Elliott is out and DeJuana, Mother and I have had a girlie evening of manicuring, pedicuring and banana-ing. We are so pitiful, but we're tired. Did I mention that DeJuana and I had walked at 6:30 this morning for an hour?

Sunday 21 August 2005
Hotel George, Inveraray

And we walked for an hour again this morning following a route under the Castle, through a cemetery (St. Cuthbert's) and the length of a park full of flowers. We get our exercise but sometimes we stop to "smell the flowers". Every city is bedecked with them. To paraphrase Winston Churchill, we live in our surroundings and we become them. It's been an honor to be in a country where they take care of things.

At 10:00 a.m. we were at the doors of Dynamic Earth, a startling new science museum with all the interactive bells and whistles du jour. We were present at the Big Bang, we were on a volcano that exploded, we went through the various extinctions and started over with new species (at this point Bushies would have been apoplectic over the science); we went to the South Pole (a real iceberg) and a rain forest (real rain). We lay on the floor on our backs and watched a movie on the ceiling, then were funneled into the gift shop where we were curiously restrained, probably thinking of trying to close our suitcases.

In fact we raced home to do just that to beat the noon check-out and almost made it. Paul rejoined us and loaded the car, then took us back to Dynamic Earth to have lunch (their café was called The Food Chain) not out of lack of imagination but because the museum was on the Pipefest parade route. Pipefest was one of the main reasons we had scheduled Edinburgh when we had.

Every five years thousands of bagpipers from Pakistan to New Mexico descend on Edinburgh and parade through town. Today they were 10,000 strong. This was a stirring sight, to see all those kilts and pipes march by. We parked Mother on a low wall and went to stand right on the street to be closer to them and take pictures. With rare exception every band had old men, little children and every age in between, and women, too. The regalia and the noise were both energizing.

At 3:30 we met Paul at a preordained spot in front of Holyroodhouse Palace to leave town. DeJuana and I were interviewed by some famous radio personality who was broadcasting from a car next to ours. Then we were off to Inveraray.

After 48 bright, sunny, memorable hours in Edinburgh it rained on us all the way to Inveraray, a two-hour hour drive almost due west through and out beyond Glasgow. We are comfortably tucked in to the Hotel George, two well-restored 18th century buildings with no lift and no phones. Mother has just fed me some fruit and soon I shall further tuck myself under my comforter for a long sleep. I feel like I have been on my feet non-stop all weekend.

Monday 22 August 2005
Hotel George, Inveraray

As I stood in the hall at 6:30 this morning waiting for DeJuana, I stared at some lithographs of Scottish clan warriors in their various tartans and tried to think of another Western culture that had had historically its own unique way of dressing. A Scotsman kitted out is a grand and glorious thing but let's face it, strange strange strange. One has to go to the Eastern hemisphere to find such eccentric clothes.

The rain had abated and we had crisp, cool, clean air and bright sunshine all day. We drove down to the Mull of Kintyre ("mull" can be a peninsula, as it was in this case) through the usual spectacular scenery that skirted Loch Fyne. As we drove down the west coast of Kintyre we were on open sea across from Ireland save for a few islands, giving us a whole new range of scenery.

Our goal, Glenbarr Abbey and Macalister Clan Centre, was halfway down the peninsula in a nice old castle that was shabby on the inside. The Laird and Lady Glenbarr, heads of the McAllister clan (it's spelled 15 different ways) give the tours themselves. From the entrance hall wallpapered in the red McAllister tartan she gave us the tour of the museum rooms full of old family stuff. She was actually from Rhode Island, married the Laird 20 years ago dressed in their respective clan tartans after meeting him at a Scottish clan gathering and obviously bought into the clan and ancestry thing in a big way. I'm always suspicious of the underlying motives of someone who is consumed by her ancestry and even though we were in the heart of the McAllister Lands I couldn't get swept up into it.

We bore up through the minute descriptions of every little thing (I say "we" because I didn't run screaming out the door) although when we entered one oppressive, low-ceilinged room in which the Lady displayed her teddy bear, thimble and quilt collections Elliott said afterward she'd been afraid she was going to have to put me on life support.

At the end of the tour we wound up in the tea room/shop and bought a few trinkets from our Lady. I escaped to the outside air and drank it in. Later I voluntarily went back inside to see her Maine Coon cat, the only thing that could have lured me back into the place. The Lord and Lady lived in somewhat reduced rooms but the cat was attractive. As we left we thanked her graciously, waving and smiling until out of sight.

We retraced our steps back up the peninsula to Tarbert, a pretty little seaside town at the top of Kintyre. There we had a tail-gate picnic in a parking space facing the harbor – bananas, yogurt and cookies.

Our afternoon activity was to drive north to Kilmartin, a village in the heart of Celt-land. When the Irish Scoti tribe drifted over to present-day Scotland this was the area in which they landed. All over Kilmartin Glen ("glen" is valley) were standing stones older than Stonehenge and burial cairns dotting the emerald green fields. We walked out to some of the stones, then drove into Kilmartin proper and went to the kirk to see its famous graveyard of burial stones dating to the 13th century, many carved with Knights Templar on them Egyptian-style, face forward but feet sideways (the Renaissance was still some way off), and some with skull and crossbones for people dead of the plague. There was a little museum next door where we used the facilities before heading home.

Back in Inveraray it was only 4:00 so we went to Inveraray Castle, the ancestral seat of the Dukes of Argyll, heads of the Campbell clan. Paul bought our tickets but refused to go in because it was Campbell. We, on the other hand, went in and were bowled over by the beauty and wealth of the castle, in sad contrast to the poor old spavined McAllister seat. It made a beautiful end to a beautiful day, the latest in a week of them.

Poor darling Paul was legally committed to buying our dinner ("farewell dinner with guide") so we all dressed up a little including him in full clan regalia (he'd been in a kilt all week) and met in the hotel bar, then the dining room for a fun dinner – for us, anyway. Paul has had the facility to act like he's having fun while he may be secretly counting the hours until he's shed of us. We part tomorrow.

Tuesday 23 August 2005
Holiday Inn Express, Glasgow Airport

As I lay awake this morning waiting for it to be time to get up, I thought of my summer ending. In this cold climate it's hard to remember it's still summer in Texas, and probably 100 degrees. As all the faces of my summer reeled kaleidoscopically by, the faces of Port Aransas and now the faces of Scotland, I was grateful for the opportunity to know more than one place. We have been in villages so microscopic it is inconceivable to think what one would do in them, yet we're atavistically drawn to them, or maybe just literarily. Now we must return to our own lives after this brief sojourn into others.

In a cold rain we walked after breakfast next door to see the old Inveraray Jail, a prize-winning museum. Skipping the torture parts, we started out in a courtroom peopled with startlingly lifelike figures in the dock, in the jury box and at the counsel table. Voices emanated from them as first a cattle rustler then a lunatic murderer were sentenced. It was eerie, and impressive.

Then we toured the old cells and the new (1849) cells and tried to think of the men, women and children we weren't, the ones who had populated this jail. It would have had a definite deterrent effect if one ever got out of it and considered recidivism.

On the road again – it had rained on us every third day, approximately – we headed in the general direction of Glasgow, our end point, but we had the whole day ahead of us. We stopped in Helensburgh, a beautiful exurb of the city out on the Firth of Clyde, there to tour "Hill House", a house designed inside and out by Charles Rennie Macintosh, the famous Art Nouveau architect of the belle époque. When we found it we discovered it didn't open for another hour and a half, so we went into the business district and found a Chinese restaurant (my request).

Full of Chinese food, we returned to Hill House and spent 1 1/2 hours poring over every little aspect of it. Notwithstanding how we previously felt about Art Nouveau, the house was enchanting and intriguing. I told the other ladies that the serendipity of getting to see it resulted from their all having been late to breakfast and late to be ready to leave. With nothing to do but wait for them, I had read the Baedeker's and found Hill House for our days activity.

We drove on into Glasgow, which is an architectural jewel. There we left Elliott on George Square to cat around and get to the airport on her own. We ogled the architecture from the windows of the van, then sadly were taken to the airport by our dear Paul and dumped to overnight at the Holiday Inn Express with sweet farewells and promises to write. Paul was a jewel himself.

Thursday 25 August 2005
Quality Inn, Minneapolis Airport

We should have been in our own beds at home in San Antonio last night but alas, we didn't make it. Air traffic control problems made us miss a connection and we wound up here in Minneapolis at what was after midnight Scotland time, too tired to go on and with no connections. We're flying home this morning in dirty clothes. We have no idea where our bags are.

As I lay waiting for the alarm to go off at 4:00 this morning, I thought of all the Scottish clan names we'd been exposed to on this trip. It was a roll call of American names. America's greatest export is the dollar (and until the current Administration, hope), but these little countries, Scotland, Ireland and England, exported their people for all kinds of sad reasons and they built the U.S.A. for us. White Anglo-Saxons may be passé now and will inevitably lose their demographic hegemony to more fecund breeders but we can thank little empty Scotland for a hell of a lot of American social history. Moi included.

CANADA
MARCH 2006
INTRODUCTION

Mother has reached a point in life where she is more interested in ecotourism than she is the intellectual pursuit of ruins and old civilizations. She has not lost her intelligence; I believe it is of a piece with her advancing age, which makes one crave those looks forward into the cosmos and the very nature of Nature itself. The embrace of Nature is in the form of a long goodbye, a rejoining, a reacquaintance if perhaps one has lived amongst the concrete, and a marriage of convenience while one is still alive so that the bonds are in place when one gives up this life and rejoins it.

We have always chased around trying to see things before they are ruined—an indictment of contemporary life—and that is part of it, too, but the craving of Nature is atavistic and far beyond our poor powers to describe in the common words of a travel journal. So we set off, Mother and me, to go to Canada to see the baby harp seals out on their ice floes. There were elements of fashionable ecotourism, of female helplessness in the face of babies, and probably that deeper, older craving and drive toward Nature, that made us go. Trips are always fun, so that would have been part of it, too.

Mother all on her own called our precious guide from our Yellowstone trip a year ago, Scott Laursen, and invited him to join us in Canada. It was the same travel company, Natural Habitat Adventures, for which he had guided us to see the wolves of Yellowstone that we were using to see the baby harp seals. He jumped at the chance for a trip outside his realm, and joined us in Canada. He was suffering from a broken heart (he is 31) so we had plenty of time to talk about Life and Love and various processes with which he was only just now becoming acquainted, but at which Mother and I were old hands.

As you will see from the following pages, our trip was not a success and yet we still had the time together, Scott, Mother and I, and a shared experience which could have been more stimulating but which we rationalized so that we could still cherish it.

THE JOURNAL

Tuesday 7 March 2006
The Lord Nelson Hotel, Halifax, N.S.

Halifax is a city name rooted in my consciousness in several ways: North American colonial and revolutionary history; Howard Norman's books *The Bird Artist* and *The Museum Guard*; my Prague roommate Joadie's hometown; Michael Ondaatje's hometown; the Titanic customers' last resting place; the largest man-made explosion before 1945. I am in Halifax for the second time, for the second time with Mother. We are en route to Prince Edward Island whence we'll fly out to the ice floes of the Gulf of St. Lawrence to see up close the baby harp seals. This nice little Atlantic Maritimes city is pilon, an extra treat, the doorway to our adventure.

Wednesday 8 March 2006
The Inns on Great George
Charlottetown, Prince Edward Is.

Scott arrived late last night. Mother stayed up to greet him but he didn't get my hug until breakfast this morning. He was a sight for sore eyes, this special boy. I don't call him boy to insult him, only to transfigure him into the grandson of Mother he could be, or the son of mine he could be. In real life he's actually very much a man.

There were sixteen of us on the morning tour of Halifax which was a standard tour by bus except for the city guide, who was an incredible character. He talked funny and fast for almost five hours—"Silence" was not his middle name. He was extraordinarily silly but so smart, quick-witted and erudite we adored him. Even I who can take just so much yammering didn't rebel.

The highlights of the tour were the fortress, built high on a hill in the middle of town, and the Protestant graveyard where most of the Titanic victims who were recovered were laid to rest by the city that sent its people to retrieve their bodies from the icy sea in the days after the sinking. Uniform grey granite headstones fanned out in long lines forming the bow of a ship. Many only had the numbers the rescuers tagged the dead with upon finding them, their names lost to the ages.

We drove southwest down the coast to Peggy's Cove, a picturesque village built on scoured granite scraped clean by retreating glaciers at the end of the most recent Ice Age. We walked around outside in the raw cold for a few minutes, down to the wharf and over to the lighthouse, then retreated into the only gift shop/restaurant to make a desultory pass through the schlock shop before repairing to the dining room for a bowl of chowder.

Back toward the city we went to pick up some more of our group at a hotel near the airport. With the full complement of 22 guests and 2 staff we drove for four hours north to Prince Edward Island, crossing the 12 km. long bridge that has obviated the need to take a ferry, and just as well as the Gulf of St. Lawrence below the bridge was full of ice. It snowed on us some.

Here in Charlottetown we are in a delightful inn in the historic downtown, The Inns on Great George. Mother and Scott have gone to dinner with the group and I, as usual, am in my pajamas pen in hand and as usual, having a banana for dinner.

Thursday 9 March 2006

No one saw a seal today because the helicopters didn't fly. It snowed several inches in the night and there was still icy rain and fog offshore, so safety trumped excitement and anticipation and we all stayed home.

What to do with us all day?

First we got into our two vans and drove out to the edge of town to a farm where we had a sleigh ride. Four of us rode in one little sleigh and the rest in a big long sleigh.

We were taken through woods that were truly a 'wint'ry wonderland', the branches of the evergreens white lacy snow fans dipping down to us, real Christmas trees not dead flocked South Texas Christmas trees. It was magical.

Back at the barn the wimps stayed in the anteroom of the stable eating chocolate chip cookies and drinking hot chocolate while a serious multilateral snowball fight played out outside. We wandered into the stalls to admire the Percherons, the chickens, a mama sheep with twins and a lonesome looking calf. The owners' collie obviously liked company but had to be kept separated from the cookies. It was fun, and when we finally dragged ourselves away it was with warm effusions between us and our farm hosts.

Upon returning to the hotel, six of us walked a block and a half to a restaurant called Off Broadway for lunch. [Ironically, the last restaurant meal we shared with Scott a year ago was at a restaurant called Off Broadway in Jackson, Wyoming.] Without any plan, each person talked about her work and life and naturally as they came into focus each was smart and interesting.

After lunch we piled back into the vans to drive to the north shore of Prince Edward Island for a beach walk. This was no ordinary beach walk for us flatlanders. This beach was covered with snow and the water at its edge was frozen—not a bikini situation. We parked in a clearing and took a long boardwalk across the dunes to the beach, then walked some way down the beach, over to the water's edge, then back. It was beautiful and took some mental adjustment, being on a frozen beach.

Scott Laursen and Mother on P.E.I. beach

Back home the daily afternoon chocolate chip cookies had come out of the oven and the smell had permeated the lovely cozy lobby of our inn. We helplessly ate as few as possible and settled in for visiting for the remainder of the afternoon. Everyone has now gone down the street to dinner and I am blissfully upstairs alone in my jammies.

Friday 10 March 2006

Another day of no seals. It was snowing when we awoke, then rained ice, then snowed some more, cleared for a short time (i.e. no precip) then began to rain. It is raining as I write at 6:00 p.m. Scott, Mother and I are going to the movies; they are joining me in playing hooky from dinner.

Our morning activity consisted of a slide show of wildlife photography by Steve, the guide in charge of us. He's a rough looking fellow with lots of brains and heart, and he made an excellent presentation of his pictures and, without being too technical, how he made them. He was followed by a PEI museum curator who 'told stories' that were interesting without being riveting.

As soon as he finished, Scott, Mother and I suited up, put our Yak Traks on our boots and headed out into the icy slush and cold fresh air to rustle up some lunch. We walked three blocks with our umbrellas blowing inside out to a place called Rum Runners where Scott, our guest, treated us to a good lunch. It was the first time the three of us had been alone all week.

The afternoon consisted of the three of us seated before the gas fire in the lobby of our inn, reading. Reading and dozing. At 4:00 we went into a meeting room and listened to a handsome young man play the accordian and guitar and sing folk songs. All the ladies were hanging on his every word and move, moi included.

We lollygagged around the lobby until 6:30, then went in a taxi to the local 8-plex cinema to see "Eight Below." It was a kid-flick, really, but a heartrending animal story that left us all in tears, and pensive.

Saturday 11 March 2006
Inn on the Lake, Halifax

We all admitted to having continuing thoughts about the movie last night. In it 8 sled dogs are left chained in front of a scientific station in Antarctica over the winter, and survive. It's hard even to write about.

This was the last day of our trip and our day finally to see the seals. The first group left at 8:00 a.m. to go to the helicopter hanger. At 10:00 they were back; they'd suited up in survival gear, then never left the ground because the advance helicopter hadn't been able to find ice thick enough to land on. The seals were cancelled for the day, which meant we would leave Prince Edward Island without ever having seen them, or much else besides the inside of the inn for that matter.

I had awakened determined to get out of Charlottetown at any cost as soon as we got back from the seals. Our group was returning on the bus to Halifax after dinner tonight, which would have put us in bed around midnight before having to get up at 3:00 a.m. to catch an ungodly early flight tomorrow morning from Halifax airport. Before breakfast I put the hotel and the tour staff to work finding us a driver, which they did. Now with our seal flight cancelled we could leave. Our driver, an attractive young woman named Heidi, picked us up at 11:15 and we were at this airport hotel outside Halifax at 2:30 p.m.

The realization of what all we went through to get to Prince Edward Island in winter to see the seals, only to have our *raison* aborted, was a bitter one tempered only by our having had, Mother, Scott and me, some quality togetherness and a few low-key shared experiences. It wasn't worth it in the end, yet we were philosophical. Charlottetown is veddy veddy quiet; the movies only run at night, for instance. We would have been happier in Manhattan, or even Halifax for that matter, as we twiddled our thumbs for three days. We are sad about the seals but not unhappy, if that makes sense, and keep rationalizing a predicament that could have made us downright mad. But who to be mad at? Mother Nature? Global warming? I'm more worried about the seals than myself.

Sunday 12 March 2006
Halifax Airport

Scott, Mother and I had a farewell dinner in the nice restaurant of our hotel and finished up our trip together. We cried in the hall outside our rooms saying goodbye, and as long as I was crying I went ahead when I got into our room and cried over the dogs in the movie the night before. I hadn't really let myself cry in a satisfying way at the movies. That done, we went to bed and slept fast, getting up at 3:00 a.m. for a 6:15 flight back to Washington. We're at the gate, our bodies slightly in shock.

At 3:00 a.m. I was more upset about our unsuccessful trip than I had been yesterday. Travel requires so much effort, and to have it turn out to be virtually for naught is discouraging. I guess in a long career of traveling something has to go wrong. Oddly, two of the most boring trips we've ever made were both to Canada. I think I'll cross Canada off the list for awhile, although Mother wants to go see the polar bears this fall. I'd rather go to Mongolia, or Timbuctu, or Uganda, but she is my precious pal and her desires count for something. We'll see. In the meantime we are happy together, even when our trip falls apart.

LEBANON
DAMASCUS
SYRIA
SAFAD
JORDAN RIVER
GOLAN HEIGHTS
ACCO
CAPERNUM
HAIFA
TIBERIUS
SEA OF GALILEE
NAZARETH
CAESAREA
JORDAN RIVER
MEDITERRANEAN SEA
WEST BANK
TEL AVIV JAFFA
AMMAN
JERUSALEM
BETHLEHEM
QUMRAN
DEAD SEA
GAZA STRIP
MASADA
ISRAEL
JORDAN
SINAI (EGYPT)
PETRA
WADI RUM
EILAT
GULF OF AQABA
AQABA

JORDAN AND ISRAEL
MAY 2006
INTRODUCTION

Several years ago I signed up to go to Israel with two well-known religious leaders from my home city of San Antonio, Rabbi Sam Stahl, head of the main Reform synagogue, and Reverend Buckner Fanning, a Baptist preacher known not just to his parishioners but to the whole city for his attractive TV spots on various life subjects. That trip never happened due to the start of the intifada.

Years went by, years of suicide bombings that discouraged tourism in Israel. Finally in 2005 a tentative peace descended and our trip was on for May 2006. Buckner's son Mike Fanning put it together. I invited my good friend DeJuana Jones to go with me and, trooper that she is, she accepted with alacrity. Mike helped us make the plan to go to Petra in Jordan before the start of the Israel trip; we subsequently met the Israel group in Tel Aviv after that pre-trip excursion.

Two weeks before leaving the country I sent a message to Mike asking for a list of people who were going to be on the trip. When he sent it there were 65 names on it! In spite of that large number, the trip was beautifully organized and went like clockwork. We all finally found our places on the buses and identified some pals to commune with. DeJuana was a kind and patient roommate as always.

In retrospect we look back on the trip as if it happened during a dream, a narrow window of opportunity before Hezbollah started lobbing missiles into many of the places we visited. The normalcy we observed was ephemeral. I was reminded once again, as I am every time I stand before the ruins of some great civilization, of the impermanence of material things that at the time seemed so durable.

I was the only "unchurched" member of our group. However, I could not help but honor the ancient lands we saw in spite of the quasi-religious nature of the tour. None of what we saw would exist without the eternal push and pull of the various religions that have a claim to the land. On the other hand their troubles and those of much of the world would not exist but for the unbending certainties of the various competing religions. Not participating in such arguments, I can only wonder at the madness of them, and hope the angry competitors don't someday fall out of the ring and land in my innocent lap.

THE JOURNAL

Sunday 7 May 2006
Taybet Zaman, Taybet
Wadi Mousa, Jordan

There were moments two days ago when I wondered if we would ever be on our way—one hour on the runway at National, another hour of mechanical problems in Newark, so we were actually grateful to lift off and begin our ten-hour overnight flight to Tel Aviv, following which we were even more grateful to have it over. Am I growing less tolerant of travel?

We landed at Ben Gurion Airport on Shabat, Saturday morning, the Sabbath, and it was quiet. An earnestly officious young man with a security badge met us with a sign with our names on it and whisked us through Immigration, baggage, customs and up to the limousine counter. I thought, wow, for a security-conscious place like this, they sure are loosey-goosey about letting guides penetrate the pre-Immigration inner sanctums, but it turned out he was an airport employee and not our guide at all. He handed us off to a van driver and disappeared.

We had five hours to kill. The van dropped us in Tel Aviv proper at a hotel on the beach. The concierge et. al. had been alerted to our arrival and took our bags into their care so we could walk the beach boardwalk and get some lunch. They said, be sure to see the Israeli folk dancing down below the hotel; it only happens on Saturday.

It was clear, sunny and windy, and not too hot. The beach was covered with brightly colored umbrellas and bathers, and beyond the breakwaters were flotillas of sailboats in the turquoise Mediterranean. We were dressed in our city/airplane clothes but it quickly became apparent we could have had on tutus and fit right in, because as we stood in the crowd on the wide pavilion under the hotel and watched the dancing, it began to penetrate that this was one of the most crazily dressed collections of people we knew we had ever seen.

The dancers were the bystanders; it was nothing formal in costume. Loud Israeli folk music came over a p.a. system and whoever wanted to came out of the crowd and did the steps in loose formation with the others. There were probably 100 people dancing on a pavilion about 150'x100'. Those 100 people, all sizes and shapes, and frankly everyone else we saw for the next couple of hours, had on the wildest, craziest, damnedest concatenation of clothing imaginable; it was Hieronymus Bosch meets Miami Beach. It looked like someone had set a bomb under a K-Mart and on whomever the clothes fell, that's what they wore.

We wandered up the paved walkway on the city side of the beach and found a nice restaurant serving at tables under umbrellas. In the cool breeze we ate and watched the people walk by, staring at them like hicks at a county fair. It was another planet, this Israel.

After lunch we went back up to the hotel and were picked up along with our luggage by another van. It took us to Sve Dov, the domestic airport, to fly to Eilat on the far southernmost tip of Israel on the Gulf of Aqaba, a finger of the Red Sea. The van driver was charming and managed to get us around barriers and up to the tiny terminal. This airport was on the beach right in the city.

And this airport wasn't loosey-goosey at all. The first thing we were asked was, do you have any weapons? We laughed, because it came out of left field. They x-rayed our luggage on the way in and we went up to the ticket counter to get our boarding passes. No, they said, Security first. Well, this Security grilled us like their lives actually depended on it. They separated us so we wouldn't prompt each other, then wanted to know how we knew each other, why did I have a Libyan stamp in my passport, whom did we know in Israel and had the bags been out of our hands at all. Oops. We said truthfully they had, so we had to open them and pore through them to make sure no one had slipped anything in them. The minutes were ticking away. Finally they stamped everything and we were on our way—all this to get on a small prop plane to fly 50 minutes to a dive resort.

We flew south and slightly east over the Negev Desert to Eilat. At another tiny airport right in the middle of town we were picked up and whisked two minutes to our hotel on the water. It had taken 25 hours to get from Washington to Eilat, and when our little heads hit their pillows it was for the first time in 30 hours.

Eleven hours of sleep later, we were ready to hunt bear with a switch.

We were picked up at 7:45 this morning and driven five minutes to the Jordanian border. There a smart, energetic young man took us in hand, walked us through the exit-Israel-enter-Jordan process in a flock of other tourists and got us all the way to the high fence at the DMZ, lined with mines on either side. We pushed our own luggage cart the 900 metres to the other side, where our guide, Mohammed, met us in the Hashemite Kingdom of Jordan. We were off in a roundabout way to Petra.

Since no one else had signed up for our trip, we had the guide and Ali, the driver, to ourselves in a taxi, not a van. First they drove us into Aqaba, the Jordanian resort town that mirrors Eilat and shares its bay at the northern tip of the Gulf of Aqaba. We did a little city tour, then headed into the desert.

After 20 or 30 minutes we veered off the highway and into Wadi Rum, the largest wadi in Jordan. (Does everyone remember what a wadi is? A dry riverbed. Wadis can be great valleys or little dry stream courses.) After some miles we went off-road and onto the flat hard sand, quickly coming to a Bedouin tourist encampment of small tents and large dining enclosures draped in heavy rug-like material. There we transferred into a 4-wheel drive truck with a grizzled old driver who let the air out of his tires with his ignition key, the better to drive on soft sand. He took us out into the dunes for an up close look at the glorious drip castle sandstone mountains separated by peachy sand and vistas muted by eternally dusty air. It was beautiful but we had already seen it: in "Lawrence of Arabia," filmed in Wadi Rum.

Lunch back in the Bedouin encampment—salads and roast chicken with rice—also eternal in this part of the world. The heat was increasing and we were in desultory, lethargic mode.

We backtracked out of Wadi Rum (if we'd kept going in our original direction we would have shortly come to Saudi Arabia, where we girls aren't welcome) to the superhighway, "The Desert Highway," we'd started on, and didn't have to do much rubbernecking once out of the famous wadi. Another 30 minutes or so brought us to the turnoff for Petra; the landscape changed and the altitude increased. We were now on "The King's Highway."

Our hotel, this hotel where I write, is 12 km. this side of Petra in Wadi Mousa, which is Arabic for Moses. Moses smote a rock and caused water to flow; that spring is at Petra. These old boys didn't know from national boundaries, but were all over the desert and perhaps understandably: it's not easy to find a comfortable place to light in these parts.

But we did. We are in a hotel that is a restored village, and an excellent restoration that people apparently come to see even if they aren't staying here. It grows organically down a hillside with a not-historic swimming pool at the base of the stone cottages. Narrow cobbled walkways separate the various buildings, and flowers in pots and beds enliven the good-looking old stone structures. We are in a huge room with two stone arches, two tiny windows and not very good air conditioning.

Mohammed the guide waited for us to check in to see if we wanted to go on into Petra but we took one look at this place and said, see you tomorrow. We lay by the pool for two hours just talking. I told DeJuana I hadn't done "nothing" for two hours in recorded memory. It was heavenly. I jumped in the pool and nearly had a heart attack, it was so cold, but I made myself persist and swim laps. Then we just kept lying there talking.

I've been home in my night clothes ever since, writing. DeJuana went to the Turkish bath and had steam and a massage, then returned trailed by room service with a tray of vegetables and flan for our supper. I'm about 'give out'; tomorrow we go to Petra which from what I understand is serious work.

Monday 8 May 2006
Dan Panorama Hotel, Eilat

Mohammed the guide picked us up this morning at 8:00 a.m. without Ali, the driver. We drove the 12 km. into the town of Wadi Mousa where the Petra ruins are, so the government is changing the name of the town to "Petra" to keep confusion at bay. We left the car on the street and walked into the service area at the entrance to Petra. There we bought tickets and had a last pit stop before starting into the funnel that is the staggeringly dramatic entrance to the ruins. First there was a wide flat sloping walkway along which one could hire a horse or a horse-drawn buggy to take one to the ruins. We wanted to walk.

For 1200 metres we walked down down down a narrow gorge, the Siq, into a state of enchantment between vaulting 300-foot high cliff walls of vividly striated sandstone—walls so close together as to allow sunlight to penetrate only barely. The great cliffs were striped vertically, then horizontally, then wavy, then in a drip pattern. At some point we were actually walking on original paving stones. If there had been nothing at the end of this walk, it would have been worth the trouble of getting there just to see this gorge. At times I was reminded of the intimate side canyons of Lake Powell, and by the colors of the Grand Canyon, but like all the great places this was sui generis and just plain awesome.

Petra as it turns out is one big necropolis, and we began to see the tombs even in the gorge, artfully cut out of the countless caves in the soft sandstone. Sandstone turns Mother Nature into a sculptress, and the Nabatean founders of Petra and their descendents followed suit and improved on the cliffs, buttes, boulders and mountains by planting their civilization right into the rock. The eye would be lured to the rock only to be jump-started by the realization that art was there, not just geology. It was a happy confluence of the natural and the man-made, both beautiful and each adding to the other.

After the Siq debouched us onto the site, the first grand thing to see was "The Treasury", so named by the locals who couldn't imagine anything else in so gorgeous a structure but which was apparently yet another tomb, only the biggest and best tomb on the site. From there we walked a couple of miles, going ever downward, to the far end of the city, gawking and photographing (although no lens in my repertoire could do it justice) and listening to Mohammed.

At the end of the ruins we plunked ourselves down in an outdoor cafe to rest for a few minutes and contemplate our future, which included a 4 km. walk back uphill in the now hot mid-day sun by two old ladies who had just hiked for two hours. We hired three donkeys without shame to take us back up to the beginning, to the Treasury, and there hired a horse and buggy to drag us up the gorge. I made the animal tenders only walk the animals, as I could not be a party to adding to the burden of our beasts of burden. Other than that I hadn't a moral qualm about using the animals to get me out of there, and discovered that having them worry about their footing obviated my having to worry about mine, enabling me to crane my neck and see everything again, in a different light and uninterrupted.

DeJuana riding a donkey out of Petra

At the top and back into modern life, we shopped a little and had a lunch of grilled meat, french fries and salads. I was tired and dehydrated and needed the food. We pondered what to do with the rest of the afternoon and settled on...nothing. We went to a bank to use the ATM, which turned into a mini-adventure when it ate DeJuana's credit card twice. Then we went to Mohammed's house to meet his wife and see his four adorable doe-eyed playful little children (turns out Mohammed was only 35 although he looked more experienced). We goofed around with them until Ali, our original driver, appeared to take us back to Aqaba, a two-hour drive back through the beautiful dusty desert. And then, strangely, it rained on us! About six drops...

At the border Mohammed took us and our cart of luggage as far as he could, then launched us into the DMZ for the reverse trip of 900 m. back to Israel. As we walked toward the Israeli side I had the fleeting sense of heading to safety although in reality the Jordanians had been much more welcoming than the Israelis. The Israelis gave us the usual third degree, polite but firm, and we gave them the usual jolly answers, our eye on the prize of our taxi waiting on the far curb to take us back to this hotel in Eilat where we started out a mere two nights ago.

We loved Jordan and the magnificent dead city of Petra, and our experiences there, but we were glad to get into a cool clean hotel room and wash the dust off.

Tuesday 9 May 2006
Carlton Hotel, Tel Aviv

I didn't sleep well. I had a nightmare wherein everyone at the San Antonio Country Club was trying to kill me. When they ganged up on Air Force One to kill me, I gave up and got up. I've had Republican nightmares before, but usually I'm awake.

We didn't have quite the deadline pressures of the last few mornings so we slept until six-whole-o'clock. Breakfast at 7:00 (in addition to eggs they served spaghetti with mushrooms, and cauliflower. I should've just eaten a plate of cauliflower; instead I stuck to the eggs, a slave to acculturation). At 8:15 we went in a taxi to Dolphin Reef to swim with the dolphins.

Eilat is a seaside resort like Aqaba in Jordan and Sharm-el-Sheik in Egypt, and like them is a destination for divers. Dolphin Reef was a commercial place on the beach just south of town where dolphins lived in the ocean in a deep hole just offshore enclosed by heavy rope-like netting. People came there to snorkel, dive and sit on the beach. It had a shop and an open-air food service, and lots of tan young Israelis walking around in shorty wetsuits to help us tourists. Also there were a lot of cats around, and I was momentarily unfaithful to Beezie as my cat-hungry hands reached out to pet them.

We put on wetsuits and walked out into chest-deep water to put on our fins, masks and snorkels. That was the moment I discovered DeJuana had never snorkled. It took her a few minutes to calm down enough to put her face in the water; I took her hand and we swam with the dolphins, who came up under us to check us out. DeJuana was touched by one of them.

The whole experience didn't last long enough. Afterward we relaxed under the bougainvillea with the cats for a few minutes, then taxied back to the hotel to dress, close our suitcases and check out.

We parked the luggage with the concierge and went out to find some lunch. We didn't get 50 feet from the hotel before we found ourselves in front of the "Santa Fe Grill" advertising Mexican food. We veered in, had a margarita, a chicken burrito and chicken fajitas and decided that swimming with the dolphins and eating Mexican food all in one day was at least one idea of heaven.

Back to the little Eilat airport where we were once again separated and grilled. We lied and said the suitcases had been in our possession at all times. They asked such personal questions it was hard not to get indignant, and to start thinking maybe you had done something wrong. Back on the little high-winged twin engine prop plane (an ATR; I asked), and in 50 minutes we landed back at the Tel Aviv in-town airport, Sve Dov. Whoever was going to pick us up didn't, so we got in a cab and came in to this hotel on the beach. As I write, the San Antonio contingent is probably checking in downstairs after flying for two days. We are smug because we are over our jet lag and acclimated. Tomorrow we tackle Israel and the logistics of traveling with 60 other people. It should be interesting.

Wednesday 10 May 2006
Gai Beach Hotel, Tiberias

The 60 people started coming into focus at breakfast. Some of them, a handful, I already knew. The rest were sweet and friendly all day, and by the end of the day we'd figured out who some more of them were. Unfortunately, the Rev. Buckner Fanning was not among them, having had a family health crisis he could not leave. This was a big disappointment to everyone. Mike Fanning, also an ordained minister, stood in for him.

We traveled in two buses. DeJuana and I got on the bus with Mike Fanning and Ruben, one of the two Israeli guides. By the time we got out of Tel Aviv I was pretty sure I'd made a mistake coming on this trip because I was already so bored. It turned out it was Ruben who was boring, talking down to us and repeating himself. DeJuana and I were rolling our eyes at each other. Also, he stood right in front of us to talk so we couldn't see forward. At the first stop, Caesarea, the other, lead guide asked me why I looked so unhappy and I told him I was bored because of Ruben. Lynn Stahl, Rabbi Sam's wife, also had a word with the lead guide. Unfortunately none of it had a good effect on Ruben, but the next time we were in the bus and he stood up to say something, I said I wish you would sit down to talk, and Mike Fanning in order to keep the peace waved me over to sit with him. He and I then talked for the rest of the day, and my attitude improved. It also improved every time Sam Stahl opened his mouth at the various sites because he was a no bullshit intellectual.

The sites themselves:

North of Tel Aviv right on the Mediterranean was Caesarea, built by King Herod. Already excavated were a theatre, hippodrome and palace. I didn't get too hopped up about this ancient city because it was so inconsequential compared to the Roman cities I had seen last year in Libya, and I wondered fleetingly if I were becoming too jaded to waste more money traveling.

The day was bright, breezy and right on the cusp between warm and cool—glorious, in a word. As the waves crashed on the rocks below the ruins I thought, that at least is always a thrill, the sea crashing on rocks.

On the same site with Caesarea were the remains of a Crusader castle. I got big into Crusader history after September 11th and had been wanting to see Crusader sites, so I responded to this. Just above Caesarea we disembarked to admire a stunning aqueduct that ran off to the horizon as far as the eye could see. This was the aqueduct that brought water to Caesarea. As a San Antonian who grew up with an ancient aqueduct, I'm nuts about aqueducts, and this one was pretty grand.

Sam Stahl lecturing at Caesarea

Next we drove farther north up the coast toward Haifa, which we skirted by turning East and inland before returning to the coast to Acco (Acre), the "capital" of the Crusaders' kingdom. After lunch in a tourist place we drove to a point of land surrounded by the crashing Mediterranean to delve into the ruins of a magnificent Crusader castle with an Ottoman Turkish community built on top of it. The great hall of the castle, now well below the level of the street, had mighty columns that became the vaulting of the stone ceiling. Gothic was flexing its muscles in the pointed arches of this huge old refectory.

We left the water behind and drove east to Sepphoris, just on the next hill from Nazareth. Sepphoris had a Roman theatre and a temple built during the lifetime of Jesus, a Roman house with beautiful mosaics as well as other mosaics in the rest of the extensive dig, and an underground aqueduct.

That was our last stop. We are now in Tiberias, 600 feet below sea level, the Sea of Galilee just outside our lovely resort hotel.

Thursday 11 May 2006

I'm a happy camper again. We had fun today and I did not have a negative reaction to every little thing, partly because we changed buses and got the other guide, Danny. And this evening, like a sign, a pair of hoopoe birds landed at my feet as I walked to the hotel beach to take a ritual swim in the Sea of Galilee.

As a secular humanist I have to take some of what is said on this trip with a grain of salt, but I knew that was going to happen and I had psychologically prepared myself. I don't really care if other people believe in God or Jesus or Maimonides or Buddha or whomever, so I'm always flummoxed when they care that I don't. So to keep the peace I have kept my lips zipped.

This morning we boarded a replica Sea of Galilee boat (it looked like an Arabian dhow) to chug across the lake (the Sea of Galilee is actually a lake). One of the deckhands ran the American flag up the yardarm and suddenly we were all on our feet, singing our national anthem to piped-music accompaniment. Singing the national anthem in a large group is one of the few times I have a visceral emotional response to something symbolic, and even though I was mildly embarrassed at the chauvinism, I wallowed in the heartstring tugging. Then of course I wanted to cry because I am so worried about my country, but that is another story.

The day was once again bright and beautiful, though warmer. We spent 45 minutes crossing the lake from southwest to northwest, then disembarked at a dock belonging to a big kibbutz. At the land end of the dock there was a museum built around a 2000-year-old wooden boat found in the mud and painstakingly restored. It dated from the 1st century C.E. and could have been the type of boat used by Jesus and his fisherman-disciples.

And indeed most everywhere we went today was Jesus Land: his Sea of Galilee, his second home of Capernum, his Sermon on the Mount mountain, his loaves-and-fishes town.

Safad was our major Jewish excursion, a medieval hilltop town made sacred by the influx of scholars who fled the Spanish Inquisition, and by the former presence of the writer of the Kabbalah, the great mystical text of Judaism. The many synagogues faced narrow lanes with stone arches and pavers, and everywhere blue paint had been applied that apparently fooled the devil. There were many art studios interspersed, adding to the otherworldly effect.

We stopped for lunch at a big tourist place, then went to Capernum where Jesus lived in adulthood and fomented his revolution. There we saw an old church, an old synagogue and a dig. No one knows for sure what any of this stuff is but one place was supposed to be Peter's mother-in-law's house. I don't mean to sound anti-intellectual but even the believers don't know for certain.

We wound around to the east side of the lake and with the Golan Heights above us on the left and the lake down on our right made our way south to the other end, crossing the Jordan River where it entered the lake at the north end and again when it exited at the south end. There we got out so those who wanted to dip their toes in the historic river could do so. No one did the full immersion thing. Then it was home in time to swim and enjoy an unpressured evening.

Friday 12 May 2006
David Citadel Hotel, Jerusalem

We left our resort hotel this morning and started zigzagging above, around and through the Jezreel Valley, a huge plain that extends from the Mediterranean Sea to the Jordan River and the only way in many respects to get from Judea to Samaria, from Egypt to Babylon, from Caesarea to Damascus—in other words, a valley steeped in blood and history.

Without stopping, we drove through the modern town of Cana on our way to Nazareth. In Nazareth we got out to take a picture of the town from a scenic turnout, there being nothing Biblical left to see down in the town itself.

The next stop was the tell at Megiddo. This archeological site had 27 layers and looked out over the Jezreel plain. It gave its name to a phenomenon we all hope to avoid, Armegeddon, and it offered up its secrets to James Michener, who fictionalized it in The Source. We climbed to the top of the tell and tried to imagine the 27 ages of the dirt and rocks before us.

At another site we all disembarked (this is a project in itself) and walked down a lane lined with bougainvillea so laden with flowers they sagged over our heads—the flowers everywhere have been spectacular: oleanders so covered with blooms you can't see their leaves, and jacaranda trees that are solid purple with flowers, not to mention wild flowers galore—to see a spring coming out of the base of a mountain where Gideon beat the Midianites, Gideon being the one of hotel Bible fame.

Speaking of things in nature, I saw several white storks soaring today.

Before we passed out from hunger we arrived at Beth Shan, which turned out to be the most extensive dig we'd seen so far, with a large amphitheatre, baths, columns and paved avenues. It was one of the oldest cities in Palestine but the part we tromped around was Roman. We didn't tromp until after we'd had a kind of sorry lunch in the snack bar of the National Park created around the tell, and it was hot, so our contemplation of an otherwise fascinating old city was sun struck and slightly lethargic.

Perhaps the most interesting part of the day was yet to come. If you refer back to the map you will see that a large part of Israel is the "West Bank", i.e. land west of the Jordan River. Israel didn't start out owning this land; it won it in the 1967 war. Now all over the West Bank is thriving agriculture in the reclaimed desert, punctuated by unkempt Palestinian villages and orderly settlements of Israelis. This may be the most controversial real estate on Earth, and we drove pretty much the length of it for two hours, north to south, hugging the Jordan River on our left, Jordan itself just beyond. All along the highway was a fence, a formidable double fence with mines between the two to keep people out. It was our first sight of the fortifications Israel has had to erect around itself to keep its neighbors from annihilating it, and we followed those fortifications all the way to Jerusalem, itself a 1967 acquisition.

On the outskirts of Jerusalem I saw a deer-like animal back in the trees and thought, with all the carrying-on going on around him, this guy has got to be getting lonely.

Just outside Jerusalem we drove to a scenic high point on the edge of the campus of Hebrew University and had a little "mazel tov" ceremony to celebrate reaching the famous city as we looked down on it.

As soon as we could get unloaded at the hotel, we went immediately to the Western Wall, formerly the Wailing Wall, entering the Old City through the Dung Gate. The point was to see the Wall as Shabat started at dusk. Women were praying on one side of a divider and men, more exotic than the women with their side curls, satin coats and generally pious airs, on the other. The great plaza out from the Wall was nicely full of people. We wandered in close to the Wall, then respectfully backed out so as not to turn our backs to it. In 20 minutes we were heading back to the bus. I thought of the 2000 years when the Jews were separated from their Wall and how very serious they must be now to keep from ever losing it again.

We are now bedded down in our fancy hotel where we will be for five whole nights. We're glad to be in such a nice nest for such a length of time.

Saturday 13 May 2006

I got loose by myself today, and it was fun.

Fifteen of us went with Lynn and Sam next door to Hebrew Union College for Shabat services at 9:00 a.m. [The Christians went with Mike to the Garden of Gethsemane for a service there.] They finally got started around 9:45 (I was reading my book sitting on the back row by myself) and after a few songs I slipped out and walked to the Jaffa Gate, the gate into the Old City nearest our hotel. It was hot and a bit of a climb to the gate so I flagged down a workman who gave me a ride up in his truck.

At the top I went to a money changer to get rid of my Jordanian dinars, then wandered across the lane to a shop with intriguing things in the window and bought four gifts, all substantially reduced in price by my excellent bargaining to what I'm sure were their actual prices. I probably left money on the table for that matter. I could've wandered all day but I dutifully went back to the hotel so as not to miss the post-services activities. I checked my e-mail and read my book (*Eichmann in Jerusalem* by Hannah Arendt) until everyone gathered and we took off by bus first to a large kibbutz on the southern edge of Jerusalem where we were fed lunch in their incredibly efficient tourist food service, following which we drove a few minutes farther south to Bethlehem.

Bethlehem is in Palestinian territory so on the edge of the town we switched into a Palestinian bus with a Palestinian guide and were taken to the Church of the Nativity, the place the Emperor Constantine's mother in the 4th century decided was where Baby Jesus was born. For want of a better idea that is where Christians celebrate the birth of their savior. We went into the church, said to be the oldest in the world, and down into the cave below to see the exact spot of the birth. In the cave we sang two Christmas carols, "Silent Night" and "O Little Town of Bethlehem."

Before we left the town of Bethlehem we were taken to an extensive souvenir store owned by a Palestinian Christian family Mike knew, and because it was for all practical purposes the first time we'd been turned loose in a store, a lot of pent up shopping took place. I even got into the spirit and spent a few bucks, both there and with the vendors on the street. We were positively giddy when we got back to the bus, which then left us off next to The Wall, the new security wall being built by the Israelis between them and the Palestinians. We had to walk a length of it to get out, and remarked on all the anti-Israeli graffiti painted on it ("Build Bridges Not Walls"; "Down With Apartheid"). On the other, Israeli side was a huge incongruous poster that could be seen through the barbed wire saying "Peace Be Unto You—Israeli Ministry of Tourism."

I thought this trip would clear my head about things political in this part of the world but I'm more confused than ever.

Palestinian side of Israeli wall, Bethlehem

Sunday 14 May 2006

We left the hotel at 8:00 a.m. for a day trip outside of Jerusalem, driving east. When we hit the Dead Sea we turned south, heading for Masada through the fearsome denuded utterly dry mountains of the Judean desert that still, here and there, people persisted in living in.

Masada, built by King Herod sometime between 37 and 4 B.C.E. (his reign), was a rugged natural fortress by virtue of being on top of a very high flat-topped mountain. This was the place where the Jewish defenders killed themselves after a three year siege by the Romans when the Romans finally breached the walls. Masada is a symbol of the old Israeli kingdom and is a symbol now of the determination of present-day Israel, too, to keep its enemies at bay.

At Masada there was a visitors' center and a cable car to take us to the top. At the top because of the heat there were intermittent areas of shade and big containers of water all over the extensive site that covered the table rock mountain. It was so hot and our group was so slow that I resorted to walking around it by myself, which enabled me to savour it without benefit of company and lollygagging. I took the cable car back down and read in the shade while I waited for the group to descend.

We backtracked up the Dead Sea some miles to Qumran, the site of the discovery of the Dead Sea Scrolls and now an archeological dig of the "monastery" of the Essenes [they think] who wrote and cadged away the scrolls. There we had lunch in their kind of shabby tourist facility-cum-shop, and everyone bought skin products made from Dead Sea minerals. I read in the shade.

Last stop was a public beach on the Dead Sea with a tacky pavilion where one could buy drinks, and dressing rooms for those who wanted to swim in the Dead Sea. This did not include DeJuana and me. We sat in the shade and read our books until we got too distracted by the passing parade of humanity in its bathing suits. It was not a pretty sight, but riveting nonetheless, like a car wreck.

Back in our cool, clean, fancy hotel room in Jerusalem we couldn't get in the shower fast enough.

Monday 15 May 2006

We had a long fascinating day of sightseeing in Jerusalem proper today. At 7:30 this morning we went back to the Western Wall, to see it again secondarily but primarily to traverse the Hasmonean [they think] tunnel that runs its length, some 1200 metres, several metres and several centuries below the present surface of the Earth. I usually get the heebie-jeebies in tunnels but this was manageable, and magnificent.

We came out into the sunlight at the Monastery of the Flagellation, the place that commemorates stations one and two of the Cross. From there we puttered along the Via Dolorosa, passing other stations (one at Our Lady of the Spasm—you can't make up names like this) until we arrived at the Church of the Holy Sepulchre, where the last six stations were and which housed under its dome the reputed tomb of Jesus. Every Christian sect had a piece of this church and a spiritual piece of Jesus they jealously protected.

There was a little shopping in the canopied lanes while some of us sat in a sidewalk cafe and shot the breeze. Then we exited the Old City via the Jaffa Gate and got back on our buses.

Next stop was the Israel Museum to see the Shrine of the Book, the stunningly original structures(s) that house the Dead Sea Scrolls. One side of this shrine was a round white ribbed tile building in the shape of a jar lid (not a Mason jar, an old pottery jar) and the other was a black rectangular box. Sprinklers shot up to bathe the white side, while the black (evil) side was left to bake in the sun. The display of the scrolls was underground under these structures in a cave-like setting. These people have a way of making their architecture speak.

At the Knesset we had a little lesson on the menorah in a garden that had a large bronze one as its centerpiece. It was close to 1:00 and I was having trouble thinking about anything but food.

Lunch we had at Yad VaShem, the Holocaust Museum, in its cafeteria. The new museum, opened only last year, was a fabulous hunk of architecture of glass and concrete and angles that again spoke to its uses. It fed the visitor through exhibits in chronological fashion like the one in Washington does, and like that one it was an agonizing process to study once more the downward spiral of civilization as the Jews were forsaken. I gave it its due and shed my tears but I knew the story, knew more than I ever wanted to know. No amount of discomfort on my part was going to equal a fraction of the squalid discomfort of European Jewry c. 1933-1945 so my respect kept a healthy check on my impatience with the repetition. Needless to say it needs to be repeated ad infinitum "lest we forget".

The last room was labeled "The Names." It was a rotunda with large photos spiraling to the pinnacle and with a deep hole in the middle and volume upon volume of books filled with names of all the victims of the Holocaust around the walls. I lost it a little bit in there.

At the end of the main museum, of which there was only one way in and one way out, we entered the separate Hall of Remembrance where Sam did a reading with responses from us. Then we went into the Children's Memorial, which was breathtaking as well as heartbreaking. The interior was an octagonal room with high ceilings and mirrored walls. In the middle was a glassed, mirrored tower with five candles stairstepped up inside it. The reflection of these five candles reverberated off the mirrored walls and off the reflections of each other until the impression was that of 1.5 million stars, one for each child lost. It was magical, and terrible. Our hearts ached.

Ruben the stupid guide didn't make matters any better by gathering us for an emotional (as if we weren't already) lecture that resulted in his claim that the Jews' faith in God had gotten them through their ordeal. I raised my hand at the back of the circle and said, "Where WAS God? He obviously wasn't in there," gesturing back at the museum. Sam neutralized the situation with a quote from the late William Sloan Coffin to the effect that God provides small protection but large support.

I wanted a drink when we got home, but had a hot bath instead.

Tuesday 16 May 2006

We had a free day today. This is the way we spent it:

8:55 a.m. — American Express office, which opens at 9:00, to get some money.

9:10 a.m. — American Express bank employee finally arrives at his job.

9:30 a.m. — Flush, we burst out onto the street, jump in a cab and go on a roller coaster trip through the narrow lanes of the Old City to the Dung Gate.

9:45 a.m. — Pass through Palestinian security to enter the Temple Mount, which we do by following an elevated covered wooden walkway that ascends to the precincts of the El Aqsa Mosque and the Dome of the Rock, the huge collection of blue mosaics topped by the gold dome that is the iconic center of Jerusalem.

We cannot go into these places since Ariel Sharon tried to enter in 2000, gumming up the works for everyone including setting off the intifada, but we hire a sweet little Palestinian guide who walks us around the vast plazas connecting the two great buildings, telling us stuff I already know from the guide book. His fee: 40 shekels for 15 minutes—we give him 50 because no one has change, and after 15 minutes of flowery talk and pledges of friendship he is off like a shot the minute he gets the money.

10:05 a.m. — We leave the Temple Mount and exit the Old City through St. Stephen's Gate. We cross the street to the Garden of Gethsemane, so small and with olive trees as old as time, walk into the Church of the Nations, climb a hill to the Greek Orthodox Church, come back down to Mary's Tomb [they think] and collapse into a taxi that takes us to the Herod's Gate entrance back into the Old City. I possess a map and am the navigator. I want to walk in the Muslim Quarter, and Herod's Gate is a good entrance.

11:30 a.m. — We wander all over the Muslim Quarter, where we have no competition from other tourists, and back onto the Via Dolorosa. Eventually we run into some people from our group and we return to the same cafe where we rested the day before. We all have something to drink and DeJuana and I eat a granola bar. When we part, we go into a buying frenzy. I want everything that is not nailed down, partly because the shopkeepers are so charming and so desperate. The intifada has hurt them.

1:10 p.m. — We reach the Jaffa Gate and go into the shop where I bought gifts on Saturday. DeJuana wants some things and I wind up with yet another souvenir.

1:30 p.m. — We walk home to the hotel and collapse, having been on our feet for five hours experiencing the Jerusalem Stairmaster.

2:00 p.m. — We get up and walk three blocks (uphill of course; everything is uphill) to a fine new Israeli restaurant recommended by the concierge to have a real meal and a bottle of wine. It's my first real food since leaving Washington. We picnic in our room every night.

5:00 p.m. — On the way back to the hotel I buy a painting we had picked out on the way to lunch. They will ship it.

5:30 p.m. — We are home to clean up and pack. It is the end of the trip. After yesterday and today, we are madly in love with Jerusalem.

Thursday 18 May 2006
On the way home

Yesterday morning we reluctantly checked out of our luxurious David Citadel Hotel and began in a roundabout way our homeward journey. Before leaving the city limits we made a brief pilgrimage to a dig Mike had worked on in his youth of a burial site from the time of King Solomon, now surrounded by the Menachim Begin Center and a Scottish church. Like all of Jerusalem, the new always sits on top of the old and the whole city is a necropolis for all practical purposes.

We left the beautiful old troubled city in the rear view mirror and headed west toward Tel Aviv. Soon we left that major highway and went south on a secondary road to make two stops.

The first was in the field on which David slew Goliath. Mike read the Biblical references he used as coordinates, then encouraged us to pick up rocks from the little dry streambed nearby where David obtained his rocks, to give to people going into battles (cancer, Iraq, etc.). Mike always read from the New Standard Version of the Bible, the language of which was so plain and pedestrian it was painful to contemplate the lost poetry. I told DeJuana that in the next, New NEW Standard Version, the story would read, "...and then he, like, killed the mothafucka."

The second was Beth Shemesh, high on a hill in Texas Hill Country-like landscape, now an archeological dig surrounded by a national park. Some of us went into a cave that had been either a columbarium or an ossuary.

It was around this time of day that DeJuana and I began to notice we were tired. Our bodies were tired. I had had leg cramps the night before from the five hours of stair climbing we'd done on our free day in Jerusalem, then after flying out of bed and hopping around to get my leg straightened out—twice—I had insomnia as my semi-conscious mind shot into the future and everything I had to do between now and September 1st.

So we were not our usual gazelle-like selves, although we managed for the most part to stay cheerful.

Lunch was at a tourist place in Latrun, back on the main freeway to Tel Aviv. But from there we went north on another smaller road to a spot in the middle of nowhere to a little Quonset hut. There for $10 each we bought baby trees, then climbed a hill and planted them. [You can't do anything in Israel without climbing either stairs or a hill.] Sam spoke of the worldwide effort to reforest Israel as an act of belief in the future, and said that in the Talmud it says if you have a sapling in your hand when the Messiah comes, plant the sapling first and then greet the Messiah. The Jews have turned much of Israel into a garden. New hills continue to be reforested, irrigated and cared for in and around the rocks and boulders, accomplishing the seemingly impossible.

Back on the main highway then, and when we rolled into Jaffa it was still only 2:30. We walked around the old part of Jaffa on a point out in the Mediterranean and could see how utterly connected as one city Jaffa and Tel Aviv are. We were in a park-like setting of restored buildings that, coupled with the view from our promontory of the Tel Aviv beach stretching out in front of us, was delightfully attractive.

In Tel Aviv proper we were driven by the Yitzhak Rabin Memorial, large black stones planted in the very spot where he was shot. Our usually irrepressible guide

Danny was unusually solemn in talking about this assassination and I agreed it had affected us hard in the U.S., too.

This was en route to Tel Aviv University, on the grounds of which was our last stop, the Diaspora Museum. We were taken through in small groups by docents. It was not a brilliant museum but it had its moments, especially about thirty models of synagogues from all over the world. Unfortunately I was now in so much pain and so tired it was all I could do to keep from lying down in the middle of the floor. My back didn't want to do one more thing.

The group was going on to dinner and the airport to fly en masse back to San Antonio. Since they were going right past our hotel, they dropped DeJuana and me off in the street. We had hurried goodbyes and off they went. We were alone, and so glad to be going to bed soon we could hardly contain ourselves.

The Renaissance Hotel put us in a room just above the Mediterranean and before we conked out we sat on our balcony and admired the manicured beach and its infrastructure. It was a far cry from our own ragged Texas beach.

This morning it was up at 5:30, breakfast at 6:30 and off to Ben Gurion Airport. After the usual grilling we passed all the tests and now await our plane.

Mike said yesterday, looking at the modern prosperous city of Tel Aviv, that (and I am paraphrasing here) the idea that Iran or the Arabs could push Israel into the sea was preposterous. As the people of Nagasaki and Hiroshima found out to their chagrin, however, these seemingly invincible human constructs are still fragile for all their concrete stolidity. We forget when things are going right that evil lurks and can be so much more powerful than good, probably because under the rubric of "good" lies passivity, the great domestic everydayness of our lives. It only took nineteen highjackers to totally foul up the works in the most powerful nation on the planet, and it may only take one or two Iranian presidents or ayatollahs to change Israel forever. It is to Israel's credit that it is as fierce and vigilant as it is, and hasn't gotten fat and sloppy like another country we know. I wish them well. I just wish we could move Israel to Arkansas, Mississippi or Canada where it would do some good, and leave the sorry desert to the Arabs who seem to want it so bad.

On this trip we have seen two sides of globalization: the side that has bought into it and thrives on it, and the other side that culturally cannot or will not compete. "Western Civ" ends just east of Tel Aviv, so the clash of cultures is not just global but is the very essence of this one tiny country, Israel. "Now we are engaged in a great civil war" within the family of humanity, and it remains to be seen who will "win." I have seen too many layers of civilization, too many ruins and too many antiquities to believe with certainty it will be us. My heart goes out to the troubled ones at the same time I wish fervently for them to leave me alone.

THE SOUTH PACIFIC
FEBRUARY-MARCH 2007

INTRODUCTION

I am in the enviable position of being able to throw away most travel brochures that come my way because I have now been so many places. The downside of that is to find a trip one wants to take, and if traveling with Mother, to find one not too rigorous. We toss trips at each other to see if we can hook the other; I long to go dangerous places and she likes to go nice places she doesn't have to work too hard to see. A year ago a brochure appeared in the mail that seemed to fulfill her part as well as mine to go someplace that, while not dangerous, was at least exotic: the South Pacific.

A World War II trip would have sufficed, because I was fascinated by the War in the Pacific. This trip had a little of that and a lot of ethnography, also a selling point. A cruise, the ship was small and attractive and the itinerary good. We signed on.

Our friend DeJuana Jones decided to go with us. She didn't have a roommate, so we stuffed her into our room. As it turned out, we stuffed all of ourselves into the room, but once we figured out how to do it, it turned out to be pleasant and fun. It's amazing how organized you can be when you have to. As for getting along, that was never an issue.

We met in Los Angeles the day before leaving so we could have a rest day, and to make sure we all made the flight across the ocean. DeJuana had trouble getting out of Washington, proving the efficacy of our plan. As a result she missed a charming dinner party at our friend Mary Davis' house in Beverly Hills at which Art Linkletter and his wife were also guests. He was 93 and as cute and funny and smart as ever. We couldn't believe our luck, getting to meet this wonderful man.

We visited with other friends the next day, then headed to LAX for the twelve hour flight to Fiji. The journal begins there.

THE JOURNAL

Sunday 18 February 2007
At sea, heading west from Fiji

At first light yesterday morning Fiji didn't look quite awake as our overnight Air New Zealand flight landed at Nadi. As dazed as I was from sitting up all night, I could still feel the New Place juices start to flow.

With some fellow ship passengers we were driven to the Westin Resort Denarau, a compound of buildings on the beach, and put in day rooms for a few hours. Mother and I immediately went for a swim in the sea. It was still so early the sky and the water were all one color, making our swim feel like it was in two dimensions. We got cleaned up and reorganized after all the stupid lengths we have to go to now with our cosmetics since terrorists have learned how to bring down planes with mouthwash. By the time that was concluded it was time to have lunch in a hotel restaurant on the beach and check out.

Our luggage was put in a truck and taken to the ship and we were taken with the other passengers in two buses to do some sightseeing. Fiji is a poor country full of sweet, gracious people who used to be cannibals. Nadi Town looked lively with Saturday afternoon shoppers. We stopped at a handicrafts place and added our two bits' worth.

We drove into countryside that fairly shouted "tropical island:" palm trees, banana trees, goats, sugar cane, volcanic soil, rain trees and villages of little concrete houses. Just under the spine of a jagged series of low mountains we stopped to see a commercial garden of orchids, bromeliads, ginger and birds of paradise that was started by the late actor Raymond Burr. The final stop was at the oldest village in Fiji, traditionally the village founded by the first arrivals on the island who may have come from East Africa. The anthropologists are still pondering that one.

In the village green we sat on woven mats and watched eight men and six women in native dress sing and dance. Their singing was melodious and may have had the influence of the Church in it. The men, in grass skirts, danced some welcoming and some threatening dances; the women, all buxom and heavy, danced lightly on their feet with clapping and little scissor kicks, singing a happy song and looking altogether motherly and graceful. I asked them afterward how old the songs were and they said, 'very old.'

Like all ethnographic performances it was touching to see grown people in the 21st century trying to hold onto or recreate folkways otherwise long gone and, in the case of this faraway island, to do it for money and probably their living. But it made me feel close to have enjoyed it, and I told them so.

The last stop in Fiji was our destination, the ship, the Spirit of Oceanus. We walked up the gangplank, checked in at the desk and were taken to our stateroom to find...utter chaos. We were so tired we were ready to drop dead, and the prospect of unloading seven suitcases into a nice but still small stateroom seemed insurmountable. I jumped into the fray like a dervish, DeJuana stayed calm, Mother rallied and we managed to get it organized before the ropes were cast off and we sailed.

We stood on the deck and watched the dock recede in the rain, and saw a phenomenon most had never seen: a rainbow that started in the water, made a tight arc and ended on the land. We could see both ends clearly. There was a second, dreamier rainbow above it, a reflection of the first I guess. Mother decided it was a good omen.

The captain gave us a safety lecture, we had lifeboat drill and made it most of the way through dinner before DeJuana turned green and got up. Mother and I jumped up and went with her. It was too late to help her but I put scopalomine patches on everyone and we went to sleep, rolling with the ship, and stayed that way for ten hours.

And we have rolled all day long. Each of us has been on and off our beds to take several naps. I went to the two lectures this morning after working out and schlepping breakfast for Mother to enjoy on our balcony. Today is her 89th birthday. DeJuana got up for lunch on the deck. Mother went to the movie this afternoon ("The Bounty"); I wrote postcards and emails (71 cents a minute). This day of sailing has put me in mind of all the aboriginals who traveled between these islands far more poorly provisioned than we, and set in motion their histories.

Monday 19 February 2007
Ambrym Island, Vanuatu

Last night the maitre d'hotel presented Mother with a birthday cake and the waiters sang to her. It capped a sparkling dinner at which we had the captain at our table, and a couple we had made friends with, Fred and Roxana Anson. Roxana Anson was named after the same Roxana that our Roxana McAllister was named after: Roxana Catto. Department of Small Worlds. We also had Michael with us, a single Englishman. The captain was a skinny drink of water from Switzerland who was smart and hysterically funny. Fred Anson taught chemistry at Cal Tech. Michael was a merchant banker. It was a fun evening.

This morning I worked out, then brought breakfast to Mother and DeJuana. The gym and the outdoor food service are both just down the hall, which is handy. At 9:00 we attended mandatory Zodiac drill in preparation for our first excursion from the ship, which took place shortly after lunch.

By late morning we were within sight of Ambrym, a large island in the country of Vanuatu, formerly known as The New Hebrides. Ambrym was named by Captain James Cook in 1774. [We will be in four new countries on this trip: Fiji, Vanuatu, Solomon Islands and Federated States of Micronesia.] The captain and cruise director went over to confer with the chief, who invited us onto the island. When we climbed out of the Zodiaks onto the black sand beach, several hundred people had gathered from villages to watch us and the ceremonial dancing ahead.

We were greeted on the beach by guides who directed us along a pathway of palm fronds stuck in the sand with flowers sprinkled at their bases, then under a palm frond arch festooned with flowers and a successive arch further on, whence we found ourselves in a great clearing under the tree canopy. The entire clearing was lined with bamboo benches on which we sat, with the Ambrym natives standing two and three deep behind us. It was hot, muddy and raining intermittently.

At the far end of the clearing we saw eight dancers mustering, then they moved out into the clearing and slowly danced their way down the length of it. From their shoulders to the ground they were covered in dried palm and banana fronds that shimmied like a grass skirt but were much more bizarre. They looked like conical hayricks. From the neck up they had on sort of bird-looking masks bound to their heads by what looked like long blonde hair but were 'strings from the banana tree' (?). Finally, each had a palm front running up and over the back of his head. The whole effect was magically weird.

In their midst were the musicians, men who were naked except for a waistband and penis sheath and maybe a flower or some leaves. The dancing was iterative, fast and hot. This was the famous Rom dance, Rom referring to the mask.

There followed some magic done by other naked men, and a flute recital by the chief, his penis sticking out above his uncovered testicles. I wanted to do him the honor of listening to his music but it was difficult to concentrate.

On the beach once more we bought some wood carvings. We didn't haggle. As the Zodiak raced back to the ship I pondered once more the clash of cultures, and as sweet as our good wishes for these people were, thought they had probably had the right idea to eat early explorers to discourage Westerners from bringing their culturally diluting ways to paradise.

Ambrym warriors

Tuesday 20 February 2007
At sea; Tikopia, Solomon Islands

Last night we dined with Michael and a couple named Sheila and Glenn, a retired nurse and doctor respectively. The conversation started out interestingly but when a wave hit the side of the ship and knocked the wine glasses over, and they poured some more, Sheila started talking and didn't stop until I stood and broke up the party. She apologized this morning.

I went to a lecture this morning on how to write a travel journal. I wanted to see how such a thing could be taught. It was a little boring for me, a longtime journal writer, but at lunch the lecturer, Vickie, thanked me for my input in a kind way and I thought maybe we could be friends.

We had lunch al fresco as usual, then dressed to go over to Tikopia, an iconic looking island at which we had anchored during lunch. In vivid sunlight it looked like Bali Hai— tall pointy hills, white sand beach, palm trees and a healthy looking reef around it.

The tide was out and the Zodiaks could go in just so far; we waded in knee- and thigh-high water over coral and sand to the beach. A bunch of little boys had come out to the Zodiaks and some of them found themselves with a job, to be leaned upon as we staggered through the water in our long pants. [We have to have our knees covered to go onto these islands, even if everyone else is naked.]

Once on the beach it was much more primitive and paradisical than Ambrym yesterday. Tikopia is a speck at the far eastern end of the Solomon Islands and doesn't get much traffic. We admired the natives' handicrafts as we walked through a bower of trees into their village; I bought two fish hooks carved from bone.

In the clearing of the village of thatched huts we ranged ourselves in a large circle and once more were entertained by dancers and a drummer who beat a piece of log laid over the stalks of two palm fronds. The dancers were wrapped in woven grass mats, and had various greenery stuck in their costumes. The chief, who was friendly, sat near us on a folding chair enjoying his dancers, a pipe in one hand, silver-rimmed glasses on and a little granddaughter fooling around behind him.

Behind where we sat, two women with nothing on above the waist and with pipes clenched in their teeth pounded tapa for cloth and wove dried fronds. All around the circle were other villagers and lots of children in grass cloth loincloths. DeJuana, who stayed on the island longer than Mother and me, said as soon as the guests began to leave, the kids began to shuck off their clothes.

The tide had come in as we left, enabling the Zodiaks to get into the beach. This was an improvement, although we were so hot and dirty it had ceased to matter what we had to tolerate at that point.

For some reason on Tikopia I didn't have that heart-wrenching Us vs. Them feeling, even though our great white ship sat offshore and we ourselves looked hopelessly touristic and bedraggled. I felt more at one with this village, perhaps because it was most definitely authentic, and more easygoing. We raced back to the ship, to the air conditioning and the showers, but we had had a good time for all the sloppy discomfort we had endured.

Tikopia weaver

Wednesday 21 February 2007
At sea in the Solomons

The first day we were on this ship we were at sea all day, and although it was comfortable to be able to rest after traveling, it still put us somewhat at loose ends mentally. Today we have sailed all day and it has been heavenly to be footloose, to read and do ones nails and try to get on top of the laundry, which clones itself. We were sailing west, toward Guadalcanal.

Around 9:00 a.m. we were all out on deck to sail past Tinakula Volcano, a near-perfectly shaped volcano rising out of the Pacific. Vapor and the occasional rock came out its vent, but most of the conical island was covered with flora.

After lunch (we eat whether we deserve to or not) I fell asleep in the coral reef lecture but was interested in the Battle of Guadalcanal lecture to learn just exactly how it went. These battle sites are bred in the bone, my having been reared by the World War II generation, but the details are another thing.

We had two women friends, Maureen and Connie, at our table for dinner. There was an empty chair so when the captain wandered in late we waved him over. Once again we were entertained by his humor and good nature—everyone on the ship adores him, men and women alike—and we came away in even more of a happy mood than usual for having had him to ourselves once more.

Thursday 22 February 2007
Guadalcanal

We were still at sea until close to noon today, heading for Honiara, the capital of the Solomon Islands, on the north coast of Guadalcanal. Vickie, the travel journal lecturer of two days ago (her husband Jay gave the Guadalcanal lecture) gave an interesting talk on cannibalism (title: "An Acquired Taste"), which was common to these South Pacific cultures until it was missionaried out of them.

We hung on the rail and watched the docking procedures at Honiara, a real live town of 53,000 people. As the gangplank was cranked down and the rails assembled, there gathered on the quai a band to play to welcome us. But this was no ordinary band.

A dozen boys and young men in loin cloths, Rastafarian wigs ponytailed down their backs, shell bandoliers, white paint markings on their brown bodies and anklets of dried seed pods that rattled, each played bamboo instruments of various shapes and sizes. There were two big sets of percussion instruments consisting of six or eight large bamboo tubes rafted together. These were played with the rubber bottoms of flip flops. There was a motheaten-looking commercial drum kit. In front of these there was a barrel on its side covered with clothes; into this a boy blew his bamboo instrument to mute it. In front of him six or eight boys blew into bamboo instruments, most of strikingly large size (ex: six, seven or eight pieces of bamboo 3" in diameter and of descending length, tied together).Some had smaller bamboo flute instruments of higher pitch. The observer had to concentrate on these individual elements because the whole effect was so strange and wonderful. One of the leaders put up a sign that said, "Karanata Reggae Bamboo Band" and they began to play. Then the fun began.

Their music was so merry, rhythmic and melodic that soon everyone on the ship was hanging off the rails clapping and shouting after every song, and grinning at each other at the serendipity of it. Some of us went down the gangplank to get closer. An old man with flowers in his hair who was dancing to the side got Mother to dance with him. Each song had the same basic beat but the boys would do something different with each one. At one point the captain came down the gangplank carrying a case of water for the band; this endeared him to us even more.

It came to a natural end and we all peeled off to have the rest of our day in Guadalcanal.

I ate lightly at lunch, then went back to our stateroom for the moment of truth: putting on a bathing suit. Of the activities available to us on Guadalcanal, I was going diving.

The divemaster picked up the four of us who had paid to go diving, and a fifth person came along: the captain. Turns out he is a very serious diver who has even dived in a dry suit under the ice in Antarctica. It was just as well there were two pros along because the rest of us were a little klutzy at first. We were driven to a beach where there was an old Japanese ship sitting in shallow water with part of the bow and some turbines above the surface. We parked under the trees and started to suit up when who should appear but two busloads of snorkelers from our ship. They managed to finish their snorkel before we ever set out, thanks to one of our party, Charlie, taking off by himself (a big diving no-no), having to be found by the divemaster, Roman the captain and Meriwether, one of our naturalists. This caused the rest of us divers to stand in neck deep water for almost half an hour until the miscreant was brought to heel and we could take off to circumnavigate the wreck. The wreck was dramatic but I was so enchanted by the plethora of gorgeous corals and fish that I frankly forgot about the wreck. It felt good to be underwater for the first time since diving in Cuba in 2003.

Before the divemaster took us back to the ship he drove us up to the American War Memorial and got us oriented in the various directions toward Red Beach, Henderson Field and Bloody Ridge, all geographical features of the two years of warfare that to this day has left the island covered with artifacts (I bought a 1945 Coke bottle) and the channel between Guadalcanal and Savo, Tulagi and the other islands paved with dead ships to such an extent it's now called Iron Bottom Channel.

Back onboard I managed to clean up before Mother and DeJuana came back from their tour of the island. An announcement was made that our band of that morning was back, and with some girl dancers added as well. The ship nearly capsized with all of us coming out on the starboard decks again.

The girls were mostly little; in fact the littlest one danced in front of the others like a leader. They had on grass skirts, flowered headdresses and had in one hand long white feathers and in the other a white rag. Also, they had on the seed pod anklets. When that irresistible music started up they danced low with their knees bent, leaning over almost to the ground. They were so precious that many of us poured down the gangway to get close and take pictures.

When they stopped dancing the boys took it up, blowing on their oversized bamboo instruments as they tried to think of variations to the dances, finally lying down on the ashphalt and blowing their instruments straight up into the air. It was witty. The captain sent word to pull up the gangplank so we reluctantly returned to the deck of the ship, and as it pulled away from the dock the dancers and musicians played their way down to the end of the quai, dancing, playing and waving. One tear ran out of each eye and down over my silly grin.

Vickie and Jay, the lecturers, joined us for dinner. We have our own table and hold court in a half-assed fashion every night. Michael, our regular, is a pretty guy-type guy, and probably didn't appreciate the kind of touchy-feely philosophical conversation we had, but it was a lovely dinner that sent us to bed, as usual, feeling full of food and full of feeling as well.

Friday 23 February 2007
Solomon Islands

This morning for the first time we had to get up early and the only reason I resented it was it meant I had a truncated conversation with Maureen, my workout buddy. We only had 20 minutes together instead of the usual 35-45. My conversations with her are deep and sometimes profound, and I've been reminded of my trip to the Arabian Peninsula with my friend Julia. We would have incredibly deep conversations early in the morning before breakfast. This is not the first time on ships I have made good women friends with fellow exercisers early in the morning.

Anyway, the reason for the early alarm was an early departure by Zodiak on a 20-minute journey into the village of Kia on the island of Santa Isabel. This village consisted of thatched roof houses on stilts, built out over the water. It was deeply tropical looking, and so remote they only have two ships a year come by and want to see them.

The village had a little dock so we were able to make a dry landing. The villagers were more smiley and friendly than the others we've seen. Mother and I were shown the inside of one of the stilt houses by the wife, who pointed out her kitchen. There were no Cuisinarts in evidence. Each house had water around three sides of it, land behind it and a purposely designed garden of flowers. The effect was pretty. At their new (Anglican) church we admired the shell inlay designs on the wood, and an altar of shells.

As usual we ranged ourselves around a clearing and as we waited for all the Zodiaks to make their long ferry from the ship, I walked around the circle speaking to the villagers until I came to a clump of two nuns and some other church-dressed women. One spoke halting but elegant English and we talked for quite awhile. They were all members of the "Anglican community"; later I learned the village goes to church everyday. I took my new friend, Lilly, over to meet Mother. When the dancing started, she interpreted.

The women danced first—a dance about a parrot and other dances of daily life. When they retired and the men gained the circle, they were trying to be serious but it was clear they were not so well prepared. Their mistakes and startings-over made the villagers laugh (naturally we didn't laugh, trying to be good guests), and we were amazed and amused by the derision. But there was something good about it, too, and gentle and open, and we left in a state of bemusement, charmed by the people and their exotic village.

As in the other villages, there were worlds of children in this one. Lilly said there were "more children than adults." I asked if that worried her—where would they live, what would they eat, what would be their work when they were grown?—and she said yes, it did worry all of them.

I told them I was 61 and single, and that many Americans lived alone. This caused their brows to furrow. I explained it was because we had enough money to live alone. It was still hard to grasp. I said 'but I have a boyfriend' and then their faces lighted up like at least we shared something.

Me and Lilly, Kia

We were back onboard at 10:30, and sailed until 2:00 when we anchored off the Arnavon Island Marine Reserve, a joint protectorate of The Nature Conservancy and several villages including our Kia of this morning who took turns protecting the three islands of the Arnavons. The Arnavons are the first "community managed marine conservation project" in the South Pacific. The islands are important for their corals, their sea turtles and birds. When we were ferried over to snorkle we had gingerly to skirt the little shell nests of the excited terns who cried and strafed us for the two hours we were near their nests. Mother showed me a baby chick not much bigger than its egg that lay sleeping on the ground next to another egg.

We snorkled over the coral and looked at the fish. I saw my first giant clams; when they're open their mantles are lined with neon blue-green algae. I was concerned about my novice snorklers, Mother and DeJuana, and kept stopping and looking up to see if I could see them. Finally when I saw them back on the beach I relaxed and finished my swim. We came on back to the ship to get cleaned up and spruced up for dinner. Our evenings are always fun.

Sunday 25 February 2007
At sea, Fed. States of Micronesia

This is our second day at sea without sighting land. This Pacific is a big damn pond. We have been running due north since leaving Kia and the Arnavons. We have left the Solomon Islands behind and entered the Federated States of Micronesia. We have also crossed the Equator and cannot be said to be in the "South" Pacific anymore.

Yesterday I went to the Sea Turtle lecture, the Tattooing lecture and the Sharks lecture. Today I've been to the Herons and Egrets lecture, the Navigation lecture and the Captain Cook lecture. I've eaten three meals a day and lain on my bed two or three times a day. DeJuana was seasick yesterday; she and Mother are championship nappers. I bring their breakfast to them every morning because they sleep later than I. I slept late yesterday and missed my conversation with Maureen; turns out she didn't work out. This morning we were both back on the treadmills, talk-talk-talking.

This afternoon King Neptune and his court inducted the Pollywogs into the Shellbacks out on the back deck. Everyone who had never crossed the Equator on a ship had to put on their bathing suits, be blindfolded, kiss a fish, have oatmeal rubbed in their hair and cold water poured out of a conch shell over their heads, then showered with sea water. It was wild, messy fun, especially since I didn't have to participate.

We arrive in Pohnpei tomorrow.

Monday 26 February 2007
Pohnpei

Pohnpei gets 300 inches of rain a year and several of them fell on us today.

We eased up to the dock at Pohnpei around 8:00 this morning. The buildings around the harbor looked more substantial than any we've seen so far, and the town less squalid. This is a well-kept secret of paradise in the South Seas: it's squalid. It rained on and off, on and off as we waited for the F.S.M. factotums to do their immigration schtick and let us disembark. That happened shortly after 9:00.

Everyone piled into six small buses to go sightseeing. The last three people on the buses were the captain, Charlie the miscreant from our dive in Guadalcanal, and me—the divers. We sat on the jump seats and I practiced keeping my claustrophobia under control. Shortly the buses stopped and Charlie, Roman (the captain) and I got off at The Village, a resort with a dive operation.

At the desk we showed our certifications, then were driven down the hill to the water. We boarded a long yellow fiberglass skiff with no seats in it; we sat on the floor on flotation cushions. Two young men tended to us, neither of whom was a certified divemaster, but we had Roman as our ace in the hole.

We had to run 25 minutes to the first dive site, the water was rough, the floor of the skiff was hard and the driver was driving fast. I thought I was going to have to have a discectomy before it was over. We were all facing backward to keep the spray and rain off us. The driver drove sitting on top of one of the two 60-horse-power motors, manuevering them both. He could have worn his goggles to good effect.

At the dive site we dropped down a wall. Charlie sucked up all his air in about ten minutes and had to be taken back to the boat. Roman and I finished the dive in a normal fashion, admiring the fan corals, one as big as a dining room table.

We couldn't do our next dive for an hour because of the surface interval requirement, so we ran to a picnic spot with a little dock and gathered under an open-sided shed to have lunch in a downpour so heavy we were forced to lollygag there for half an hour before we could even get back out to the boat. Lunch was steamed rice, fish and boiled eggs wrapped in a banana leaf.

The second dive consisted of sitting on or hovering above a sandy bottom as manta rays glided by above. This was a manta ray cleaning station and the graceful, mystical animals slithered out of the gloom, into view and back out, silent, leaving the diver filled with longing.

When our skiff dropped us back at the ship, no one was sad to get out of it. I was tired beyond the telling, yet managed to get cleaned up and get through the evening. As the ship passed through the channel in the reef at dusk, with breakers crashing on the coral on both sides of us and little inter-island freighters lit up at their anchorages, The Last Day of Pohnpei receded and we gave ourselves back over to the sea.

[What follows is DeJuana's description of the trip the rest of the passengers took this day to Nan Madol, a brilliant archeological site that is considered to rival Easter Island in its mystery. I was sorry not to see it.]

While Taddy dived, Edith and I took a guided tour which filled the better part of the day. Our morning destination was Nan Madol, an ancient stone city built around 500 AD, still studied by archaeologists and engineers seeking to discover more about the the race who constructed the island city, once a thriving, royal civilization. What began as light rain turned into a downpour as we trekked a mile and a half over large wet stones and small rickety bridges with a single railing. Michael, our British friend, provided tender guidance and care on the treacherous paths. When we reached the Nanpil River, we crossed by boat to the island and climbed up 50 or 60 feet to the top of the ruins where we listened to our guide tell of the strange practices of this ancient culture. Stone pillars formed the residences of kings and sorcerers. Basalt rock logs, brought to the islands by rafts, were used to construct steps, paths, and a tall temple of worship. Some us remarked about magic spirits sending the rain to discourage our invasion. Soaked, even under umbrellas, we lunched on fish, rice and an egg served inside banana leaves.

In the afternoon we hiked along a steep, wet, rocky ledge above white water to see the famous Keprabi Waterfalls, which proved to be a spectacular site but far too large and forceful for the planned swim below. Two wholly innocent, beautiful, naked children about 8 years old danced for our entertainment on a bridge while we waited for transportation.

[Here endeth DeJuana's portion of the tale.]

Tuesday 27 February 2007
Oroluk Atoll

This morning we rotated beds. Every five days we have slept counter-clockwise on the three beds in the room because one of them is not as good as the others. That was our domestic adjustment of the day. Last night our domestic adjustment was to get to bed as fast as possible because we were so tired we fought over the bathroom, but the flip side was we got to set the clock back an hour for the second time this trip. We are moving west. So we slept long hours and woke up happy again.

Around 7:30 or 8:00 a.m. we began to run parallel to the reef of Oroluk Atoll. We chugged slowly along it for an hour. It was mind-bending to see this endless reef out in the middle of the ocean. Finally a decision was made as to where we would stop, because we were going to snokel along the wall of the reef.

When it was the Coconuts' turn to go over in the Zodiaks (we are Coconuts; the other half of the passengers are Sea Cucumbers) we clambered down the gangway and into a Zodiac, dressed only in bathing suits and our gear. [DeJuana didn't go.] It was rough going over to the reef and Mother got scared and wouldn't get in the water. After swimming along the wall for fifteen minutes or so, I signalled her Zodiak to come over and convinced her to come in. Then she had a good swim and snorkle and admired the clear water and the myriad fish and subsequently the idea we had all swum a reef that no other human had probably ever seen the underside of.

By the time we returned to the ship we had to hurry to have lunch before the kitchen closed, then fiddled around all afternoon trying to get ourselves put together in between lectures (Vickie and Jay on their teaching in Fiji, Jay on the World War II campaigns in the Pacific). Now we are in the bar relaxing before dinner.

We have five more nights on this ship. It has been a long trip, but it's been a true vacation in that we have never known what day it was and wouldn't have known what time it was if it weren't for meals and scheduled activities.

Wednesday 28 February 2007
Truk Lagoon (now called Chuuk)

At 6:00 a.m. I was hanging on the rail of our balcony admiring the neon peach colored sunrise behind lavender cumulus clouds as Truk Lagoon came into view. In this enormous lagoon, 40 miles wide and with 80 islands in it, the American Pacific fleet had a turkey shoot and destroyed masses of Japanese ships and airplanes. I thought about all the young men, ours and theirs, who saw magnificent Pacific sunrises on the last days of their lives and then went to sleep with the fishes.

Mother and DeJuana took the land tour and I went diving. Our dive boat picked us up at 8:00. It was only Charlie and me, no captain. Later I was sad he hadn't seen what we had seen. We ran about ten minutes, then anchored on the wreck of the Fujikawa Maru, a 426' long airplane transport ship sitting upright from 40' to 120' deep. We swam over, around and into it, and saw the best corals I personally had ever seen. The way Nature colonizes these dreadful things is one of the top reasons to be optimistic about life. Long after we have spent ourselves trying to destroy each other, Nature calmly takes over and rebeautifies her world again, makes it livable again.

Peering over the side of the ship I got distracted from the corals by a huge school of large fish swirling in a circular pattern near the bottom. It may have been a bait ball.

The second dive was a shallow dive on a Japanese "Betty" bomber. Here again was Nature at work. The hatch was up on the cockpit, and there where the pilot would have sat were masses of minnows, hidden in the ombre shade from predators. Larger fish filled the fusilage; fan corals grew upside down from the undersides of the wings. A tomb had been reclaimed by the living, heartening an imagination that harked back to a fateful morning in 1944.

We sailed at noon and fell into a lethargy that required us to lie on our beds until it was time for an afternoon cookie snack, a lecture on wayfaring and then the evening, which is always fun and full of good talk.

Friday 2 March 2007
Ifalik Atoll, Yap

We had to take a rain check on yesterday. After steaming for 24 hours from Chuuk to Satawal, when we arrived it was raining heavily and waves were crashing on the shore of the island, preventlng our landing. Ironically, we had picked up Chief Leo in Pohnpei and were taking him to Guam. Chief Leo was the chieftan of Satawal, and then we couldn't even land on his island after reaching it. [Last night at the cocktail hour wrap-up, Chief Leo had on a pink souvenir T-shirt from Guam that had hearts on it.]

In the morning we had a talk by Chief Leo on Wayfinding as it has been done by islanders since time out of mind. Jay then lectured on Micronesia and the other "-nesias" (mela-black; poly-many; mega-large (like Australia) and austra-south) and explained the differences (racial, location). It was helpful to me for whom the South Pacific had always been a mishmash of island names and clusters with no real identities except those given us by Marlon Brando and Rogers and Hammerstein.

After lunch when we couldn't go ashore we napped, then watched a sickening movie on fishes of the extreme deep sea. None of these animals would you want to encounter in real life nor have in your aquarium. They were the ugliest creatures I've ever seen. I announced afterward I didn't want to buried at sea after all.

We fiddled away the rest of the afternoon (Mother is zeroing in on finishing writing her Christmas thank-you's, it now being March) and had a fun dinner, as always, this time with Vickie and Jay. We have gotten close to them; they are a remarkable couple.

This morning we arrived at our day's destination, Ifalik, in...rain. Rain has been our constant companion on this trip, and we have marvelled at a whole category of people, islanders, who live wet. To us it is dirty and uncomfortable, but at least it explains their lack of clothing.

Ifalik was the most beautiful, charming village we'd been in to date, and this time we were able to make it to the beach in Zodiaks because the village was inside a lagoon. It turned out our Chief Leo lived in Ifalik even though he was the chief of Satawal. These are matrilineal societies and the man goes to live with his wife's people.

We were greeted on the shore by beautiful, half-naked children in sarongs (lava-lavas) with flowers in their hair who gave us leis. We walked around their village and bought handicrafts, admired their outrigger canoes and themselves. They were the best looking people we'd seen so far, and not a one of them was dressed above the waist.

There was the usual dance performance, this one in the yard between two long school buildings. We huddled under the eaves while the women performed for over 45 minutes. Having little patience for repetition, I was ready for it to be over sooner. The men danced briefly and half-heartedly with a kind of 7th grade attitude of cool disdain for the process. As soon as it was over I pulled Mother back to the beach and in short order we were in the first Zodiak to return to the ship. We were wet as drowned rats.

DeJuana and children of Ifalik

Mother and Ifalik boys

Jumped into dry clothes and had lunch on the deck as the rain poured around us. We had finished and were still visiting when Alistair, our leader, came up the outside steps trailed by ten chieftains from the island who had expressed an interest in seeing the ship. In their lava-lavas and palm frond decorations they went through the line and got lunch. It was an exotic sight to have them on our territory. Later I saw them being taught to use the elevator. I notice I've stopped worrying about the juxtapositions of Us and Them, but seeing those chiefs eating our food and exploring our ship brought back the poignancy of the differences. However, it appeared to be my problem because the chiefs seemed very secure. In the village this morning it was we who looked horrible in our wet clothes and thrown-together ensembles and funny hats and umbrellas, and the villagers who looked like they'd stepped off a movie set. It was difficult to be patronising in word, thought or deed.

After lunch I went over to some shallow water to snorkle with a Zodiak load but the rain on my back was cold and I came home to the ship and a hot shower at the first opportunity.

As we heaved anchor and left this genuine little corner of paradise, the captain warned that we would be in heavy seas due to a depression over Japan.

Sunday 4 March 2007
Guam

The captain wasn't kidding. The ship pitched all night in 10-12' seas. DeJuana got sick and had to leave the dining room; she remained more or less comatose until this morning.

Saturday we were supposed to stop at a little island called Gaferut to do some bird-watching early in the morning. We diehards were up having early breakfast and watching the Zodiaks go to shore to check conditions. The gangplank was lowered but the rollers were so big they crashed over the bottom of the gangplank, so the safety officer nixed our leaving the ship and that was that.

The rest of the day was spent bouncing around the ship in now 15' swells, packing and visiting and gathering in the lounge to watch another Blue Planet movie on the "Open Ocean," a slide show by our beloved naturalist Meriwether of pictures she had taken of us during the trip, and a lecture by her on spinner dolphins (I now know the difference between a porpoise and a dolphin).

We had to have lunch in the main dining room instead of the aft deck because it was too wet and dangerous to be outside. Mother and I, Todd and Margaret, and Maureen and Connie, four women with whom we had developed special relationships, gathered at a table for a baccalaureate lunch, only to have the ship lurch about half way through it and the lunch land in Mother's lap. Crockery, silverware and glasses crashed all around us. We managed to get the poor waiter to bring us some dessert in and around his trying to clean up the mess, then we retired to let the wait staff tote up the losses.

After that experience, they delivered ham sandwiches to our staterooms for dinner. I took mine down to the bar and ate it with a glass of white wine.

We levitated with every crash of the ship and so were relieved when it reached our final destination, Guam, around 4:00 a.m. I slept through it, and awoke to find us tied to the fuel dock, bunkering. We had almost run out of gas.

Guam officialdom came aboard and we ran the gauntlet of their makeshift immigration operation in the bar. Then we sat interminably, in our rooms and in the lounge, some four hours until the bunkering was done and we could change over to the people dock and disembark. We had been up eight hours at that point.

At the Hyatt Regency Guam we wolfed down a Sunday brunch buffet before Mother and DeJuana went on a prearranged tour of Guam. I took to my room to contemplate the end of this very special trip.

Monday 5 March 2007
In the air over the Pacific

In trying to dissect why I have such a happy picture in my memory of this trip, I see that every element was good: the ship, its crew and the naturalists; we three roommates and the other passengers we enjoyed and even began to feel like family with; the various island destinations; the food and the diving; the antipodal Otherness of the Pacific island societies; the water (rough or calm). It was hard to think as we moved along, and now briefly in retrospect, what could have been improved. We have laughed and talked and hung on the rail, and been fed and led by the nose and cared for like precious babies. We have read and napped and swum in beautiful waters. We have gossiped, and found soul mates. We have had darling smart naturalists who let us love them, older person to younger person. We have had crew who memorized our eccentricities and were always there with what they knew we liked. We have the memory of the precious curious wide-eyed children bedecked with flowers and smiles. And we have had each other to share all this with, to help and to love as we have moved along. The wonder of such good fortune, such luck causes a 'why me?' reaction along with the pure comfort of it, and helps one, I hope, keep her perspective.

IV.
EDITORIALS

EDITORIALS

INTRODUCTION

In 1989 I was the Development Chairman of the San Antonio Festival, the annual music festival held in the spring in my home city. The Festival always had money problems in spite of our best efforts to obviate them.

One morning a well known critic had a piece in the San Antonio Light derogatory to our effors. In a case of having had it "up to my eyeballs," I called the editor of the paper and complained that this kind of thing made my job much harder, and with every arts organization in the city hanging on by its fingernails, we all needed support. I was not naive enough to resent the critic for the pure execution of his duty; I was just tired and mad.

The kindly editor listened and then said, simply, why don't you write something for us? Thus he inadvertently launched me on a random, half-baked career as an op-ed writer. Some of the results of that "career" follow; some are embedded in the Letters from Prague section of this book.

CRITICS' ILL-TIMED BARBS CAN OFTEN CUT TO THE HEART OF THE STRUGGLING ARTS

March 3, 1989 — San Antonio Light

My old friend, author and editor Willie Morris, used to say that he was a liberal because he was a conservative, by which he meant he wanted to see preserved the best of the American system, starting with the Bill of Rights.

I, too, cherish the Bill of Rights, and would practically defend to the death the right of a newspaper critic to exercise his rights of free speech and free press by publishing criticism of an organization. I may be unhappy or disturbed by what a critic says, and may fear the results he may engender, but I would still be on the front lines defending his right to do so.

With that in mind, I will now confess that there are times when I would dearly love to tear from limb to limb a couple of art critics in San Antonio. My reasons for this rather violent desire are parochial: I am the development chairman for a major performing arts organization. When I open the paper and see a negative piece about my organization, I get a sick feeling in the pit of my stomach. It is hard enough to raise money in this city in this conomic climate without being cut off at the knees by a critic with the imprimatur of his newspaper all over him.

We don't have in America the European tradition of kings and royal governments patronizing the arts. In the United States, until Lyndon Johnson became President in 1963, we didn't even have a National Endowment for the Arts. It has really only been in the past 25 to 30 yearss, since the inception of the NEA and the arts council movement, that there has been serious, steady funding of the arts by government. That funding has been eroded in recent years by the Reagan revolution on the national level and by the increasing demand for social services spending on the local level. Government spending on the arts has never equaled private sector spending, and that is the American way of doing things. That is the system in which we who are involved in arts funding have to operate.

So I would say to all those busines people to whom we go for contributions, if you cheered on the Reagan revolution, don't be surprised when you are now asked to fund directly arts and social services programs partially or wholly defunded during that revolution. The hitch in all this, from the organization perspective, is that we don't have the power of the federal government to make you fund us. When the feds assess you, you don't have any choice but to pay up. When we "assess" you with our fund-raising appeals, you have the choice to ignore us.

When you ignore us, however, I believe you do so at your peril. The very nature of a city is that it has everything: one could almost say that is the definition of a city. Much of that "everything" is tangible: architecture, transportation, people, food, parks—things you can see at a glance. But much that is important in a city you cannot see: what goes on in the heads of all those people, what goes on inside that architecture, what's moving inside that transportation.

Yet surprisingly, when creativity manifests itself at its zenith, which is to say in art, many otherwise intelligent people have difficulty understanding that this "intangible" is important to this organism called "city." Their eyes glaze over as you try to make the connection between the reality of their life and the larger needs of the complete "city."

In our beloved city, San Antonio, some sobering facts emerge as one moves around asking for money for art. Fact one is that much of the old money which traditionally underwrote the arts has dried up. Fact two, and this comes from an arts professional with her ear to the ground and statistics at her fingertips: there are only about 10,000 arts patrons in San Antonio and they can each be counted on to attend at least one thing in the course of the year.

That is slim pickin's for the earned income side of the ledger. So we fund-raisers for the arts repeatedly request funding from the business community and the new industries which have replaced oil, cattle and banking, and we scramble to address "audience development" as a critical issue.

As we work and agonize on the road to arts funding (earned and underwritten), we duck and zigzag past the critics, who have the luxury of pretending they live in New York City or Los Angeles where all wishes and demands are met in the arts. I wish that were true here. I wish we could pick and choose amongst a plentiful offering of avant- garde, mainstream, experimental and in between. Since this is not the case, not yet, anyhow, I would ask two things: one, that the critics be more realistic in their demands on our fragile arts scene, and two, that their readers understand their hidden agendas and make a leap of faith over their words and beyond to the larger picture.

I believe there is a way for the critics to be true to their craft without pushing over organizations struggling with funding problems—and there is not one organization which isn't, not today, not here, not in San Antonio. In the meantime, I shall put my trust in the inherent good judgment of the readers to sort through the negativism and ride with us on our road to solid funding and eclectic programming. The trip will be worth it.

AUDIENCE DEVELOPMENT IS REALLY AUDIENCE EDUCATION

S.A. Light, 5-30-89

Audience development is a big issue in the performing arts because the arts take so much work, cost so much and make so little money that to produce art and have a smaller than deserved audience is dispiriting indeed.

It is hell to sit around doing things for noble reasons while most others go around doing things for realistic reasons, like because they're hungry, thirsty, cold or lonely. Art is one of the few massive projects we do for other than economic reasons.

While marketing technocrats, Ad Age gurus, arts administrators and even early-childhood education experts work over the issue of audience development, I would like them to consider a theory they may find depressing: The standard issues of audience development are loosely parallel to those of racism and ethnocentricity and will not be ameliorated beyond a point. It doesn't have to be that way.

In arts programming, there is a lack of understanding of those whose taste doesn't coincide. In audience development, there is a secret belief that others have a screw loose if they do not appreciate what is being presented.

In arts programming, there is the very real fear that someone else's "trash" will overwhelm limited support resources. In audience development, there is a high regard for and use of celebrities to overcome resistance to an art form. And one must commit to the goal whether or not it is reachable, for the sake of the higher "good" which is art.

Accepting these shortcomings of human nature does not mean giving up on achieving the admirable and beneficial goal of audience development. Indeed, it is also human nature to rise to a challenge, the harder the better. It does not subvert the process to admit that certain WASPs are not going to be drawn to salsa festivals or musicals about Malcolm X, or that conjunto musicians will probably not throng the opera. But let's stop looking down our noses at each other!

Every idea on this earth has some reason to it, even if only to the person who has it. Beyond that, there are more widely accepted and, in some rare instances, universally accepted ideas which have lots of room in them for shades of difference. New York City has an anti-racist, anti-defamation campaign on right now that goes under the rubric "A World of Difference." That is the reality of life, but it should be a source of pleasure, not conflict. Boundaries should exist to be breached, not defended.

Audience development for the various performing arts should start in babyhood, but of course it mostly doesn't, except insofar as television has utterly leveled discrimination by showing benignly every awful thing imaginable. Shoot-'em-ups and blue movies unfortunately do not thereby create audiences for opera and modern dance. The shared aesthetic of most people doesn't get much beyond police drama. But it could! Audience development for the fine arts is really audience education and is therefore theoretically possible and available on a universal scale.

We're not working at it nearly hard enough. Education could provide the shared cultural conditions which would make it seem perfectly natural for salsa musicians and '09 matrons to be in the same audience.

Goetz Friedrich, the Director of the Berlin Opera which will perform here next week, speaks of a phenomenon which enlivens and vivifies his work, which he calls the "community of audience."

Friedrich has a spiritual feeling for the public gathering of peaceful people who will see the same thing, yet receive it each through his or her private perception. He feels the challenge of opera (in his case) is to provoke these individual feelings within the larger context.

This is extremely close to a religious attitude toward art, and Friedrich compares opera to a form of religion for some people in that it creates a place for them to gather together, step outside themselves and have an uncommon experience. It is a way, in other words, to transcend some of our natural but ignoble instincts, to ameliorate the harsher reality of our fears and prejudices. The "community of audience" can overwhelm distrust and competition.

So audience development remains a worthy goal but a goal fraught with a certain built-in failure rate. It is important to continue to seek audiences for the performing arts.

The transforming nature of art is critical to the whole body of civilizing influences on which we all depend for peaceful co-existence. Whatever it takes—from modern marketing techniques to encouraging the more profound amorphous "religious" feelings about art and its audience—should be employed in audience development. It is in the best interests of everyone.

LOCAL ART PATRONS DESERVE RECOGNITION
S.A. Light, 9-3-89

Light columnist Rick Casey wrote a couple of months ago on how our relatively low tax rates multiplied by our low per capita income makes us a poor city.

Those of us involved in fundraising for nonprofit organizations know how shallow the sea is in which we do our fishing. So it's timely before the new performing arts season starts to say thanks to some people who have helped bring us things we might not otherwise enjoy in this poor, yet wonderful, city.

San Antonio may be poor and off the beaten path, but it has three things other cities don't: the Metropolitan Opera, the Berlin Opera and the Joffrey Ballet. That these three major international arts organizations have a special relationship with our city is due to three major local arts patrons: the late Margaret Batts Tobin, Gilbert M. Denman, Jr. and Margaret King Stanley.

Mrs. Tobin got the Metropolitan Opera National Council auditions moved from Dallas to San Antonio some 30 years ago when she became regional chairman. She prevailed on the Junior League to sponsor the auditions for the multi-state region which includes Texas and which is one of 16 National Council regions. There is a large Texas presence at the Met today thanks in part to that "audience building."

Gilbert Denman founded the San Antonio Festival in 1981 and, for three of its seven seasons, we have seen the Berlin Opera in our city. This is helpful to those of us not inclined to go 10,000 miles to other cities to see an opera company, no matter how famous and provocative it is. Denman and Berlin Opera Director Goetz Friedrich had a meeting of the minds sometime early on. It became a genuine friendship, and it grew to include everyone around it.

Margaret Stanley made friends with Bob Joffrey in the '60s. No one was presenting dance companies of his magnitude in San Antonio at that time, but in 1976, the Joffrey came to the city at Margaret's instigation under the auspices of the Arts Council. Louis Harris was polling the cities in which the Joffrey appeared, and the results of the San Antonio poll helped to develop the San Antonio Performing Arts Association the next year. The association helped build its audience with appearances by the Joffrey, which has been to the city seven times, performing three local premieres and one world premiere.

Two good things come out of appearances of these highly regarded groups. One, each member of the audience gets to have the delicious, private pleasure of receiving that which is being presented. For the cost of a theater ticket and a parking garage ticket, individuals get to see things they would have to spend large amounts of money to travel to see. Two, famous groups generate audiences for less famous groups. A person recalcitrant about ballet might go see the Joffrey because it is so famous, only to discover that he or she actually likes it and next year buys a ticket to SAPAA's New Directions series.

In San Antonio, we have ongoing philosophical arguments about how to allocate limited resources in the arts. But we must be careful that "poor" does not breed "parochial." We must nurture these worldwide relationships. San Antonio is so charming that the Met, the Berlin Opera and the Joffrey actually like us for ourselves now, but one cannot be too careful with treasures.

In another economic age, Victor Alessandro and Max Reiter made us a premier city producing opera. Their legacy is a city full of opera lovers who, unfortunately, do not have a local opera. It would be great to see this city say we want our ballets folkloricos, our 24th Streets and our Urban15s, but we also want grand opera and great dance.

Until that glorious day, I just want to say thank you to those who have brought us this far.

LET'S STUDY POPULATION CONTROL

S.A. Light, 1-29-89

In Jesse Trevino's "Who will pay for a surge in state poverty?," I was pleased to see him address the necessity of bringing up to par Hispanic and Black education so that as those two minorities become majorities, they are brought into the economic mainstream and do not drain the wealth of the state.

But as I read along, basically agreeing with what he said, I still got this sense that something was being absurdly omitted from his argument—something that is absurdly omitted from all social arguments. That is the subject of the birthrate.

I would like to see the subject of birth control opened up for general discussion. I would particularly like to see it opened up in this city of Catholics, to see if we are capable of talking about something with such crushing societal consequences without accusing each other of racism or bigotry.

Because, if we don't start to do something about the birthrate—and I mean everyone's birthrate—we are going to wind up living in a kind of middle-class version of China or India.

In China and India, you see a lot of people standing around looking unemployed or underemployed, and while these countries take certain admirable views toward human life, they are also so wildly overpopulated that individual human life does not carry the enormous importance we have been able to give it with our Judeo-Christian ethic and great wealth.

If our birthrate proceeds apace and we follow our Judeo-Christian liberal ethic to its logical conclusion, the demand on the social services dollar will become so great that the tiny amounts we now spend on "quality-of-life" will dry up. The City Council still has the luxury of appropriating $2 million a year to the arts, but in 20 years, when the economically deprived population is substantially greater, it will be hard to justify spending money on music and museums when our streets are looking more like those of New Delhi.

Sheer math shows that there aren't enough jobs selling hot dogs in domed stadiums to support even minimally all the people we are going to have for neighbors in the next few decades.

So, while we must, as Jesse Trevino points out, educate a skilled work force, we must also be talking about how to slow our population growth.

And I'm not talking about slowing it just for poor people. I'm talking about slowing it for everyone.

Rich people are pretty good at sucking up resources, too, although in pure economic terms they obviously produce more. But they take up just as much space as the next person—more, usually.

The issue of population control has to do with space and the environment, as well as the social and domestic concerns of education and welfare.

I am 43 years old, and there are 12-year-olds who are right now having babies.

If their babies have babies at 12, I am looking at a new generation again when I am 55, again when I am 67, again when I am 79 and again when I am 91.

That's five generations of children who will be born to children just in the second half of my one life.

Who among us truly believes we can support all these unsupported children of children?

All the hamburger franchises and amusement parks and laundries and hotel kitchens in this great theme park we call San Antonio cannot support all these people.

I'm smart enough to see that we have a problem, but I am not wise enough to solve it.

I am simply calling for us to open the discussion, to bring the subject of population control out of the closet, to see how humanely and carefully and Americanly we can start to solve the problem

Because if we don't start to work on it now, while we are still slightly ahead of the game, we will have to solve it drastically when it becomes a crisis. And it will.

ROAD TO LEARNING
S.A. Light, 10-19-89

In the mid-1960's during the Cultural Revolution in China, Chinese schools and universities were closed for some years and their students, teachers and intellectuals "re-assigned" to the fields and mines for a little cross-cultural punishment.

I was in university at the time and madly in love with learning, and I remember thinking with shock and empathy that a whole generation of Chinese society would be profoundly handicapped by having had stolen from it a critical chunk of education.

Twenty-odd years later, in our big, safe, free, stable United States of America, we have our own lost generation. I use the term "generation" loosely to mean part of the one ahead of us, a sizeable part of the one to which we belong and the beginning of the one behind us. The lost generation comes in all colors, sexes and degrees of wealth.

San Antonio Youth Literacy, an organization for which I do some volunteer work, is a pioneer effort of the business community to influence the outcome of the education of teenagers whose schools do not have the resources to make the herculean effort to push them over the finish line successfully. In partnership with the schools, we intervene to help students reach their full potential.

Our theory as business people is that we must help, or we will face a bleak future of an uneducated work force, ignorant consumers and thoughtless fellow citizens. It is a logical tack that literacy providers all over the country are taking, right up to the President and Mrs. George Bush. It is wonderfully American in its rational, bottom-line approach. It makes sense, and from a practical point of view, it is also useful in fundraising for literacy. Business people would rather pony up $1,000 now to see someone through school than $10,000 later to support that person in a homeless shelter, a job training program or jail.

But let's talk heart-to-heart about what else we lose when we produce a generation of illiterates. We lose the knowledge that each of us carries within about a myriad subjects encountered on the road from birth to death. A child born to educated parents learns actual facts from them: names, concepts, theories, history, ideas—memories of knowledge that explains the vast store of phenomena to which the child is exposed. It is clearly possible for an illiterate parent to know the names of things, but the child raised by an ignorant parent will also clearly miss possessing a large fraction of the available knowledge.

A 15-year-old relative of mine told me in all seriousness that he could know everything there was to know without reading. As calmly as possible, I pointed out to him that he was wrong, and when I recovered from my apoplexy, I mused that people who don't read don't know what they don't know. Each thing you read widens your limits, including knowing just a little more what you don't know.

My 15-year-old relative is a typically ignorant teenager who one hopes will eventually suffer the shock of recognition the rest of us have experienced as adults looking back on our callow youth. But in the meantime he will have missed the joy of learning, the rush experienced when one more thing becomes clear; when words are put together so beautifully they take your breath away; when an idea is expressed so clearly your life is changed forever.

I weep for what they lose, and I fear for what we lose when our collective memory becomes tenuous through disuse. Let's not just tell people they won't get a good job unless they're literate. Let's tell them that they will miss the longest-lasting, most predictable source of joy in life: the pleasure of the brain at work, expanding. And let's tell them that the history of the world needs them to keep it alive.

LITERACY COULD WIPE OUT RACISM
S.A. Express-News, 3-30-90

One night recently I watched a multicolored crowd whirl around the dance floor to the tunes of a society orchestra.

It was a beautiful, peaceful sight. The occasion was a fundraiser for an organization of literacy providers, and the guests were participating in a common rite: partying to raise money.

There was really nothing remarkable about this fundraiser except the interesting crowd. As I savored the memory of the party the next morning, it dawned on me that the literacy battle could spell the end of racism.

The crushing seriousness of illiteracy and its consequences means educated people are going to have to reach out to uneducated people—no matter their color. We have fiddled around in America and put off for decades, centuries even, ensuring equality for everyone, and what they have done is gone and had millions of babies who are minus generations of memory because of the poor educations afforded their predecessors.

Now the economic producers, many of whom in their hubris and economic interests have subscribed to a politics of exclusion, are facing a dangerous and possibly bleak future—one full of neighbors who are too ignorant to work for them and, therefore. too poor to buy from them.

Not withstanding how poor and ignorant they are, the Judeo-Christian ethic to which most Americans subscribe requires that we take care of our helpless, and so we have and so we will, at least until the drag becomes too great.

The consequences of the drag becoming too great could be a left-wing or a right-wing revolution, both too horrible to contemplate. That is why most thoughtful people, particularly business leaders, are hustling to play catch-up before the next generation, exponentially bigger than the last, spawns.

Business has taken the lead in private sector intervention in public education. What has happened in the process is that a lot of different kinds of people who would never have known each other have become friends and allies.

WASP Dan Webster III, a literacy organization board member, sups with Mexican-American Edgewood Superintendent Jimmy Vasquez. Anglo GOP activist and CPA Harriet Marmon makes her way through swarms of her black and Hispanic San Antonio Youth Literacy kids, smiling and encouraging. Clark Mandigo, CEO of Intelogic Trace, powwows with black teens fascinated by his work. Edith McAllister, San Antonio School District Superintendent Victor Rodriguez and State Rep. Karyne Conley dance past each other.

Universal need requires universal handling. Of all the noble causes to which people give their time and their lives, the one that touches and seriously affects every single one of us is literacy. Our prosperous, advanced society will not survive massive illiteracy, and we've got it. The economics of illiteracy is untenable, the terrifying birth rate of illiteracy insupportable. Neither the social order nor the environment can afford the arithmetic we are experiencing.

Our precious friend John Henry Faulk says that racism is the worst problem of society. It is, in its way, because it is a result of ignorance. I believe that the literacy movement can put a big dent in racism because of all the kinds of people who must reach out to one another in the fight for better education. It almost goes without saying that if we are successful, the children of that better education will approach the world and act out their lives with the tolerance and moderation that come from knowledge.

It is an old saw that just because perfection is impossible is no reason not to strive for it. In the case of literacy and its concomitant benefits—a higher standard of living, a lower birth rate, and the racial tolerance that comes from knowledge and exposure—perfection is not the issue: survival is.

Lots of brains housed behind lots of black, brown, white, pink and yellow faces are joining forces to ensure that survival. They already know that racism as an issue pales in comparison

---

COULD THERE FINALLY BE PEACE AFTER GROWING UP WITH BOMB?
S.A. Light, 1-9-90

The atom bomb and I arrived on Earth within a week of each other. This was entirely coincidental. The former was certainly a more portentous event than the lattter, but chronilogically it means that this baby and the bomb grew up together.

From 1945 until the Cuban missile crisis in 1962, the bomb was the most intractable social malignancy we had to deal with. The Korean War abroad, McCarthyism at home—even these were manageable compared to the terror inspired by the bomb.

I can remember cruising up and down the Austin Highway with my friends in our early teens, smoking cigarettes (the worst thing we could think of to do), eating hamburgers, looking at the boys and talking about the bomb. We were not yuppie baby boomers. We were born to people who were either fighting World War II when we were born or were just coming home from it. We were raised on patriotism. When my brother Reagin and I were little, we used to bounce on our parents' bed and play "Bombs Over Tokyo," crashing into the pillows in freefalls.

We were raised by two generations of people ahead of us who had seen it all, and had their values firmly in place. Depression and war made home and hearth and education and peace mightily important. There was just one thing wrong with this rosy picture of post-war hunkering down, and that was the bomb.

As teenagers we were sure that the world would end before we were grown. Oddly, this did not turn us into glazed-eyed existentialists. But all the terror we had shivered with in our contemplation of the destruction of the world was justified for a brief moment in 1962 with the Cuban missile crisis, a moment which in its way was more memorable than the assassination of the president the following year.

Somehow after Cuba the terror subsided. It looked like maybe we wouldn't blow each other up after all. But for the next 27 years there were enough geopolitics, armament and disarmament, war, famine, genocide, social disruption and religious hatred to keep us stimulated. Russia and the United States kept up their tense competition, aided at times and hindered at times by their fickle allies but always the two of them arm-wrestling to a draw, their free hands swatting at the Ho Chi Minhs, the Chairman Maos, the Indira Ghandis, the Golda Meirs. Then Gorbachev came to power.

I did not realize how long I had been holding my breath or how excited I had not let myself become until last November 9th, when the Wall came tumbling down. The German Ambassador to the United States was in San Antonio that day to address the World Affairs Council, and he and his wife came to tea afterward. They were in a state of high excitement about the news from Berlin. At the end of the day, after they had left, I turned on the television news and there they were, the ecstatic, cheering, weeping crowds gesturing from the top of the Wall. A dam burst in me.

A week later Gilbert Denman and I saw Goetz Friedrich, the director of the Berlin Opera, in New York. He spoke of the incredible emotion of his city. His opera and the Berlin Philharmonic were giving free concerts for the East Germans. Everyone was helping each other. His secretary had been awakened early one morning by an East German family knocking on the door. They needed to warm the baby's bottle. The pure ingenuousness of that story says it all: there's a chance the human family can get back together. Anyway, I cried over each succeeding news story and human interest story. What finally put me over the top, crying-wise, was the sight of Russian soldiers standing on the stage of the Kennedy Center at the Kennedy Center Honors singing "God Bless America." I lost it.

For 44 years, since the week of my birth and Hiroshima, we've been living with Russia and the bomb. I've learned to worry about other things, things which my friend and Chief-Worrier-About-The-Bomb Ronnie Dugger might find relatively parochial compared to the utter horror and finality of the bomb. Now I feel this delicious slipping away, this shedding of an enormous weight.

I know it's too soon to declare the millenium, I think that talk of cutting the defense budget is premature, and as much as I hated it that George Bush didn't dance a little jig before recomposing himself, I understand why he has had to remain straight-faced throughout this joyous time.

But for the moment I think I shall float happily in this warm sea of tears.

I hope we can all remember how good it feels when the going gets tough.

CONFESSIONS OF A RIVER RESIDENT
S.A. Express-News, 5-4-90

Twenty years ago Texas-born author and humorist Larry L. King wrote a serious book called, "Confessions of a White Racist." In it he described his coming to terms with his own racism.

He said it was incumbent on civilized people to deal with the racism which was inevitably in them and not to pussyfoot around claiming it didn't exist.

I suffer from another social vice: snobbery. I admit it, and I try to deal with it. I'm not a snob about critical matters such as equal justice under the law. On the contrary, I'm almost suicidally pinko on social Issues. Rather, I'm a snob about social matters such as brains and taste, which brings me circuitously to the subject of the San Antonio River.

Recently, I ended a seven-year residency on the San Antonio River. Let me hasten to say that the Paseo del Rio Association band festivals did not run me off, although the noisy activities of this commercial trade association are certainly capable of running residents off the river.

The city has not made up its mind how to reconcile its desire for people to live downtown with its look-the-other-way boosterism, but that is the subject of a whole other essay. Suffice it to say it would be hard to run me off, as most people who know me would agree. Something else is luring me away, but before I go I want to say farewell to my river.

There is something about geography that enters the mind, the emotions and the bloodstream as surely as love for a human being or an animal does. How many of us love a ranch or a beach or a favorite vacation place or a romantic city or our own back yard? How many of us enjoy that rush of feeling that imitates love when we arrive at our cherished "place"?

That is how I feel when I walk down onto the San Antonio River. It is so beautiful and smells so good and feels so good that even from a great distance it is remembered as if it had a persona.

I have walked the river from El Tropicano to Pioneer Flour Mills, and I have never ceased to be astonished at how beautiful it is. It is like the city decided to make one thing perfect. I've seen birds, mammals and fish. I've watched the seasons change, and the plants change and the flowers come and go. I've seen the river flood, and I've seen it drained, and it has always amazed me.

Like all great entities it has its warts: an occasional bogeyman lurking in a deserted stretch; too many kids under the bridges in the afternoon kissing too passionately to make it through school unpregnant; too many tourists walking four abreast as if the sidewalk were one-way; too much one night stand bad food in restaurants that do not have to cater to repeat business; too many ignorant boat drivers as sources of San Antonio history; and far too much hollering and carrying on down in that echo chamber/tunnel of the River Walk.

But the joys! The cypresses surrounded at their bases with little beds of cypress root stumps; the smell of aerated river water in the waterfalls; all the secret nooks and crannies of the flower beds and architectural flourishes; the ancient stone backs of buildings that have tacky, modern fronts; the early morning steam rising off the water. All this is made mine by my experiencing it, and I'm a snob about it.

It is irrational to be a snob about a public place. I know this but I can't help it. The river belongs to all of us, and, speaking literally, one might say it really belongs to future generations because all we can do with such a gift is hold it in trust.

There is a painful dichotomy in living in a cherished place that everyone else loves, and having to share it with them. But "everyone else" is not going away, nor do we want them to.

The river, as part of the Earth, is theirs as well as ours.

One of these days when life quiets down I will have a good cry over leaving my beloved river.

In the meantime I want to thank the good guys, including the Park Rangers, for their contributions to my well-being for the past seven years, and to tell the bad guys that I'll be watching. So will future generations.

TEARS FLOW AS MAJESTIC CITY CRUMBLES
SA Express-News, 12-30-03

One morning two years ago, I had the city of Bam, Iran, virtually to myself. Five of us and a guide parked in the shadow of the wall, walked through a tall arched entryway and onto a dusty lane, took a hard right, went up some stairs, turned around and screamed.

There before us was an immense sand-colored city from antiquity, the early morning light not yet bleaching the color from the mud buildings.

Sunday morning I put my head down on my newspaper and cried for Bam.

When our little group arrived in Bam, we had already been in Iran for more than two weeks, going from one famous archeological site to another. We prepared by reading our art history and guide books and listening to the scholars who were with us. In most instances we were prepared for magnificence, only to be disappointed upon finding nothing more than a mound of dirt or a hole in the ground. The working archeologists who had come before us had excavated, and Mother Nature had taken care of the rest.

Persepolis was an exception; it was impressive but still woefully incomplete.

Thus at the very end of our trip, to come on the vast intact city of Bam was to be thunderstruck by its dimensions. It was not untouched; the restorers had obviously worked a long time not just to put it back together but to keep it in shape.

The two miles of wall that enclosed it embraced hundreds of dwellings, mosques, public buildings and the great citadel. It was said that 200,000 people would have lived in it at one time.

We were so excited we spent the entire morning combing around it. We became crazed with thirst because we had left our water bottles in our van, not realizing this would not be just another indecipherable site.

At the end of our tour of Bam we bought bottled water and pomegranate juice from a vendor and sat in the shade in happy contemplation of the most outstanding ruins we had seen in all of Iran, a country built on thousands of years of skeletons of history.

Now Bam is gone.

I have pored over the newspaper articles hoping to find a list of aid organizations to which one can send a contribution to help the poor souls of Bam. Even though Iran had a State Department warning out on it when we went there—and still does—we found the people friendly and glad to see us.

They missed their old prosperity, with which they associated us, and they were tired of their isolation from the West. They are like billions of people all over the world— and I would include us—who are better than their governments. Being poorly served by ones leaders should not preclude sympathy on a personal level.

When I determine how to send aid to help the people of Bam, and subsequently to begin the restoration of Bam, I am going to be as generous as I can. I hope other Americans will see past the mullahs and the ayatollahs and remember their suffering human beings in Bam.

V.
MISCELLANY

EXCERPTS FROM A NOVEL

INTRODUCTION

In the fall of 1968 I began my last semester of college at the University of Texas. Having achieved all the standard requirements for my degree, I indulged myself in some advanced, experimental and conference courses. For one conference course I wrote a novel.

I subsequently worked on the novel some more after graduation, but it never came to fruition as a published work and I finally put it aside and joined the rest of the human race as a working person.

I carried the attached excerpts around for years as writing samples. They are the writing of a woman in her early 20's, and they are representative of an autobiographical novel in which the young woman, rich and careless, discovers her humanity.

THE EXCERPTS

Burton Gill dreamed he was a lion who fell out of a tree to the earth's floor and propagated a race of animals who thought they were supreme in the world they saw. When he awoke he was sitting on the side of a draw surrounded by deer; his gun was across his lap, and it was dawn. He rarely fell asleep out hunting, but Christmas had been hectic in the city as usual, and he had not caught up on his sleep. He was mildly uncomfortable in his sitting position and realized he must have dreamed about falling out of a tree because that was the way he felt. As he came up out of sleep he held on to the dream and when he was fully awake he recalled it. All his life he had mused on the contradiction of ownership of land, and had tried to instill in his children a lack of regard of property for the sake of it, but it was a lesson poorly taught because the family owned such an immense piece of earth, and were so rich because of it. Burton's consolation for not having raised a family of utopians was that at least they took the land for granted, and having so much they would not be inclined to fight for more. He hoped ...

Burton pictured a supranatural force ignoring fence lines and open spaces, reaching out for his dependents, tugging at their loyalties, urging them to free themselves for a higher loyalty and a greater dependence. Burton the employer was irritated and concerned; Burton the worldly historian was fascinated and amused. No cause he had ever been acquainted with had enchanted his imagination enough to make him wish the stakes were low enough to let life as he knew it slide, so that he might take up with the new movement. He was only a little sorry this was true. Life without conflict had been smooth and luxurious and full of happiness. Still, a man had to envy those whose humanity was best drawn out by an idea, no matter how nebulous, and who signed on with that idea for the duration, no matter what they had to leave behind to do so ...

His instinct was to hold to life as it was in the memories, where the future held no terrors, but his sons had already plunged into the life of their generation and his daughter lived most of her time in a life he could only guess at, and while he was proud of their seriousness it also made him sad. Life would be a matter of sustained seriousness from now on, he felt, and the old kind memories would truly be a thing of the past ...

"In my world there aren't any helpless neighbors," Judson said.

"Christ!" he exploded.

Judson was taken aback. "I suppose that was a pretty naive thing for me to say but it was completely uncontrived. There's just no poverty in the lives I'm intimate with."

With some restraint he said, "Did it ever occur to you that unfamiliarity with the world carries with it a kind of curse, like blindness, that handicaps you every step of the way? That people who live isolated from the bulk of humanity are the ones who stand blindfolded in front of a wall at dawn and still can't figure out what they've done to deserve their fate? That the vast majority of people suffer every day of their lives? Maybe you know all that, but has it ever struck home to your heart? Has it ever made you ache at the very core so bad you know it will never stop hurting? Have you ever had the sensation of being one tiny man against an Everest of thoughtless humanity and been so angry you had to laugh to keep your head from exploding? Have you ever watched a man muster courage for a fight he knows he's going to lose?"

He stood up and went to her, and put his hands on her arms. She started to draw away, but it felt good for him to touch her in a friendly way, and she stood still. A vision of Nicholas and the governor flashed to her, the way they had complicated her life, their selfish, insouciant demands on her time and her body, the manner in which they had jeopardized their own friendship by both sleeping with her, their faulty and aggressively thoughtless masculinity and contempt for weak things, their hatred of opposition to what they thought was right and proper in government and society, their powerful insolence and pride, their detachment from and indifference to life as it welled up all wrong and askew around them. Stanley put his arms around her and she crumpled against his shoulder ...

The act of making a conscious decision to stop what you are doing and do something else or to change the way you are living often derives its strength from the mental drawing of a line of demarcation which indicates that everything in the head up to the moment of the decision will now become memory, even if there are some things there which had up to that moment been plans for the future. To make a decision like that, to leave something behind in order to move ahead more freely, is exhilarating because there are gaps of interest left and only the future can fill the holes. But you also feel a kind of gentle sorrow for time past, for the places you can't go back to and the people you won't love daily any more. The sorrow is not for time wasted but for time loved. The filament of continuity of days is not broken, but knotted to indicate change.

In retrospect there are a thousand tiny ideas, doubts cast on tradition, which prepare the way to change and explain it. Decisions which seem abrupt are the conscious culmination of unconscious fermentation that rumbles and bubbles in the head below the level of normal awareness. The realization that abrupt change was arrived at naturally and logically is a solace for the mind confused by loss of the past...

Is this where we all started? Somewhere the original seed bloomed full blown into poverty, naked as birth, to establish with copulation and human intelligence a line whose names and fortunes changed over eons to burst into the twentieth century on a floodswell of oil, cattle, machinery and electricity, peaking out in a year in the second half of the century to spill me and my generation over the top ...

It was never men I thought about, but cosmic forces and grand contexts into which fit ruins and monuments, arts and letters. My heart was disengaged from the daily tragedies; I looked at the laborers on the side of the highway and wondered not at how they loved and died, but rather how they were said to be the only people who could dig a hole straight down or build a stone wall straight up. I stayed in splendid isolation in intimate little hotels, but never went home with the maid to her neat barren hovel. I bundled in furs for an elegant evening, and never thought that someone else was cold. I travelled with ease over the surface of foreign lands, but never burrowed any deeper than aristocratic recountings of national history at candlelit dinner parties. I missed the whole point of humanity: its burdens, which you assume when you realize the verity of someone else's existence. Innocence indeed becomes shocking.

SPEECHES

WHAT CAN I DO?

INTRODUCTION

During most of the 1980's I worked with an unusual literacy program in San Antonio. It was applied to high school students and included the use of video equipment and peer tutoring to encourage students to read, write and stay in school.

Each summer the core 'leadership' students from each high school attended a two-week workshop which we ran to teach them peer tutoring techniques and how to use video equipment so that when school started in the fall they were prepared to execute the program.

In the summer of 1988 I was asked to be the closing speaker on the last day of the workshop. The following is the speech I gave. There was utter silence when I finished, and I left dejected and feeling like a failure. Later, however, I was told that they had rated my talk the best of their two-week experience.

THE SPEECH

Your Aunt Harriet [Marmon, founder of the program] asked me to make this speech entitled "What Can I Do?" on this, the last day of your two-week summer workshop. I like the idea of thinking, "What Can I Do?", but I think a more appropriate title for the speech would be "What Can't I Do?"

I would like to take you on a logical trip through the minds of the adults who conceived of this program and run it. The first leg of this journey could be entitled, "Why Be Literate?"

After breathing, eating and sleeping the next most important thing in the world is words. Words sort out and identify things. The difference between knowing words and not knowing words is the difference between knowing this world and not knowing it. Knowing the words for things gives us power over them, and makes us at home with them. If we know the word for something we bring it into existence and make it stand separate and of itself. If we can look at a bush and say, that is a pyracantha bush, then we have that piece of knowledge and we possess it, and the world is clearer and more understandable because of it.

The words which identify ideas are equally important. The ideas of love, transcendence and fear, of something being provincial or modern, of things being right and wrong, all require words to understand them. Not only do we want to walk through the world knowing the names of things, so we are at home with them, we also want to know feelings and ideas so we can communicate with and try to get along with our fellow humans. If you know and understand the world, and you know and understand your fellow humans, the chances are excellent that you will do less harm and more good than those who don't.

Here's an example: Let's say you go on vacation to the coast. You sit on the beach and swim in the surf. Well la-de-da, so there is sand and there is water. But what if you knew the word "estuary" and you understood the physics of an "estaurine system." Believe it or not there would be no coast, no islands and no beach in Texas without our estuaries. Knowing one little word, estuary, can turn you from a thoughtless sunbather sitting on a beach to someone who really knows where he is in the world, and why it looks the way it does, and how it works.

Here's another example: You are on a field trip to a museum. For you it is a day away from school, so what. But you may be about to walk into a building whose lintels, columns, windows, arches and decoration might represent an enormously important school of architectural thought, a school of thought which has much to do with the way our world looks. Your teacher stops to discuss the architecture of the building, but you are slouching around at the back of the crowd having a nicotine fit and acting cool. Well let me tell you something, there is nothing cool about ignorance. Learn those architectural terms and get inside the heads of the smart people who figured out how to make such a building, because that is one more thing you will know about this world and the more you know the smarter you are, and the smarter you are the easier life is.

Do not think there are subjects you can skip. Do not think you can have knowledge if you say, I don't need to know about estuaries and I don't need to know about architecture. You need to know about everything, because the world is made up of everything and not just a few things.

Now, how do you learn words and their meanings? By reading, of course. Get out from in front of the boob tube and read a book. Read a thousand books. Gobble books. If you don't have a book in the house, hoof it down to the nearest library and get one. Stop being a passive consumer of the unrealistic silliness on television and do something to expand your brain. The feel of the brain expanding is an ecstatic feeling. The feel of the brain subsequently using its knowledge is also an ecstatic feeling.

I could go on but I think I will conclude this first leg of our logical journey to discover why we should be literate. Simply put, we want to be literate so that we can think, talk, know and understand, so that we can be at home in the world, and so that we can have power over it.

For the second part of our journey I will pretend that we are all literate, and show you what happens when you are. This part of our journey could be entitled "Getting Free." I should perhaps call it "Becoming Free" because that is more proper, but sometimes it is appropriate to use a slightly less proper word or phrase because it has more emphasis.

Your job at your age is to become educated, and you go to school because basically you have no choice—grown ups make you go. But you are at a very egocentric age where you have discovered the concepts of self and consciousness, and you are probably questioning a lot of what you think of as the b.s. that grownups make you do. As a grownup who still thinks of herself as a kid, and can see both sides, let me tell you why you have to become educated: because life is long and the preparation for it is short. You have approximately fifteen years in which to prepare to live eighty. If you think school is work, wait until you really have to go to work. School is a piece of cake compared to working for a living.

But working for a living is fun because it is how you 'get free'. It is fun to work and get paid for it because the money is your ticket to freedom. Money provides for our basic needs and so frees us from want. Money stands between us and fear for our ability to survive. Money helps us get free and live free.

But you can't earn money if you're illiterate. You can empty garbage cans into garbage trucks if you are illiterate, but most other jobs require the ability to read and understand instructions, or to listen and understand instructions. Most other jobs require you to communicate with your fellow workers in a clear and understandable way. You cannot learn to type, you cannot learn to fix an engine, you cannot learn to argue a case before a judge, you cannot learn to run a printing press, you cannot keep a ledger, you cannot tell the difference between a stock and a bond, you cannot mix concrete, you cannot pull teeth, you cannot drive a forklift, you cannot perform brain surgery, you just plain flat cannot do much of anything that earns decent money unless you are literate. And unless you earn decent money you will never 'get free'.

Are you sitting there thinking to yourself, what's the big deal about getting free? In case you hadn't noticed it, my little fledglings, the whole impulse of life is to get free. Parent birds push their baby birdies out of the nest. Tiger mamas push their babies off the tit and out into the field. Mama cats drop their babies off in other people's yards. And your parents go to an awfully lot of trouble and expense to get you ready to be free, because they know that the instinct and the soul of us as human animals is to seek freedom. God, aren't we lucky to live somewhere where we can actually be free? Don't waste the opportunity.

Are you all enjoying my preaching?

Now we're literate, and we've gotten free. "What Can We Do?"

Remember, that was the title of my speech. "What Can I Do?" I still say it should be "What Can't I Do?" As far as I'm concerned, with the kind of preparation I've been talking about you can do anything you want to do. When I was your age I used to keep a motto on my desk. It said, "Success is never final, failure is never fatal, it's courage that counts." You can know what you know, and know how to do what you know how to do, and know how you look and know how you act, and know who your people are and know what you come from, but you don't know whether you have courage until you've had to use it. And believe me, you'll get a chance to find out. Life is replete with opportunities to find out if you have courage. The main opportunity will be, do you have the courage to gut up, work hard, achieve and be the best that you can be? Do you have the courage to fall flat on your face on the way to your goal?

When I was building my restaurant, Taddycake's, I had many dark nights of the soul where I would lie in my bed late at night and wonder if I would succeed or fail. What if I built a restaurant and no one came? What if the food was bad and people came but hated it? What if I turned out to be a lousy manager and the business lost money? You know how I handled those dark nights of the soul? With courage. I simply decided that if I failed, I would do it with dignity and my head held high, and I wouldn't curl up and die but would go on and try something else. Life can be pretty darn scary but with courage it is manageable.

Do not think that the first thing you do is the only thing you will ever do. You may start out as a secretary in a law office and wind up a lawyer. You may start out as an orderly in a hospital and wind up a doctor. You may start out cutting grass and wind up owning a tree service. You may start out as a teacher and wind up mayor, like Henry Cisneros did. You may start out as an actor and wind up President of the United States.

Whatever you do, though, don't spend these precious years goofing off. Have fun, play and enjoy your friends, but when you think about life know that it is a deadly serious proposition which requires preparation, and which lasts a long time. Don't spend the last sixty or seventy years of your life doing some dead-end thing because you didn't get properly ready for it.

I'm going to end our logical journey here and give you a couple of pieces of my famous advice. The first is, keep your pants on. Now don't get insulted when I say this, but any fool can have a baby. It takes a really smart person to keep from having one. It is difficult enough to become a literate person, learn how to do something, earn money and get free without having to take care of a baby. Life is plenty long enough to have all the babies you want after you get free and are able to give them the life the poor little things deserve. Don't use babies to try to solve your problems. That's not what babies are for. You meddle around with babies' lives and try to make them be something for you and you will wind up with a very screwed up little person. Babies represent the hope of the future and need to be raised very carefully and frankly you teenagers just aren't smart enough yet to raise a good baby.

My second piece of advice is, stop saying 'you know'. Do you know how many times you say 'you know' in the course of your conversations? "I'm going out the door, you know"; "I'm going over to her house, you know"; "We were at the movies, you know"; "I was down on Houston Street, you know". Some of you say "you know" at the end of almost every sentence. It sounds ignorant, and people who sound ignorant don't get good jobs.

You'll be pleased to know that that is all the advice I am going to give you.

On behalf of the San Antonio Youth Literacy Board I want to tell you that we have watched you with pride and joy these past two weeks. You have been a wonderful group of students to work with and we will look forward to visiting you in your schools this coming year. You are fine, intelligent people and you give off some powerfully good vibes. I expect to see you out in this city doing good things for a long time to come. Thank you.

TALK TO GIVE AT THE SULGRAVE CLUB
WASHINGTON, D. C.
MARCH 11, 2003
On the Subject of WANDER LUST by Taddy McAllister

There is perhaps no place else in the country with more people per capita who understand the efficacy of foreign travel than Washington, D. C. Therefore, looking out at your sophisticated faces causes the sinking sensation that whatever I say will be preaching to the choir.

I see among you many faces I know, some of them Texas faces who prefer to live here in Washington. One of them is Marta [Miller Dunetz, who arranged the occasion] herself, whose dear late parents were famous for taking us Texas neophytes under their wings, treating us with dignity and respect and exposing us to the social life of the capital. We should all be so hospitable.

But knowing that this room and indeed all of Washington City are filled with expatriates of every stripe, I am reminded of Theodore Roosevelt. I've been listening on the treadmill every morning to Edmund Morris' biography of him. When Roosevelt was U.S. Civil Service Commissioner he told someone in a letter that he liked Washington because he could be around big men with big ideas, and I have a sneaking suspicion we all feel the same way. Washington is the least parochial of American cities, and I include New York in that assessment.

But enough about us. Let's talk about the world, the world we see when we travel. How superficial is our perception of it? How much can you know as you move around countries as a tourist, living the artificial life of a traveler from another culture, present only temporarily? I study like mad when I am getting ready to go to a new country, reading history, art books, current political nonfiction and the novels and stories of that place. Before I ever leave home I have ingested a lot of knowledge about my destination. But one could say that for all the nobility of that preparation, it is still academic and not the same as, quote, "living" deeply and realistically in the destination culture.

In the introduction to my book I cockily point out that I have always traveled first class (which p.s. is not totally true) and that I make no excuses for touring as opposed to the down-and-dirty, go-native type of travel that other writers are famous for. How useful intellectually is this kind of travel? What are we missing? Are we indulging ourselves and coddling ourselves and in the process missing the reality of the places we visit?

The answer is yes, we are frequently missing the reality, if by reality you mean the squalor and hardscrabble day-to-day eking out of a living that most people on the planet do. By the same token we could say that, as connected as we feel to our city of Washington, we are missing the reality of it by not going regularly into housing projects and across the river to Anacostia. However, I believe one does not have to trade places with other people to project oneself into the reality of their existences. If you're focused on the other and have an academic base from which judgments can be made, you can extrapolate and reach some viable conclusions about what you're seeing, or not reach any conclusions for that matter but simply accept the Other with a capital "O".

Let me inject here that I am actually turned on by squalor, decay, ruins and filth and like seeing them, but that may be because they are "Other" with that capital "O". I like travel to places that make me step outside myself.

Stepping outside oneself is not sometimes as easy as you might expect. I can remember one day in Bhutan a learned woman in our group exclaiming after seeing an ancient monastery, "Why don't they just paint these places and fix them up!" My reply was, have you seen anyone in a car yet? If they could get paint they'd have to carry it straight up the mountain on foot. I personally was getting ready to walk across the Himalayas and felt pretty strong but even I would quail at such a task. If I were a poor monk the idea would be even more formidable. How much extrapolation did that take? A smidgen at most.

In the year 2000, walking in a village in Yemen, a man caught up with and walked with us for a few moments before leaving us and moving ahead at a faster clip. When he got flush with me he looked over and, like every single other Yemeni who spoke to us, said at first, "Amereeka?" I said, "Yes." Next he said, "Beel Clinton." That was always what they said after "Amereeka." I said, "Yes, he's our President." Now, usually the next thing out of their mouths was, "Monica Lewinsky," which for some reason they pronounced correctly. Not this guy. He stepped out in front of me in order to look back at me and, still walking, held his hand flat down near the ground. "Beel Clinton," he said with contempt, then immediately raised his hand way above his head as if measuring something extremely tall and said, with almost a love-light in his eyes, "Madeleine Allbright." And with that he was gone.

Madeleine Allbright was Secretary of State and was at that time trying to broker peace between the Israelis and Palestinians. We discussed this amazing performance for some time afterward and concluded, truly or erroneously, that this man approved of the peace process. Of course we wondered how representative he was of his fellow Yemenis and we didn't hazard a guess in that direction, and he may have only been an odd duck, albeit well-informed. But the tourist can put a kaleidoscope of such encounters together and get a picture fragmented but made up of true experiences.

The story illustrates another observation about touring, and that is no matter how rarefied the air you move around in as a tourist, you are still constantly relating to people on the street, in restaurants, hotels and shops. With the exception of Russia in 1997, I have never been anywhere—Hanoi, Aden, Tehran and other godforsaken so-called enemy redoubts—that people weren't friendly. It makes one think that if our country spent some of its incalculable wealth on life-improvement projects in poor countries instead of writing so many checks to the military-industrial complex, our world would be a safer place. People are the same everywhere in spite of their governments. I'm the way I am in spite of MY government.

The seond efficacious thing that happens when one is abroad—and you need never leave your Ritz Carlton for this experience—is the lucidity with which you look back at your own country, the good old USA. I knew a tough Texas guy in Washington back in the '70's named Lee Swift who said he thought all members of Congress should be required to travel abroad extensively. This was in counterpoint to the ever-recurring newspaper exposes about junketeering. I understand his ornery stand now after watching my country in the rear view mirror during several decades of globe trotting.

Two things have become apparent to me from watching my country from afar, and those are, one, how others perceive us, and two, how incredibly important we are to the rest of the world. I do not mean militarily or politically so much as the idea of us. Thomas L. Friedman said the rest of the world may hate us but if they opened their borders their countries would empty and everyone would be here. I relate this not in a chauvinistic manner—I'm much too realistic and kind-hearted to be a chauvinist—but only because I believe, hyperbolically, it is true.

The other aspect, though, holds equal weight, that is the business of we travelers seeing our country through the eyes and the press of other countries. One wishes today certain of our leaders had looked more through foreign eyes before taking office. Doing so helps explain a lot of otherwise mystifying things one reads in the Post, the Times and the San Antonio Express-News, i.e. why are they tweaking us, why do they hate us, why did we get bogged down in that war, why didn't we know that in their culture they do thus-and-so. Hell, even reading the International Herald Tribune or English newspapers offers one a whole other slant on the United States. This is eye-opening stuff you don't get out of the news box in front of Wal-Mart. And television! This is a subject for another essay. In Arabia they are either aping us with busty, sexy women doing soap-opera behaviour, or they're earnestly discussing what's wrong with us. The juxtapositions one encounters in travel can be delicious, and they can be terrifying.

The ultimate thing that comes from this perforce superficial pleasure of touring, after the experiences themselves, the cogitation and empathy they cause, the ability to see ones own country in clearer perspective, the extrapolation—to keep working this word over—are the understanding and proprietary interest with which the traveler looks back at the countries visited. I remember going to Sri Lanka in 1980 and reading ever after the newspaper stories about it, stories I would have skipped had I never gone there. I admit that I skip some now, a function of their interminable civil war which broke my heart when it started because the people there were so touchingly sweet. In the same vein, I can remember putting my head down on the kitchen counter one morning in my apartment at the Watergate and frankly crying over a front page story in the New York Times that much of Srinagar had been leveled in the Kashmiri war, because I had loved Srinagar so much.

So often we don't care at all or only care about the world in the abstract until we've been there, and then we care painfully about it as if it were ours. And it is. It's ours. Let's get out there and show we care about it. I want to go to a dangerous place and walk the streets, as stupid as that sounds, because I've been places with State Department warnings out on them and had some of the best times of my life. My heart breaks everyday now, and all because I've been on the surface of 57 countries. Fifty-seven countries extrapolated out is the world, my beloved world, now so endangered. Thank you.

"BEEZIE AND THE DOGS"

INTRODUCTION

For those of you who missed the marketing blitz of my second book, "Beezie," the volume consisted of four stories about Beezie, the First Lady's cat. Beezie started out as a stray and became the most famous cat in the world. His personality was based on my actual cat Beezie, who only thinks he lives in the White House, and acts accordingly. The other Beezie stories, while sophisticated, were basically sweet. In the story that follows, Beezie is a little more of a hellion. I hope his fans won't be shocked.

"Beezie and the Dogs"

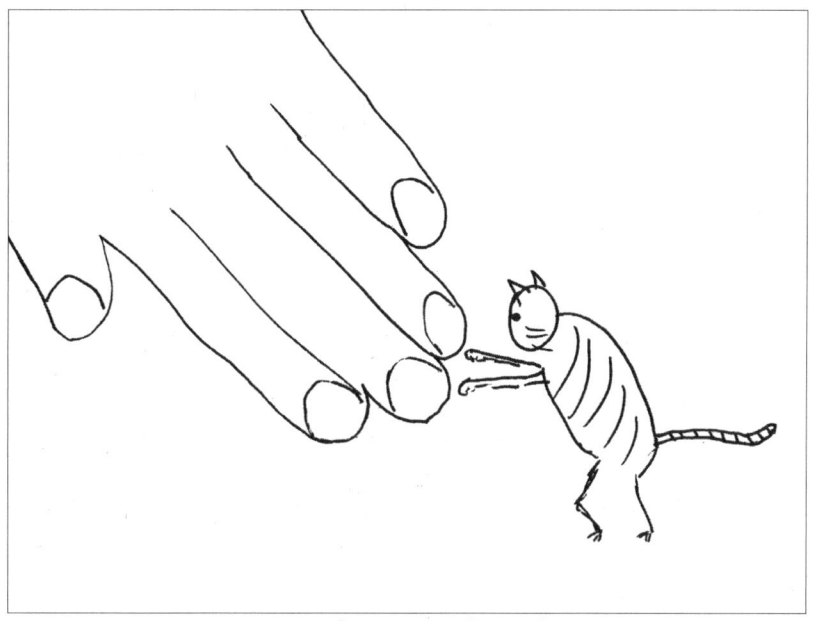

Beezie the White House cat lived in the lap of luxury. But it was not always so. Beezie had been dumped on the street as a kitten. When he was rescued, he still had some fight in him.

Beezie wasn't a bad kitty. Like all kittens he found a lot of trouble to get into as he explored his world, but he was also a sweet, loving little guy with a very loud purr machine. He was like the grownups around him: good, but capable of mistakes.

Beezie was a "cool cat" and not afraid of anything. Well, sometimes a loud noise would make him jump. But Beezie was not afraid of dogs. They were afraid of him.

When Beezie decided to scare a dog, he got all puffed up,
his ears lay flat, his fangs were bared and he made growling noises.
He would turn sideways and tiptoe toward the dog,
looking like evil incarnate.

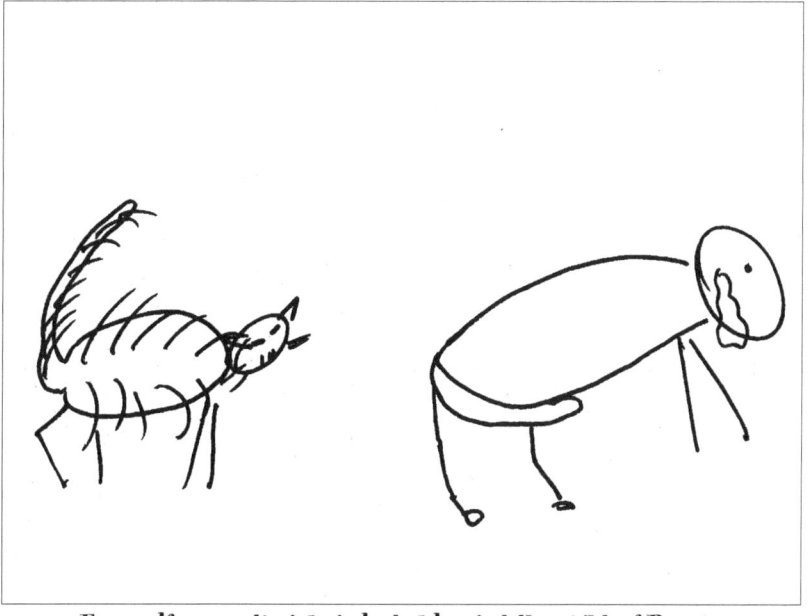

Few self-respecting dogs lasted long at the sight of Beezie in full-race-woolly mode. They would slink away with their tails between their legs, whining pitifully.

Beezie would stare at the retreating dog, then sit down and start to lick himself nonchalantly. His fur would flatten out, and he would go back to eating his crunchies or lying on his pillow.

Mrs. K., Beezie's person, was the First Lady. One day her best friend from school days came to spend the night at the White House. With Mrs. K's permission, the friend brought her dog.

Mrs. K. warned her friend not to let Beezie hurt her dog.
The dog had fluffy red hair and looked like a fox.
She wiggled a lot and danced around in circles.

Beezie looked upon this dog with utter disdain. What a silly animal! What a useless animal! Beezie lay on top of a wing-back chair in the family quarters upstairs in the White House looking down at the idiot dog.

The dog had not noticed Beezie yet. Casually Beezie rose and stretched his back. That was all it took. The little foxy dog started crying and backing up to the feet of its master.

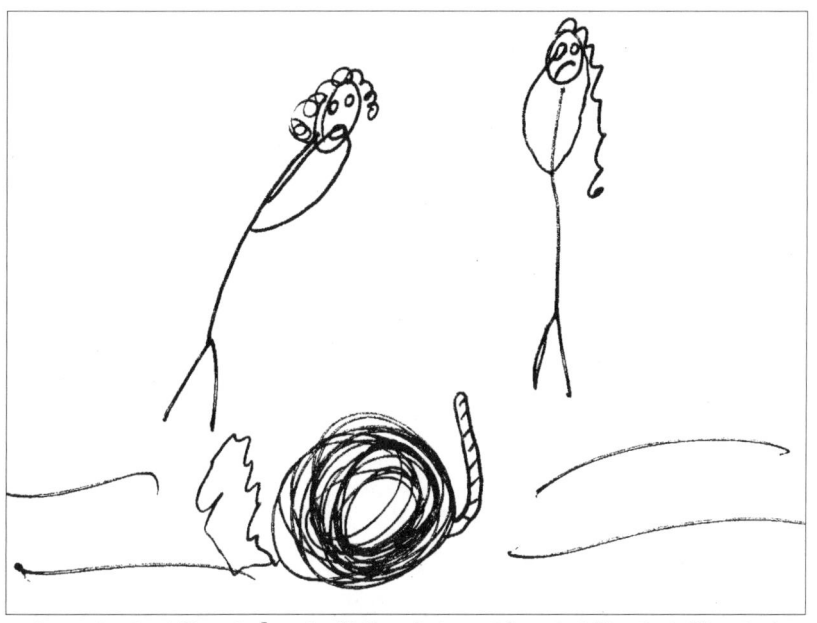

In an instant Beezie leapt off the chair and jumped the dog. The dog screamed. The women screamed. The fur flew.
The guards came rushing in.

As quickly as it started, the fight was over. Beezie hopped back up on the wing-back chair. The little red dog cried and cried, even after its person picked it up. Mrs. K. was mortified. Beezie had not been hospitable to the guest dog.

A maid came in to vacuum up the fur. The little dog had also piddled on the floor. As the women tried to calm the dog, Beezie washed his face and paws.

Mrs. K. apologized over and over to her friend, and they talked about living with animals and how animals sometimes acted like people and sometimes acted like the wild animals they used to be.
They agreed that part of the mystery of living with their pets was wondering what they would do next.

That night Mrs. K. had some pillow talk with Beezie as they lay in bed in the dark. "Beezie boy, what got into you this afternoon? You scared that little doggie half to death. That doggie was our guest, and you were mean to it."

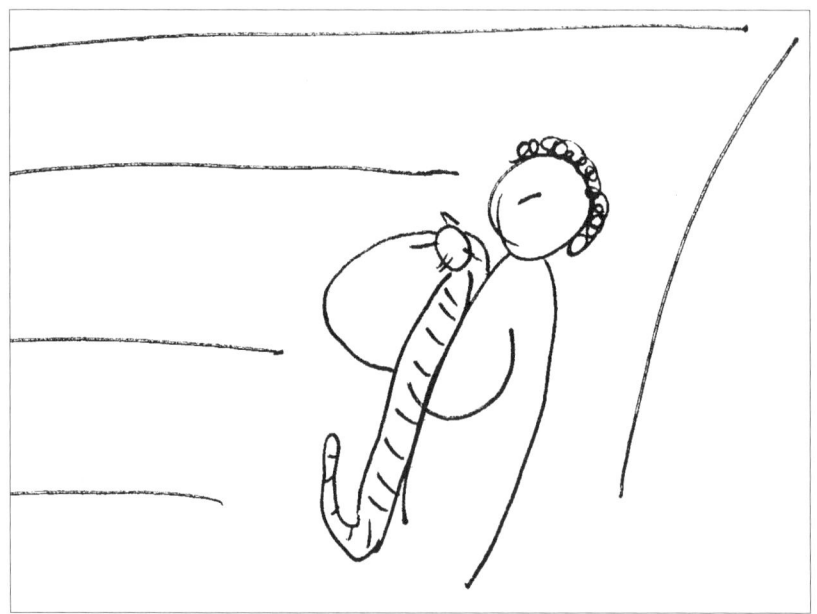

Beezie in his cat way stretched out against the front of Mrs. K. It had been a good day for him, and now Mrs. K. in her low, quiet love talk way was talking to him just like she did every night. It always put him to sleep in a happy, secure mood. He did not know he was being forgiven.
He only knew he was loved.